BORSTAL GIRL

BORSTAL GIRL

EILEEN MACKENNEY

with

JOHN F. MCDONALD

SIMON &
SCHUSTER

London · New York · Sydney · Toronto

A CBS COMPANY

First published in Great Britain by Simon & Schuster UK Ltd, 2011
A CBS Company

3 5 7 9 10 8 6 4 2

Simon & Schuster UK Ltd
1st Floor
222 Gray's Inn Road
London WC1X 8HB

www.simonandschuster.co.uk

Simon & Schuster Australia
Sydney

A CIP catalogue record for this book is available
from the British Library.

ISBN: 978-1-84983-475-9

Typeset by Hewer Text UK Ltd, Edinburgh
Printed in Great Britain by CPI Cox & Wyman,
Reading, Berks RG1 8EX

This book is dedicated to the memory of my dear brother Johnny, who fought with the 14th Army in Burma during the Second World War. Also to my beloved 'Sixer', who stood by me to the end.

I will never forget the people I have lost, who meant so much to me – Johnny, Sixer, Tommy, Gracie, Jimmy and Bill. You are always in my heart.

I would also like to thank my wonderful granddaughter Shelley for being my right hand and doing so much hard work to make this book a reality.

To my sons and my daughter for being who they are and always standing by me and each other – blood is thicker than water!

And a big thank you to my little brother Ronnie for reminding me of the antics we used to get up to.

Finally, to all those people who didn't believe I could do it and thought I was talking rubbish – I told you so!

CONTENTS

1

EARLY DAYS IN LONDON

People say you ain't a real cockney unless you were born within earshot of Bow Bells. I don't know about nowadays, with all that noisy fucking traffic round Cheapside, but when I was born, on 15 April 1931, the sound just seemed to drift across the River Thames on the reeking fog, and you could hear it on a quiet Sunday morning all the way south to Rotherhithe.

I came into the world as Eileen May Killick, and I had four brothers and one sister – Tommy, Gracie, Johnny, Jimmy, me, and Ronnie, in that order. All of us were tall and blue-eyed and Tommy and Gracie had blonde hair. Johnny, Jimmy and Ronnie were darker and I was fair. Jimmy had freckles like my mother, who had long wavy auburn hair, like that film star Maureen O'Hara. My father was a well-built man and the boys took after him. Me and Gracie liked to think we looked dignified and womanly in shape – Gracie was even offered a job as a model once, but she turned it down.

When I was young, I slept in the same bed with Gracie and my mother, who had tuberculosis. The rooms were small and dingy, like something out of Charlie fucking Dickens or Sherlock fucking Holmes, and the street was no better – it was a tiny little lane, with tight rows of terraced houses and no room to move. My mother didn't go into hospital or anything to have me, you didn't do that back then. Women had their babies at home, in the squalor and dirt and dog-fleas, that's how there was so much infant mortality. But I was a healthy enough baby, even if I was a little underweight, and I came into the world kicking and fucking screaming!

Rotherhithe was classed as a slum area in those days, with massive overcrowding and very high crime rates and unsanitary conditions and vermin everywhere. I can't remember exactly where I was born, except that it was near a tannery or wool merchants or something, and the rotten place stank up the whole area, especially in the summertime – it was the smell of death, dead animals, dead skins and dried blood and it stuck up your nose and on your clothes.

We didn't have any electric or central heating or stuff like that, we had a gas lamp in the front room and we used candles for light everywhere else. There was no bathroom, no place to wash, so we traipsed off down the street to the public baths once a week, carrying our towels under our arms. I was only little and it was a pitiful sight to see, especially in the winter, walking down the street with my towel under my arm, come rain or come shine. And when I came out, I'd be fucking freezing all the way home. Sometimes, if we didn't get there early enough, there'd be a huge fucking queue, so we'd turn round and come back – then we'd have to wait till the following week.

People didn't have any carpets on the floor, just lino-leum downstairs and bare boards upstairs. There was no wallpaper, just distemper to cover the walls – I'm not talking about the dog-disease, this was yellowy stuff like whitewash, made of powdered chalk and lime and white lead, and it came off on me if I brushed against it. The houses were alive with fleas – big red bastards, because everybody kept dogs and cats to kill the rats. The fuck-ing fleas got everywhere, especially in the beds, and I'd be covered all over with flea bites every morning. It was so bad that sometimes the rotten old mattresses would nearly walk out of the rooms by themselves. No matter how we tried, we couldn't get rid of the fuckers; they'd get into the joints of the beds and bite me raw while I was sleeping. My father put paraffin on everything to try and kill them, but it didn't work and they once bit my brother Jimmy so bad he became infected and almost died.

I remember all the houses having black iron railings round them, I don't know why I remember that, it must be something to do with my dad's sister. But these railings were all removed during the war – because they needed the iron to make weapons, I expect. And there used to be terrible poisonous grey-green fogs – smog they call it now, like you see in the pictures – because everyone was using coal for their fires and the smoke would collect and some-times I couldn't see my hand in front of my fucking face. The fog smelled too, like the dead skins in the tannery, like something stagnant and polluted and rotting, and a lot of people died from pleurisy and bronchitis because of it.

When I was about four, we moved to a three-bedroom house in Cyril Street, Camberwell, which we shared with another family. Conditions weren't much better there. The infamous Richardsons lived about two streets away and my older brothers got in with them and other local gangs and there was a lot of petty crime and the coppers were always down on us. Cyril Street ain't there no more, of course, because it was blown to bits during the war – and when I say 'house', it was more like a fucking chicken coop. It was so pokey I could lean out the window and shake hands with my neighbours. The rooms were always damp and we had to get the chimney swept every week and everything got covered in fucking soot.

There was no garden, just a yard, with an outside khazi that regularly got blocked up, because we had no toilet rolls in them days, just newspaper – and the newspaper didn't flush if you had diarrhoea and used too much, which was most of the time, and it would block up the bog and overflow all over the place. One of my brothers bought a cockerel once and kept it out there, but the fucking bird was so aggressive nobody could go to the bloody lavvy without being attacked, so some cunt set his dogs on it and they killed it.

Everybody knows there was a lot of contagious diseases around in them days, because of the unsanitary conditions and because everyone was living on top of each other in the slums and the germs were having a fucking field day. We got every fucking thing that was going. The house always smelled to me of damp and must and overcrowding, like it was on my skin or something, like I just couldn't get away from it, no matter what I did. We had old coats for bedclothes and the pillows were sacks stuffed with flock and hard as fuck. It's like the old joke that comedians tell – 'I was fourteen before I found out that blankets didn't have sleeves in them.'

When I was very young, I had trouble pronouncing words. When people asked me my name, I'd say 'Dileen Dillick', instead of Eileen Killick. They'd laugh and think it was funny to hear a little kid saying silly things. My mother thought it was how I was going to speak naturally and it was just me, so she never paid much mind to it. The other children started taking the piss and mimicking and making fun of me and I'd end up running away in tears. I talked like that for a long time. My mother had so much other things to deal with in life that I never got taken to a doctor or a speech therapist or nothing like that. I just got on with it.

I was in bed one day feeling ill with a sore throat and that night I woke up choking on the blood I was coughing up. I couldn't breathe and was so frightened my eyes were bulging. My mother was too ill herself with the tuberculosis to do anything and Dad was at work on the night shift. So my sister Gracie ran to a neighbour's house, a man who had a lorry, and begged him to help. They both took me down to Evelina Children's Hospital in Southwark and I remember her carrying me in and that's all – I must have passed out. When I woke up they said I had quinsies really bad, abscesses on both sides of my tonsils and they'd burst. If Gracie hadn't done that what she did, I'd have died.

Evelina Children's Hospital was a little Victorian building and they kept me in there for two weeks. There was a matron who had the biggest hat I'd ever seen in my life and all the nurses were dressed in white. The thing that struck me most was how clean it was, with women scrubbing the floor on their hands and knees. I was on a small ward with a window and I used to look out and see the big buildings all around. I had a little bed and a little side table with a drawer for my belongings, which wasn't much. People were allowed to visit, but not very often, because the matron was very strict and a bell would ring and she'd make all the visitors leave. Gracie came to see me a few times, but my mother didn't, because she was so ground down with all the things she had to deal with in her life.

I actually liked being in hospital, to be honest. It was like a holiday after sharing a bed with my mam and sister in a cramped, damp house and all the fights and arguments between my brothers – and here I was, in my own little bed. Everything was so clean, no bugs to bite me and they served the most wonderful food I'd ever had in my life. At home we had to share everything and there was never enough to go round – here they served good portions and I could have a whole plate of minced beef and potatoes to myself and it was like a fucking feast. It was like I'd been starving my whole life and this was the first time I'd eaten properly. The nurses must've thought I was a fucking feral child, the way I scoffed the lot and licked the plate after.

After a few days of treatment, I was allowed out of bed and could look at the few children's books they had there – it was the first time I'd seen a book, at least one with pictures in it. I wasn't allowed outside until they sent me home, but the strangest thing was, I found it so much easier to talk after that. I never again spoke words funny and I pronounced all my words correctly – so I must have had the abscesses in my throat for a long time, it must've been something to do with my tonsils why I couldn't talk proper to start with.

They said it could've been something to do with diet – there wasn't a lot of food back then, no processed stuff like today and, in a large family, everything had to be shared round. I didn't get a lot of fruit – I never seen a banana nor a fucking pineapple nor nothing like that. I mostly ate liver and streaky bacon and onions and potatoes. Pigs' trotters and jellied eels were a treat, like something you'd have on a Sunday. I did have lots of greens, though, like cabbage and spinach and broccoli, but there was no tinned food for the dogs, so we had to buy manky horse meat and sheep's heads for them. The sheep's heads had to be boiled and they stank the whole house out for fucking days.

There were a few luxuries every now and then, like butter and chicken, but it was mainly at Christmas time from our neighbour, Mrs Moyes, or some other special occasion. I hardly ever saw an egg and I mostly had to eat stew. My dad liked fish bloaters and he used to eat them a lot. He'd cut off their heads and cook them up, but they stank the house out worse than the fucking sheep's heads and I'd have to get out somewhere until the horrible smell went away.

My mother, Grace Maud Fryer, was from Camberwell and my father, William Killick, was from Rotherhithe, so I suppose we weren't strictly Eastenders, more south-east Londoners. My mother was a seamstress before she got sick, and worked in a factory up Bermondsey way, sewing pinafores, and my father worked on the railways. I had it hard when I was growing up, there were six of us and my mother was ill a lot of the time – she caught the tuberculosis from my father, who had it before her and passed it on, even though he recovered himself. We would hear her coughing up blood and mucus at night, Gracie and me, as we tried to sleep in the room with her. It's a fucking miracle we didn't get it as well.

My father caught the tuberculosis from working the night shift on the railway. The depot was at the Bricklayers Arms at the bottom of the Old Kent Road and he used to load cargo onto the trains. One night, it was so dark he fell down a big pit and no one knew where he was. All his teeth got knocked out and he lay there all night long, till they found him the next morning. He was really ill after that and he had to stay at home for a long time, with my mother looking after him. We didn't know he had tuberculosis in the beginning and Mam was doing everything for him and was very close to him all the time. When she found out what it was, she made sure we were careful and didn't get too near him, but it was too late for her. He had his own cup that was marked with a piece of thread and she'd make us wash our hands and faces all the time. She worried so much, she put herself in danger to protect us. She eventually had to take him to the hospital, because he wasn't getting any better – by which time she'd caught the disease from him. But she didn't know it.

This was one of the worst times for us because, even though we were used to being poor, with Dad out of work, we had no money at all coming in and the house was falling apart too, with distemper peeling off the walls and damp and draughts everywhere. They were very dark times and my brothers tried to help out, even though they were only young, and Gracie too. Mother was getting ill, but she didn't let on, like she was pretending to herself it wasn't happening. She just carried on as normal and got a job scrubbing shop floors to try and earn a bit extra for us, even though she was beginning to spit up blood. She might have survived if she'd been treated sooner, but if she was in hospital she wouldn't have been able to care for Dad and look after us. She was the heart and soul of our family.

Every little bit of money counted, from wherever it came. My mother was a strict Catholic and frowned on villainy of any kind, but I think she might have turned a blind eye to what my brothers got up to while Dad was ill. As the saying goes, a gift horse is never a bad colour! My father did get better and was released from hospital and went back to work on the railway as soon as he could, because we needed the money. But the damage to my mother was already done.

My eldest brother, Tommy, was sixteen years older than me and he was a right tearaway, make no mistake. I remember so many times being sent to fetch him from billiard halls and pubs and he wouldn't come and, when he did, he'd have a fight in the street on the way home. It made the rest of us tough as well, though, because he'd pick on us too and sometimes we'd get a hiding from him. Tommy was a heavy drinker and he loved fighting. He was always picking on my other brothers and then it would kick off, and I mean real fighting, not just arguing – glass would get broke and chairs smashed and it'd be fucking bedlam.

Tommy would get into fights in pubs every time he went into one, and I don't think he ever lost and he never got into trouble with the law – which was a fucking miracle, wasn't it? Or maybe it was just because he was a lucky cunt and never got caught. But he was a right bastard, there's no two ways about it – I always got on well with Gracie and my older brothers, Johnny and Jimmy, but not with Tommy. He was aggressive and violent and brought a lot of trouble to our family. There was never any peace in the house with Tommy around.

So you see, I grew up seeing my brothers fighting, it was as everyday as eel-pie and liquor to me. My mother was a bit of a fighter too, I suppose it was because her mother was Irish. I remember once we had a Welsh woman living next door to us and she got into an argument with my mother and set three Alsatians on her. Mam got away from the dogs and back into the house, then she started throwing ceramic flower-pots through the window at them. I remember the fuckers yelping and running off down the street, then she ran back out and grabbed hold of the Welsh sort, just as she was going back into her house. She dragged the bint back out by the barnet and knocked two types of fuck out of her! When Tommy came home and found out, he went round the house and done over her old man. The Welsh bird ended up having my mother arrested and she was bound over to keep the peace. But the cunt didn't dare grass Tommy, because she knew he'd only come back for her. This was normal for me growing up – I thought everybody lived like this.

My mother was a tall woman with thick brown curly hair and blue eyes. Like I said, she was a devout Catholic, like the Irish she came from, and always slept with a rosary above her bed. Tommy and Gracie both went to Catholic school, but times got so hard and life got so difficult, by the time the rest of us arrived, we couldn't go to the same school – I don't know why, maybe it had something to do with money, but it wasn't something that was of much concern to me at the time.

As I said, my mother was very strict before she got really ill. She didn't smoke nor drink and was brought up strict herself. If I got out of hand when I was young, she'd get a big cane and beat me, so I wouldn't do it again – or she'd lock me in the coal cellar until I learned my lesson. I remember when I was five or six, I let the dog out the front of the house and he chased a geezer who was riding past on a bicycle. The dog tore all his trousers and my mother had to pay for them to be invisibly mended. While she was walloping me with the cane, it caught me across the face and split the front of my lip, which swelled up and made me look a right fucking sight for a long time after.

My mother ruled the house with her cane, but she wasn't a bad woman – it was just what she was born into. I remember seeing her washing the clothes in a big tin bucket on the table. She'd scrub them on a washboard, then put them through a mangle, with a bucket behind to collect the water. Sometimes she would sit at the front window and eat peanuts. We had no electricity and, one night, it was so dark I tripped over a heavy metal shovel and knocked it onto her leg – the wound never healed properly and she had an ulcerated leg for the rest of her life.

I don't remember much about Mam's family, except she said she had a brother who stole some butter from the docks and, as a punishment, he was put in the army and sent to the front line during the Great War, where he got

killed. She also had a sister called Lizzy. Lizzy had five children and she used to have to clean steps and shop floors to
earn money to feed her family. One of her sons was called
Dennis and he liked listening to a radio programme called
The Man in Black; it was a geezer with a spooky voice telling
creepy stories for boys. One show described how the man
in black escaped from a trap by using his belt and, when
Lizzy went home that day, she found Dennis hanging from
his bunk by his belt. There was a little pool of water on the
floor underneath him. Lizzy was never the same after that
and she died herself within a year.

My father was a tall man with dark hair. He fought in the
Great War too and was gassed in the trenches and nearly
died. He received the Mons Star medal for bravery. He
was always working – he had to, to keep six children. The
bigger the family grew, the longer he worked. He would
bring home bundles of wood for the fire and anything else
he could scavenge from the railways to keep us going, and
I was his favourite. He wasn't strict like my mother and
I could wind him round my little finger. I got away with
murder when it came to my dad; he was always kind and
I used to try to play Mam and him off against each other.

All I know about dad's family is he had a sister who also
lived in Rotherhithe – she was married to a violent drunk
who ended up throwing her out through a window and
she was impaled on the iron railings outside. She died.

My sister Gracie was fifteen years older than me and
very prim and proper. She never liked all the violence
and criminal activities that went on with my brothers; she
and Tommy hated each other. They were close in age and
she couldn't stand the way he got drunk and threw her

make-up and stuff all over the floor for no reason. He did it just to get at her and make her walk out of the house. Gracie always used to work. She'd come home after school and scrub stone steps and run errands for money and, when she left school, she went to work in a factory making tin cans, where she had an accident and lost one of her fingers and, for some reason, she was never able to have children after that. Don't fucking ask me why – maybe it was some kind of shock or trauma thing.

Gracie got a little bit of compensation money for her finger and she done one of the only things in her life that went against her practical nature, she bought Mam a second-hand piano. Now, Mam couldn't play the piano, but Gracie could – don't ask me where she learned it, but she knew how to bang out a few tunes, so maybe she bought the piano for herself and just said it was for Mam so no one would think she was being extravagant. No one else in the street had a piano and you should have seen the neighbours' faces when it was delivered. They must've thought we'd won the fucking football pools or something. They all came round to have a look at it and Mam used to polish it like it was a diamond. She was so proud of it because it was the kind of thing only posh people had and she loved to tell everybody how her daughter bought it for her.

Sometimes, when Tommy wasn't fighting, he'd do a little tap dance while Gracie played and people would come in the house and gather round it and have a sing-song. There wasn't any television in them days and a piano was some-thing special. Gracie left the tin-can factory after her finger got cut off and she went to work in an ammunitions factory for a while, before being hired by Woolworths, where she got herself promoted up to the grade of supervisor – that was Gracie, always on the up-and-go.

She also worked as an air-raid warden when the war started, going round with a torch at night. It was a dangerous job, but Gracie didn't mind that, she had to always be doing something. I suppose it got her out of the house, away from the violence of my brothers and the coppers coming round all the time. She met this geezer called Mark, who was another air-raid warden. He was from Sheffield and, because of his accent, my mother though he was a foreigner. Mam would answer the door when he knocked – 'Is Grey there?' That's what he called Gracie.

'Gracie, the foreigner's 'ere.'

He took me and Mam and Ronnie up north to Sheffield once and they gave us tripe to eat. We didn't stay there long.

Jimmy was four years older than me and the quietest of my brothers. He tried not to get involved in the crime stuff, but that was impossible when Tommy was around. Johnny was my favourite brother and one of the nicest people you could ever hope to meet. He was ten years older than me and he joined the army when he was eighteen to get out of the poverty. He was sent to Iceland first, then he was posted to Burma and fought in the jungle with the Gurkhas. He loved my mother and he always sent her gifts and cards, and when he came home on leave he always brought her something expensive from his travels with the army. Once, he brought back a locket with his photo in it and Mam gave it to me as a keepsake. I always wore that locket round my neck with the picture of Johnny in it, all through the war and even when I was evacuated. I never took it off.

Here, listen to this – Sir Michael Caine was born in Rotherhithe and moved to Camberwell like us. He was two years younger than me and went to school with a mate of mine called Patrick Connolly, whose nickname was 'Sixer'. Caine was called Maurice Micklewhite then, and his nickname was 'bubbles', on account of his curly hair. His mother was a charlady and his father was a Gypsy fish porter. I knew him when he was growing up in Camberwell because he used to hang round Camberwell Gate and the Elephant and Castle. My brother Tommy chased him down the street with a shotgun once – I don't know why, it didn't take much to get Tommy going. He trained as a boxer and that's what he should have become, if it wasn't for the fucking war. I'm not sure what was said or what happened so, if you want to know, you'll have to ask Sir Michael.

I went to John Ruskin Street Primary School in Camberwell when I was five years old – in 1936. It was an old Victorian grey building, painted with distemper on the inside. I had a small wooden single desk, where I could lift the lid up to put stuff inside. I had one pen, which had a nib and there was an inkwell in a hole in the desk. It was a small school, with only three teachers and no school nurse nor office people nor anything like that. There was two classrooms, one for boys and one for girls, a tiny assembly hall and a yard for playtime. The yard was bare, with no trees nor grass nor shrubs and with outside toilets in one corner that were in a frightful fucking condition – no wonder the kids got sick all the time.

The school was very overcrowded, as most of the children from my area went there. I used to go to school in cut-down Wellington boots that left marks round my legs. All my clothes were made from fabric and rags that my mother got from the ragpickers, I never had no clothes that were bought new from a shop. All the boys had patches in the arses of their trousers and the collars of their shirts got turned round when they got frayed. Sometimes I'd get hand-me-downs from jumble sales that the better-off people had donated, but that wasn't very often, because they went very quick. My mother worked and, by the time she got there, they'd all be gone.

There weren't any school dinners either. I used to go home for dinner – I had half an hour, then back again afterwards. I was only taught the basics – reading, writing and some arithmetic. All the lessons were dictated by a teacher at the front of the class, with a big blackboard and the floor was made of stone. I learned how to tell the time from a big clock in the centre of the room and I also learned how to count and how to spell. As well as the reading, writing and 'rithmetic, I was also taught manners and how to be respectful. This didn't really sink in with me, because I thought, why should I be respectful to people who're trying to fuck me about? Anyway, I went through the motions, just to avoid getting belted with the fucking cane.

I didn't do no tests nor exams back then, they just taught me what they believed I needed to get by. They probably said to themselves, all them girls will just get pregnant and have chavvies and the boys will go into factories or prison or the army, so it was just a matter of doing it because the government said they had to. But they weren't all that worried if we learned the stuff or not.

Disease was a big problem. There was no antibiotics around then and, even if there was, we didn't have any way of getting them, and I can't remember ever seeing a doctor the whole time I was going to school. There were some terrible diseases about – tuberculosis was a major problem and pneumonia and scabies – they used to paint us with some home-made concoction that was blue if we got scabies and everybody knew if you had it, because you went around looking like a fucking smurf. Impetigo was also rife and was called 'school sores' because you could catch it easily from other children. Many kids had polio and I remember them having to wear heavy iron braces on their thin little legs. The braces kept their legs straight and they'd have to drag the fucking things along. I was running alive with nits and fleas – my mother used to use vinegar and paraffin to get rid of them, but it never worked all that well. Most of the chavvies were suffering from some kind of skin disease, due to the poor hygiene and poor diet and poor living conditions.

But, despite all that, I liked being at school. We used to have morning assemblies, where we'd sit on the floor and sing songs. I had a lot of close friends and, even though they were very strict and I'd often get punished, I still used to enjoy myself. I'd play whip-and-top, where I'd balance the top on a drain and pull the whip to get it spinning. I'd build little go-carts with old pram wheels and bits of scrap timber and run down the road in them, screaming and laughing. I had four or five good years at school, before the war started – that's when everything changed.

There were really big windows on either side of the assembly hall and they had to be taped up criss-cross from the inside, in case they got blown in during the bombings. They started teaching me how to use a gas mask and what to do when the air-raid sirens went off and I had to do role-playing on how to behave if I got evacuated – I was all the time taught about 'community spirit' and 'battling on' and 'doing the best for the country'. I tried to carry on as normal, but no two days were ever the same. Attendance wasn't regular, because we didn't know what the fuck was going to happen next. I'd go to school on a Monday and then the next day three or four pupils would be missing because they got killed. There were no social-welfare people to make sure I got proper schooling and, with so much destruction going on, it ain't any wonder that a lot of us didn't go there regularly.

In the end, I was expelled for beating up a big ginger girl who was older than me. You see, we were all living on rations and we didn't have much food to take to school with us. She was bullying the younger kids to get hold of their bits of food and she tried it on with me. I'm not being funny, but I'd seen so much violence I wasn't scared of anyone, so I hit her as hard and as fast as I could. Well, she never seen it coming and she was on the floor before she could even think of doing something about it.

I must have been about nine or ten at the time. They expelled me for it, but it didn't matter anyway, because education wasn't really a priority no more. I was soon to be evacuated and I never did go back to school after that.

The thing about it was, although south-east London was full of poverty and crime, everyone was in the same boat.

Everyone was suffering in the same way. Nobody had anything, so nobody lorded it over anyone else. We had respect for each other and we were friendly to each other and trusted each other, as long as nobody took liberties. Even the criminals had a code they lived by and everyone tried to pull together to get by.

As some geezer once said: 'It was a good life, if you didn't weaken.'

2

HOPPING DOWN IN KENT

We could never afford a holiday back then so, to get away in the summer, we'd all go hop picking in the fields down in Kent. I first remember going 'hopping' when I was about five. The whole family would go, except my father – he always had to work on the railway. Most of the people we knew in south-east London went too, everyone around us was poor and hop picking was a way to get away from the smog and the rats and earn a bit of money. My mother had to book in advance to go, if she didn't book in advance, someone else would take our place and she didn't want that.

Hopping would be going on all over Kent, and you could go to a different place every year. We went to Canterbury and Faversham and Sittingbourne and we stayed for the whole season. London families did this every year, from old grandmothers and grandfathers to young kids and babies. We had a song that went:

'If you go down hopping, hopping down in Kent
You'll see old Mother Riley, a-putting up her tent
With an e-i-o, e-i-o, e-i-e-i-o.'

We'd go at the end of summer, late August and September, for about six weeks. We would go on the train and we looked like refugees, because we had to take pots and pans and all the stuff we needed to cook our food over an open fire, like camping. There'd be loads of us on the station platform, waiting for the trains, all sitting on our bags like fucking hobos.

We'd get on the train in London, where it was dark and grey and noisy and dirty and we'd get off in the country, where it was all misty and quiet in the early morning. It looked like a foreign country to me, I never got used to the contrast. I was used to rows and rows of buildings close together and people everywhere and, all of a sudden, I was surrounded by open fields and trees and the sound of birds and animals. Even the air was different, you could breathe better, but the mist coming off the fields when it began to get warm and the size of the sky being so big fucking scared me.

The first few times I went down there, I used to go to the top of a hill and look round at all the fields and the little farmhouses and cottages dotted here and there. It was like I was Alice and I'd fell down the rabbit-hole and come out here. I'd never seen rows of apple trees nor seas of wheat, nor so many green-coloured things all together in one place.

We were allocated a 'pickers' hut', where we lived and slept. It was like a garden shed with windows, made of wood and full of hay. There were rows and rows of these huts, like some kind of concentration camp, and we were always given a big un, because of the size of our family. We didn't have any beds to sleep on, so my mother would take big sheets and sew them together and stuff them with hay to make a kind of huge mattress. And the only light we had when it got dark was from a small oil lamp.

There was never no shortage of hay, and the stuff was alive with bugs. I know we had bugs in London, but they were nothing compared to these fuckers. The spiders were so big they were wearing striped jerseys and the flying ants and horseflies bit us to fucking death and my mother put cotton wool in our ears at night to make sure nothing crawled into our brains. There were stories about earie-wigs getting into people's ears and sending them mad and, to this day, I can't stand them fucking earie-wigs. We didn't have any heating neither, but that wasn't so bad because it was summertime. It was mostly warm enough when we got up, which was always at sunrise – the earlier you got up, the more money you earned.

The Gypsies would come round and sell us rabbits and other stuff they'd poached. We were wary of them because they were fucking rough and they could handle themselves. They were always fighting – it was a way of life to them, bare-knuckle stuff – and the Gypsy boys would learn how to fight as soon as they could walk. Sometimes the hoppers would try it on with them for a bit of a wager, my brothers included, but they seldom won. It wasn't like fighting in London, where it could get right fucking evil at times and people would be tooled up. It could be brutal, but there were rules; if a man went down, the other man stood off him until he got back up. If he didn't get back up, then the fight was over.

We were a bit like Gypsies ourselves and I think that's how the country people looked on us, like thieves and urban Gypsies. We'd cook everything in a big pot over an open fire and we'd get cheap vegetables from the farmer and sometimes we'd have fish too, but not often. There was a little huckster's shop, where we could buy sterilised milk for the tea and a tiny pub that the men could go to. The local country people didn't like us much, because they thought we were dirty criminals. But it was good to get away from the slums and the dirt and the fleas and the rats for a while. However, I'd always be bored by the end of the six weeks and want to go back to London.

Although it was a break from the filth of London, the picking itself was hard work. The hop plants were called 'bines' and they grew up along wires or poles, which were arranged along drills called 'alleys' or 'aisles', that seemed to go on for fucking miles, like in a ploughed field. These would be divided up into 'sets' or 'drifts' and the pickers worked in gangs. I picked the hops in a gang with the rest of my family and we had a big cradle thing, like a kind of hammock that was held in place by two wooden beams. It was called a 'bin' and I was so little I had to sit on the side of it to pull the bind down and pick off the hops with the others to fill it. We'd be working for hours and hours in the sun and I'd get dents in me khyber from sitting on the thin wooden beams. I'd be too sore to sit in the same position the next day, so I'd sit on the other side of the bin and make new dents.

The vines were really tall and sometimes I couldn't reach to the top of them, so my brothers would pull them down for me and, once they were down, you had to be quick to get the hops off. The vines grew up along wires that sometimes cut into my hands while I was stripping them. I had to make sure no leaves got into the bin, otherwise the farmer wouldn't take them. A tallyman would come round to measure the hops and collect them in a 'poke', using a basket called a 'bushel', when the bin was full. He'd give us tally-sticks to prove how much we'd picked. We were paid according to how many bushels were in the bin. We always had to watch the fucking tallyman, because sometimes he'd be ordered by the farmer to take them heavy, meaning he'd try to squeeze a bushel tight down to a quart in the basket. But my brothers were wise to that scheme and he was afraid to try it on too often with them.

The 'tally', or rate, was usually about thruppence a bushel, that's three old pence, which would be just a little bit over one new penny today. I worked from seven in the morning till six in the evening and a good picker could earn about two quid for a sixty-hour week, taking breaks and rain into account. It was hard to pick the hops if it rained, because the rain made the fucking things slippery and that meant you didn't earn so much money. As well as that, the size of the hops varied all the time; on some vines they were as big as crab-apples and on others they were as small as fucking peas. The bad vines took longer to strip than the good ones and they were always more tangled and it could take five or six of them to make up a bushel.

The hop fields seemed huge to me when I was little. I was always frightened of getting lost in the aisles of tall vines. There were hundreds of aisles, up and down and, when I first went in there, it was so fucking dark it was like

I was in some limbo-land or something. The vines blocked out the sun until the hops were stripped off, then the light would shine through like a revelation. I always stuck close to my brothers, just in case they mislaid me and I couldn't find my way back – I felt so small in such a big place.

We'd have a little lunch break in the middle of the day, when we'd eat sandwiches my mother made with big thick slices of bread that looked like they were cut with a fucking hatchet. I could hardly get my mouth around them and they'd soon be all black and stink of hops from my hands, like I'd been boozing all day long.

At the end of the day, my hands would be all chapped and torn and my clothes would be filthy and my back and legs would be aching, but that's when me and my brothers would fuck off on the foraging, as we called it. That's when the fun started. We began by just scrumping the apples and pears – my brothers would shove me up the tree and I'd pick the fruit and throw it down. My brothers would sack it up and we'd carry it back – the carrying was the hardest part for me, the apples were heavy and I looked like one of Fagin's boys from *Oliver Twist*. Whatever we couldn't use ourselves, we sold to other pickers and we saved the money for when we got back to London.

Now, you must remember that my mother was a strict and devout Catholic and she would have had a fucking coronary if she knew what we were getting up to – and it wasn't long before we were going to the neighbouring farms to nick eggs and tomatoes and carrots and cabbages and turnips and parsnips and potatoes and onions and anything else we could find. It was like being in a free fruit-and-veg shop! We also got blackberries and strawberries and we never stole from the farm we were working on, because that would've got us thrown off. It was always a long walk to the other farms – we'd be gone for hours into the twilight and the dark. My mother was suspicious when all this stuff started coming back with us, but we told her we just done extra chores for the farmer. I don't know if she believed us or not, but she liked boiled egg sandwiches so she said no more.

Most of the pickers would all eat together round a communal cooking fire, singing and stuff. It was a way of sticking together and getting through the hard work. But we stayed on our own when we were eating, because we had so much stuff and I think Mam didn't want people asking where we got it all. She'd build a fire with bricks round the base and firewood on the inside and a big pot like a witches' cauldron hanging over it. She'd throw all the vegetables into it and boil them up. After we'd eaten, we'd go across and join in the singing about the hopping and about missing London.

'Now some say hopping's lousy, I don't believe that's true
We only go down hopping, to earn a bob or two
With an e i o, e i o, e i e i o.'

We found a dairy once and I tried to get away with a milk churn, but it was too fucking heavy and I had to leave it – broke my heart! We also came across an idea on how to catch pigeons: we'd nick bits of wire and string from the farms and wind them through the tree branches, with plaits and knots, over and over. It took fucking ages to do, but it worked like a kind of home-made snare or gin, as they used to call it. We'd put little bits of bread inside and once the birds went in for the bread, they wouldn't be able to find their way back out. I'd get up the tree and hand them down to my brothers, who'd wring their necks. My mother would make pigeon pie with them – this was a kind of pigeon stew thing and Mam would make a makeshift pastry from flour and sterilised milk from the local huckster shop, which was miles away and sold stuff like the porridge that was like fucking gruel and loose tea and it was always my job to walk there. Mam would serve the pigeon pie with potatoes and it weren't half bad sometimes.

Once, my brother Tommy got the bright idea to steal a pig, so we could have pork. My mouth watered at the thought of it – roast pork, what a fucking feast that would have been. Anyway, we went to this farm and selected the biggest pig there. We tied a rope round its neck and tried pulling it, but the fucker wouldn't move. Tommy kicked it up the arse, but it still wouldn't move. I even sat on its back and tried to ride it out of the farm, but that didn't work neither and the bastard thing was grunting and squealing all over the place and made so much noise it alerted the fucking farmer. He came out with a shotgun in his hand and we had to leg it before we caught an arseful of buckshot. When we thought about it later, we agreed we were too fucking greedy – it would have been easier to nick a piglet; we could've just grabbed it and ran.

We also tried to nick chickens, but they made more noise than the fucking pig and the farmers and their dogs always kept a close eye on them because of foxes and the like, so we gave up trying. No wonder the locals didn't like us – we fleeced them of anything they didn't have nailed down.

What they didn't understand was, it was a way of life to us. We did it in London to survive and we couldn't stop just because we were in the fucking country. In London, we had to fight to get the things we needed to survive; if we didn't do it, we'd have starved, because nobody was going to hand it to us on a plate.

A lot of people in the hopping huts had 'principles', which meant they were too scared to go stealing and they lived on potatoes and porridge. You should have seen the state of them, they were half starved and gaunt and feeble-looking and filthy – and so were their children. They didn't realise that the fucking farmers were exploiting us as slave labour, which amounted to stealing the fair wages we should have been paid, so it was only fucking right to steal stuff back from them – that's what my brothers said, in any case.

There wasn't much in the way of hygiene while we were hop picking, because there was no baths or washing facilities. If I wanted to wash, I had to use the local streams and I was usually too busy working and stealing for that. There was one outside tap between so many people and there was always a queue. My mother would wash our clothes in a tub which she kept in a barn. She'd boil some water in an iron kettle and then wash the clothes with a bar of soap and a scrubbing board. There was an old wringer in the barn which she used as well. It was hard work and Mam did most of it at night, when we were away pilfering.

There was no proper toilets neither, just an outdoor makeshift thing and it stank and was unhygienic, even to us, which is understandable, considering how many fucking people used it. I usually ended up going in the fields; it was cleaner and more private that way. But still, in spite of everything, hopping was all right. We found ways to enjoy ourselves, no matter how small – there was a little local pub in the main village and the men would go there on a Sunday, which was the one day off. My dad would sometimes come down on a Sunday to see how we were and he'd go to the pub with my older brothers.

By the end of the summer the villagers fucking hated us – I mean, with a vengeance. They saw us as vermin, worse than foxes and rats. You'd think we were foreigners or from another fucking planet, the way the cunts looked at us. I'd hear them saying out loud to each other as I passed them by: 'Watch them cockney bastards!'

It made it all the easier to steal from them. If they were a bit more civil and not so fucking rude and ignorant, we might have thought twice about robbing their vege- tables. If I went into the horrible little huckster shop to buy milk and butter, it was like a bad smell had come in the fucking door. They'd grab all the stuff and put it behind a wire partition, so I couldn't touch it without asking. They never did that to their own people, just to us. And they'd never touch me, like when they were giving me back change. They'd put it on the counter, as if they might catch some fucking London disease off me or something. It was the same in the pub for the men, the locals would pass remarks and this wouldn't go down well with my brothers and there'd be a fight. My brothers always got kicked out and then they'd be banned for the rest of the season.

Sunday was a holy day to my mother. We'd have to put on whatever 'good' clothes we had and traipse off to the village church and say our prayers and sing. Then, after we'd thanked God and begged His forgiveness for our sins, we'd go out in the afternoon selling the stuff we'd stolen during the week.

'Now the hopping's over and all the money's spent
I wish I never ever went a hopping down in Kent
With an e i o, e i o, e i e i o.'

When the hopping was done and we'd been back in London for a few days, it always seemed like our trip to the country was a dream and it never really happened. In the last week or so while I was down there, I'd be getting fed up with it and wanting to get back home. But, once I was back to 'normality' for a while, I'd be wishing I was back down in the open fields and fresh air. By the time Christmas came, it would have faded from my mind like the mists that used to rise from the fields.

Christmas wasn't like it is today – we were very poor and we couldn't even afford a Christmas tree. I remember the first time I saw one all lit up, when I was invited to the house of one of our neighbours, Mrs Moyes, whose first name was Violet. She'd just moved into the area and we thought she must have been rich or something – well, better off than us at least, because she had her own telephone and everything. She said her husband died and left her some money and I think she felt sorry for my mother, not having anything to give us. The tree went right the way up to the ceiling and the smell of pines filled the whole room and it was decorated with little wooden Father Christmases, tied on with red ribbons. I can remember it to this day, it was the most beautiful thing I'd ever seen, with the room all lit by candles because there was no electricity and everything looking so cosy and warm.

I often visited Mrs Moyes at Christmas time after that, and I'd sit and help her make paper-chain decorations and she'd let me take some home to our house to brighten things up. We didn't get presents at Christmas, we didn't have enough money for things like that, but we weren't sad because of it; we knew the score and we knew not to expect anything. The best my mother could do was a chicken sometimes on Christmas Day for a treat, and bread pudding for afters, which was easy to make with the left-over bits of bread.

I have fond memories of Mrs Moyes, she was nice to me and she seemed to be able to get anything she wanted. She owned the whole house she lived in with just her daughter, who had lots of uncles who used to visit all the time and she taught me how to dye my hair with peroxide and get it right. When I was eight years old, she took me to the Regal Cinema in Camberwell Green to see *The Wizard of Oz*. I'd never been to the pictures before and it was amazing. This was in the days before television, so seeing a film at the cinema was unbelievable. Here I was, sitting on these cushioned seats, with loads of people about and a great big screen in front of me with pictures and sound and, when the film changed from black-and-white to colour, I just couldn't believe my eyes.

It was so real to me that, when the house fell on the Wicked Witch of the East, I was so petrified of her that I started screaming and ran out of the cinema. Mrs Moyes couldn't catch me and I ran all the way home, not stopping even once. I suppose you could say, at a push, that I was a bit like Dorothy myself, even if I wasn't exactly an orphan.

But I liked Mrs Moyes; she was such a lovely woman.

3

THE WAR IN LONDON
AND EVACUATION

As I said, my eldest brother Tommy was a very violent man. I remember being about eight or nine, the war had just started, and me and my mother were out looking for him. We found him in a local pub and he was beating up some Canadians that had come over here. They came rolling out through the pub doors, as we stood there – one, two, three, four, then Tommy after them. He was a right fucking hooligan. He went into the army when he was called up, but he jumped ship, just as it was pulling away from the quay, and swam ashore. He said he didn't want to leave our mother, because he was worried about her, but he ended up bringing her more stress, because the redcaps, the military police, were always after him.

They'd come to the front door and he'd run out the back, through the yard and over the guinea-pig cages he'd stacked up against the wall. He was convinced a woman down the road, who delivered wet fish, was grassing him up. They eventually caught him and, after doing time in the glasshouse, he was put on the guns – that meant he was made to work the anti-aircraft guns. Being on the guns meant you were a direct target for the German planes and you had no cover from the falling bombs and the mortality rate was high. Tommy survived, with nothing worse than a perforated eardrum. I told you the bugger was lucky.

Johnny was in Burma with the 14th Army, fighting in the jungle, Jimmy was in the RAF and Gracie worked in an ammunitions factory on the Old Kent Road. She told me she was assembling tanks for the front line, but she wouldn't talk about it to Tommy because he kept asking her if she could get him a couple of machine guns. She got fed up of Tommy being on at her about guns, so she left the weaponry and joined the Land Army – she was good at it too, because she was well bossy and she went quickly up through the ranks to become a forelady. She really should have stayed home to look after Mam while she was ill, but she had to get away from Tommy's violence and drinking.

I have vivid memories of the war – we didn't have a shelter in our street, so we used a brick outhouse to escape the flying shrapnel. Shrapnel was very dangerous and was always falling from the shot-down planes. Once, in 1940, our house was hit by an oil bomb. Most of us were in the brick shelter, but my dad worked nights and, when he came home, he saw the house ablaze and thought we were inside. He rushed into the flames and only realised we weren't there when he heard my mother screaming: 'William! William! William!'

She was falling apart at the thought of losing him. When they carried him out, his clothes were on fire and he was burned all up his legs and was taken to Lewisham Hospital. Then the fucking hospital took a direct hit and he was buried alive. He had to be dug out and, luckily, he survived, but he had to walk with the aid of a stick for the rest of his life.

The smell of oil and burning is branded into my memory for ever – I'll never forget it. I can smell it to this very day and I'm afraid of thunder as well. The fire brigade came and put the fire out, but it left a huge gaping hole in the roof and we had to carry on living there for three months, as there was nowhere else for us to go. The rain came down and saturated everything and it was just plain fucking miserable. Eventually, the council gave us another house, down the road in Camberwell Gate. Camberwell Gate ain't there no more neither – because they tried to clean up the slums after the war and knocked everything down and built new houses and roads.

Camberwell Gate was a wider road than Cyril Street, with bigger houses. They were tall, townhouse-style places and we shared a garden with the neighbours. By this time, my dad was feeling better and he went back to work on the railways. I used to play with my friends in John Ruskin Street, where I went to school – we'd go there and pick up bits of shrapnel and stuff from the German planes that had been shot down. It was all over the place after the air-raid wardens gave the all-clear, and we were able to sell it for a few pennies to the scrap-metal men and we could also sell the strong glass from the cockpits, which could be recycled. Sometimes when my brothers took the glass off to sell it, they'd come back with rings that were made out of the stuff for my mother. They weren't kids' rings or anything like that, the glass had been melted down and re-formed and moulded with a tiny stone in the middle. They were real pretty things and my mother loved them. Everything was re-used and nothing was wasted.

We had this old two-channel British Relay Wireless for news about what was going on with the bombings. I don't know why they called it 'wireless', because it had wires coming from it all over the fucking place. We had to pay so much a week for it and it was really just a speaker in a wooden casing with an arched top. Ours was kept on a little shelf on the wall, so we wouldn't damage it. I don't know how much it cost, but everyone on our street had them. It had two little knobs on the front, one for the volume and one for the tuning, and it played music in the mornings and news and stuff at intervals through the day. It had to be charged up with an accumulator and Dad used to take it down to the local oil shop every couple of days. The oil shop sold stuff like coal and coke and oil for lamps and everyone would go there to recharge their wirelesses.

As well as the news, we'd get a few programmes like *Music While You Work* and *Family Favourites* and sometimes we'd hear famous people like Gracie Fields and Anna Neagle and Glenn Miller and even Winston Churchill. Now and again, a broadcast would cut in from Lord Haw-Haw, who was really a Fascist geezer called William Joyce. They called him Lord Haw-Haw because of his posh voice; he'd come on the radio and say: 'Jairmany calling, Jairmany calling. I know where your Elephant and Castle is. I know where to get you, we are coming for you.'

It was mostly propaganda and it didn't scare the adults, but it frightened the shit out of us kids because it was like he was saying, it don't matter whether or not you have blackouts, we'll still get you.

We also had a magic lantern – a very primitive projector box with an oil lamp inside it. Dad turned the handle on the side that changed the pictures in a slide and the light projected the picture onto a white sheet that we used to hang up for a screen. There wasn't many of them around and we were lucky to have one. It was another form of family entertainment for us, like the piano, in the days before television. We had to find ways to occupy ourselves, especially during the blackouts. Some people would go to the pub and stay there all night – you couldn't walk around the streets or nothing because you couldn't see where you were going and you might end up getting blown to fucking bits by the Luftwaffe. People who went to the pub couldn't just go in and out when they liked – once they were in, they had to stay in till closing time, then the lights would all be switched off and they could leave. But my mother, with her religious rules, wouldn't have none of this going to the pub. Only Tommy was a drinker in our family and nothing could be done to stop him.

There were always dead bodies around the next day, after a bombing. I remember walking over towards the railway once with some other kids and I could see what looked like a massive black sheet. We went to take a closer look, but the soldiers wouldn't let us get too near. We were able to see arms and legs sticking out – pieces of bodies, just lying there – everywhere. It was all the dead people from the previous night's bombing.

Another time, I remember coming home from somewhere for dinner. I don't know how, maybe they'd forgotten to put up the barrage balloons or something, but this fucking German plane flew down low and started machine-gunning us. I remember all the people, including me, running for our lives and the sound of the bullets hitting the street and the chunks of masonry and brick and shrapnel flying everywhere. I remember the screaming and I don't know if anyone got hit or not, because I just kept running and running and running – until I came to my house and ran inside and put my hands over my ears until the noise stopped. I was to see some of my friends die like that, when they were just trying to get home from playing or from the shops or wherever they were, trying to live normally.

A lot of people died in London during the war and special clean-up crews would come round the streets to gather up the bodies, if there wasn't any family left to do it. They'd take the bodies off to be disposed of and the rag-and-bone men would come after them and collect everything they could from the destruction. They'd sift through the debris for clothes and anything else they could find. If they got there before the clean-up crews, they'd even take the clothes off the dead people. You might think this was a despicable thing to do, but people in London were surviving any way they could and the clothes were no use to the dead, but they could be put to use by the living, that's the way they looked at it. Everything was in short supply and nothing could be wasted. When a house got bombed, a big black sheet thing was put up outside, so we couldn't see the carnage until the house was cleaned out and the bodies removed. Sometimes the rag-and-bone men helped the clean-up crews to do this, in exchange for the clothes.

We got used to the sight of death everywhere. Once I was playing in the park with my brother Jimmy and the sirens went off to warn us the bombs were coming. As we ran for home, I could see this German plane dropping bombs not so far away from us – then it suddenly erupted in flames like a ball of fire and the noise was fucking deafening as our guns shot it down. I stopped running and stood watching, like I was mesmerised, and I could see the German pilot coming down with his parachute. Instead of running on home, I ran to where he was coming down and, when I got there, the people were all round him like animals. I believed I hated the Germans for what they were doing to me, but I was too young to really understand what real hate meant – now I could see it for myself. The crowd steamed into him and almost tore him apart. There were so many people round him in the end that I couldn't see him at all. By the time the police came, there wasn't much left but a big bloodstain on the ground.

I knew why they did it – or I thought I did. The German pilot represented everything we hated. He represented the reason why we'd suffered so long in the slums of southeast London. It wasn't nice to watch, but it was only one of the many things that weren't nice in those days. It hardened me, in a time when I wasn't much more than skin and fucking bone, living on my nerves. I looked so bad that people would say to my mother: 'Is Eileen all right? Are you sure?'

It wasn't just the physical effects of the war; the psychological effects were just as bad. The Germans would bomb us and send us running to the cold, dark shelters in the middle of the night – then the all-clear went and we'd come out from the shelter and the skies would be completely red.

It was like you'd emerged from the belly of Jonah's stinking whale – into fucking hell. The air would be thick with smoke and fire and I can't remember seeing the stars at night until I was evacuated. We'd trudge back home, tired and weary, but, no sooner than we were back in our beds, the sirens would go off again and we'd have to get up and run back out of the house. It was meant to break our spirit, along with the constant noise and shooting, and I was a nervous wreck all the time and as thin as a fucking rake.

It's a little-known fact that many people killed themselves during the Blitz in London. People were terrified and their nerves were shattered and some of them thought that gassing themselves and their families was better than having to put up with it any longer. It happened all the fucking time, but the authorities kept it quiet, because it was bad for public morale.

This was the worst point of the war, with doodlebugs and screaming bombs and all sorts of shit being dropped on us. You sometimes see television programmes showing all the people down in the Underground, happy and jolly and singing like Vera Lynn – it wasn't like that at all. Oh, we shared what we had, like jam and tea and stuff but, if people sang, it was out of fucking fear. Lots of us would be crammed in there, some even down on the train lines. It smelled of sweat and urine and the young chavvies would be screaming and the women praying and it seemed like the whole world was coming to an end outside. They used to say, 'You won't even hear the bomb that gets you.'

The bombings maimed a lot of people too, and you'd see cripples everywhere, missing arms or legs. The mental effect was worse, people were walking around all gaunt, because they didn't get any sleep and were ... properly. They looked drained and worn from consta... waking in the night and running to the shelters. We had to run in the wind and rain and snow and a lot of people died from pneumonia. To this day I can still tell the different types of bombs that were dropped, just by the sound – the memory never leaves, of all the fear I felt back then. It comes back to me, just to think about it – the screaming bombs, the V2s, the oil bombs, the doodlebugs. The German planes made their own noise too, they didn't sound like the British planes – when they came it was like 'bom bom bom bom bom' and, as soon as we heard that sound, we'd all scatter.

One of the hardest things was the blackout. Across the whole city, every light had to be covered, every window and lamp. It was literally pitch-black and you couldn't see a fucking thing, even the smallest crack of light would be seen by a German bomber. Walking down the road in the blackout was near impossible, you couldn't see anything, and it was really dangerous because you could get run over or walk into things. So, when it was blackout time, we tried to stay indoors as much as possible and tried to make sure the blackout sheets and curtains were in place before it got dark, otherwise the wardens would come round and give us a bollocking. The wardens started putting white paint onto trees and lamp posts because loads of people hurt themselves bad by walking into them. They also painted the edges of the kerbs white, so you'd know where the road finished and the pavement began.

When the war started, my mother didn't want us to be evacuated – she didn't want to 'lose us', as she said. She

physically, and she tried to keep
...e summer of 1940 the bombing of
...d worse and we were constantly up
...nning to the shelters. I think the final
...he oil bomb hit our house and we had to
...in the roof for so long. I think it dawned on
her ... couldn't keep us safe, no matter what she did
and we ...be better off out of it. So, she sat Ronnie and me
down and explained why we were going to be sent away,
for our own safety. I remember crying and being scared I
was never going to see my family again.

The first time I was evacuated, it was 1941. I was ten
years old and Ronnie was seven. Mam got our few bits
of stuff together and I remember us standing on the platform of Liverpool Street station. The smoke and steam
was coming from the massive old locomotive and the
platform was packed and it seemed like we were so small,
in the middle of something that was very big. Parents
weren't allowed onto the platform with their children,
because there were just too many people. I remember
seeing hundreds of other kids just like me, standing on the
station, waiting to say goodbye. We had little cardboard
boxes with our gas masks inside, and some sandwiches
and a little brown case with all our worldly belongings,
which wasn't much because we only had a few clothing
coupons given to us each month and they didn't go far,
so everything got mended over and over again. Ronnie
had an old pair of shoes on, little short trousers and an old
shabby coat that someone gave to my mother. I remember
he was shivering and I don't know if it was because of the
cold or because of the fear. I was wearing an old dark coat

with a dress underneath and the usual cut-down Wellingtons. Our clothes were old, but Mam tried to get them as clean as she could so that we wouldn't look bad and be embarrassed at the other end.

We had tags round our necks with our names and other details on, like pieces of luggage. We all looked the same, confused and bewildered, and some kids were crying and begging for their mothers. Ronnie was worse than me because he was younger and didn't understand what was going on and why we had to leave home. I held on to his hand tight, because he was trying to run back off the platform. I remember looking round and seeing my mam behind a fence with loads of other mothers. They were all pressed up against the wire, trying to see their children and trying to wave goodbye. The mothers were crying too and that only made the kids worse. The level of feeling at that station was massive, because we were all thinking that this could be the last time we'd ever see each other. Nothing can describe the feeling of being ripped away from everything that was familiar to you. To make things worse, a siren sounded while we were waiting to board the train, but nobody moved, nobody ran for cover – we barely heard it and, to this day, I don't think I've ever felt anything like the emotion of that first evacuation.

There were care workers on the platform; they were called wardens who were there to help get the children out of London. They were going up and down and they must have had a register or something, because I heard them call out my name and Ronnie's and we had to go in single file onto the carriages, like sheep. Even though we were going single file, I never let go of Ronnie's hand for a second. One of the wardens came along and asked if we were related and I said he was my brother and he had to come with me. Ronnie was nearly hysterical and, after being taken away from his mother, there was no way I was going to let him be taken away from me too.

The train was packed. There were rows and rows of big seats with tiny little people, whose heads you could hardly see, sitting all forlorn on them. Nobody looked happy, although it was a lot quieter on the train than the platform. But you could still hear the muffled sobs while we waited for what seemed like for ever for the train to leave. I sat next to the window, with Ronnie beside me and the longer I sat, the more I wanted to jump up and run with him back to my mother. Each carriage had a woman warden and we weren't allowed to look up or down the train and we weren't allowed to move from our seat, only to use the toilet.

I was relieved when the train finally did get going. I couldn't bear to hear any more fucking crying and, after a while, I started to see fields and countryside come into view and I remember a huge sense of relief coming over me. Ronnie must have felt the same, because he began to brighten up as he started to see cows and sheep and things through the window. We had little cheese sandwiches that we ate on the way and I told Ronnie to pretend we were going hopping again like we used to do. The journey was a long one and it felt like we were on the train for fucking ever, because it kept stopping and names would be called out by the warden and children would get off at remote villages.

We never knew where we were going until we got there. Our stop was Bishop's Stortford, although we didn't know that at the time. To us, it was just somewhere in the country. Names were called out by the warden and about ten or fifteen of us got off the train in single file, with me still holding on to Ronnie's hand. The station was nothing like Liverpool Street, which was packed and noisy and full of smoke and steam and grey and grimy. But here it was different – it was all open and I could see the sky was so blue. That wasn't something I was used to seeing because, more often than not, the sky in London would be red with fire from the bombing and shooting and dusty and full of smoke and searchlights shining every fucking where.

There was a small station-master's office and nice wooden benches all painted green and it was so quiet, I could actually hear the birds – I half expected to hear the bombs falling on London in the distance, but there was nothing but silence, apart from the noise of us kids – like London was in another part of the world. We were led down a little country road and I could see so many trees in the distance and huge fields. I felt happy, which might sound strange after all we'd been through, but it was so peaceful and it looked like a brand-new world to me. We had to wait at a country crossroads for our bus to arrive, it was like a black minibus thing and I had a window seat again and I held on to Ronnie's arm. We drove along little country byways with fields on both sides and we saw all sorts of wild things, at least to us they were wild things, like goats and horses and ducks and pheasants and geese. I was actually excited – our mother was always with us when we went hopping, but this was different, this was like our very own private adventure.

The minibus took us to what looked like a church hall. I remember it being very dreary and not very exciting at all, not like the journey there. We were all led off the bus and into the place by the warden and all us little boys and girls were made to stand in rows to be looked at by the prospective 'fosterers'. There was loads of people in there waiting for us and they were sitting in the pews. It was very intimidating for us kids, being on display like that and being looked over like we was a piece of furniture or something. We weren't allocated to someone, like we thought we would be; the people were allowed to pick which children they wanted, like they were browsing in a fucking jumble sale.

They showed no emotions, not even a smile – it was fucking horrible. I've never felt so lost in my life. They were looking to see how useful we could be to them. It was like being an animal in a pet shop, the people had no regard for us at all, and you could end up anywhere. Also, because we'd come from the slums of London, we were treated like vermin, like we were covered in dirt and didn't know how to wash. The reason we were dirty was we didn't have baths, like the people in the country had. So, the first thing they did when they took us home was to make us wash ourselves from top to bottom so we wouldn't contaminate their fucking houses.

Ronnie and me were picked by two old maids, old spinsters, two grumpy old women who must've been in their sixties. They were never happy, all they did was sing hymns all day, and they only picked us so we could work for them on their old farm. They got us up and down cleaning constantly and they half starved us, the horrible cunts. It was non-stop, Ronnie had to clean out the chickens every day before he went to the school they sent him to, and I had to wash the floors and the dishes and the clothes with a washboard. We had a room in the attic and it was covered in cobwebs and running with spiders, like nobody had been up there in thirty fucking years, until we got there. We were fucking miserable.

It was a really old farmhouse; I reckon it must've been built when fucking Methuselah was a boy. I mean, I know we never had much in London, but this was like the land that time fucking forgot to me and Ronnie. They had oil lamps that they were too stingy to light, so we spent most nights in the fucking dark, which frightened Ronnie. They were strict too; they used to pull me by the hair into the kitchen to scrub the floor, when I wouldn't go. They'd only feed us porridge, nothing else, and the last straw came when we were out in the fields one day and we came across these apple trees. We were fucking starving, so I climbed up and chucked some down to Ronnie. We didn't know the trees belonged to the spinsters and they used to make crab-apple jam to sell in the village and, anyway, they said they couldn't walk far and the trees were a good ways away from the house.

Well, they could walk all right, because the fucking old cunts came and caught us. One old bitch got her walking stick and started trying to beat me out of the tree, while the other one had Ronnie by the ear on the ground. I tried to kick the stick out of her hand as I hung on tight to the branch, but she kept on swinging it and was literally

beating my fucking legs black and blue. I tried to grab the
stick and she grabbed my arm to pull me out of the tree,
she pulled so hard it felt like she'd yanked my arm out of
its socket. I fell out of the tree and on top of the old hag, she
broke my fall and I knocked the wind out of her. The other
one let go of Ronnie and grabbed me by the hair, then the
two of them marched us up the hill to the house and called
the authorities.

I swear to God, my arm hurt for weeks after that and I
really think she done me some damage. We were moved
on from the old farmhouse and the two stingy spinsters.
Needless to say, I was glad to go.

We were sent to live with a Mrs Cox, who also lived in
Bishop's Stortford, just down the road from the old hags,
and who was blind as a fucking bat. Mrs Cox wasn't as bad
as the spinsters, her heart was willing but she just wasn't
able to look after us. She was probably only in her fifties
or sixties, but to me she looked like she was a fucking
hundred. She was only small and had really thick glasses,
like milk-bottle bottoms, that made her eyes look weird.
But she was all right and I used to help her mix up batter to
make sausage toad and help her cook, because she couldn't
see fuck-all. She lived in a tiny little cottage, set back in
a lane in the middle of nowhere. But there was flowers
everywhere – she liked them and let them grow wild all
over the place. I think her husband died years before and
we did all the work for her, but we didn't mind too much,
because she treated us all right.

She had a mystery room in the cottage that she kept
locked. When you're young, your mind runs away with
you and I imagined all sorts of fucking things behind that

locked door. I tried to find out what it was, but every time I talked to her about it she'd just shut up and wouldn't say. So one night, after she went to bed, I crept round the cottage, trying to find the key that would let me into the room. I was trying all sorts of things in the lock, when she came up behind me and caught me red-handed. I thought I'd be in for it now and me and Ronnie would be sent on somewhere else, but she wasn't angry or nothing. Instead, she opened the door and took me into the room. It was like a shrine to her dead son inside. It had fine Persian carpets and the medals he'd won and other things that he played with when he was a boy. It was beautifully kept, nothing was dusty or dirty and she must've gone in there every day when we weren't about.

Mrs Cox liked me and I liked her. She even sent me and Ronnie to school for a bit. It wasn't a proper school, just something that was thrown together for all the children who'd been evacuated, because now there was far more kids in the village than before and they had to do something about it – but not much. It was just a church hall or community-centre type of place and there was only one teacher, who'd sit at the front and tell us off every few fucking seconds. If the teacher caught us talking, she'd come down and whack our fingers with a stick. There wasn't much talking, though, because us evacuated kids had been worn down so much we just kept quiet. The school officials looked on us with distaste and mistook our silence for insolence and called us scum. As well as the finger-rapping, they used to beat the evacuees a lot. But I didn't have no problems with them, because they couldn't keep me pinned down. They couldn't hit me if they couldn't catch me and I made sure the fuckers never did. But they complained to the authorities that Mrs Cox wasn't able to control me and I suppose they were right. So we got moved on again.

Mrs Cox had a friend called Mrs Plum. She was a horrible fat old bag who ran a pub down the road that had a massive picture of Lord Kitchener with his big handlebar moustache, pointing his finger and saying 'Your Country Needs You', and it had a candle underneath it that was always lit. The pub was called The Hoops and was more like a country inn or something and there was no electricity. I remember it was full of wooden tables, where people would come and sit and Mrs Plum would take their orders. Customers would ring the bell and she'd come out with a jug of ale for them. Mrs Cox spoke to her one day when she went to visit and Mrs Plum agreed for us to come stay with her, because she had a daughter and she wanted some company for her.

Her daughter's name was Barbara and she was four years older than me. She was really timid and quiet, the complete opposite of me. But she was nice to me and I had some fun there because, for the first time in my life, I actually got to be a girl. I'd grown up with a load of brothers and my mam never had the time nor the inclination to teach me about girlie things and Gracie moved out as soon as she could, so this was a kind of a revelation to me. Barbara showed me her make-up and her nice dresses and gave me a pair of silk stockings. Even though I was only about ten or eleven, I felt proper grown up. I tried all the lipsticks and different styles with my hair, using homemade rag-rolling. The dresses were too long and the shoes were too big, but I still tried them on and admired myself in the mirror.

Shoes were a special thing with me. I never had a proper pair, only old hand-me-downs from the jumble sale with holes in the soles, or cut-down Wellingtons. I always wanted a pair of shoes with heels – I remember in London I used to go past this shoe-menders and there was this gorgeous pair of tap shoes in the window. They were black and shiny, with a little heel and a big black bow in the front. Every day, on the way home from school, I used to press my nose up against the glass, just to get a good look at them. Until one day they were gone – someone had bought them, and I was heartbroken.

Mrs Plum was married to an ignorant old farmer. He was a miserable cunt and never talked to me and Ronnie – he talked at us. He'd shout and holler at us about cleaning out the chickens and milking the fucking cows, which I wouldn't go near, because I didn't trust the big fuckers. And God fucking help us if we messed things up, because he'd swing his great fist at us and try to clump us, but I was always too fast on my feet for the bastard.

Mrs Plum was all right, I suppose, though she was very strict, but at least she fucking fed us. By this time, my rebellious side was coming out bad in me. I didn't like the pub that much, apart from Barbara's clothes and stuff, and I showed it. Mrs Plum kept loads of geese and it was my job to get them into their pen. The fuckers never wanted to go in and I'd have to chase them round all over the place. After a while, they started to chase me back, horrible fuckers, pecking and biting at me, so I had to whack them with a stick and they made a hell of a fucking din. Mrs Plum didn't like me doing this and she didn't like me dressing up in her daughter's clothes; I think it offended her country morals or some fucking thing, because she used to tell me off about dressing above my age and would constantly nag me and preach to me about it – it was no wonder her daughter was so timid, if that's what she had to put up with all her life. It all came to an end when I started going through the clothes and stuff when they weren't looking, even though I'd been forbidden to – and I started nicking bits and pieces, like lipsticks and bows for my hair. Mrs Plum called me a little 'tea leaf' and she got in touch with the authorities, who contacted Gracie. She slagged me off rotten to Gracie, telling her I was going to grow up to be a right handful. What a fucking understatement! There was nothing else for it – we had to go back to London.

Although me and Ronnie was made to work and weren't fed properly by some of the people who took us in, I suppose we were quite lucky in a way, because that wasn't the worst thing could've happened to us. I met other children later who were badly abused while they were evacuated – it was a fucking disgrace! Remember, the government never did any checks on those people, like would be done today, it was just a case of you went with anyone who'd have you, regardless of how you got treated. Yes, we weren't bombed or dead, but they could beat us, starve us and abuse us whatever way they liked. When I think about it, I don't know how some of the kids who weren't as strong willed as me ever got through it.

When we eventually got back to London in 1943, the Germans were bombing worse than ever and we were always running down into the Underground for shelter.

We spent most of our time down there and it was like a fucking refugee camp. We'd be all huddled together, waiting for the bombs to fall, with the rats running everywhere. This really took its toll on my mother and her health was getting worse and worse.

My dad couldn't take care of us, because he was working and trying to look after my mother at the same time. So my sister Gracie was given leave from the Land Army to try and sort us out. While she was back, our garden was hit by a whistling bomb and it took all the windows out. We all ran into the street, but the buildings were getting hit all around us – it was lucky we wasn't all blown to bits or killed or maimed with flying debris. This was such a close fucking thing and Gracie decided me and Ronnie couldn't be left there – it was far too dangerous.

Gracie had us evacuated again, to a family called Duffield in Cutbush Lane, Reading. Mr Duffield had some high-ranking position in Huntley & Palmers biscuits and they had a daughter called Doris, who was twenty-four. Mrs Duffield had these long plaits in her hair, one each side, and she'd curl them up to look like spirals. They didn't talk like the other country people; they had posher accents and spoke like they had something hot inside their mouths. I was so thin from moving around, I looked really ill, just like a little twig. But Mr Duffield treated us like human beings, not like little slaves or subhumans to be abused, and me and Ronnie began to put on some weight and look normal. Mr Duffield and his wife lived in a huge house with five bedrooms and they owned it outright. The house had a really big front room and a beautiful garden with an apple orchard in it. I'd never seen anything like it before and I wasn't used to having such nice things and living in such beautiful surroundings.

We stayed with Mr Duffield for about a year and I even went to school there for a while. It was also where I got my first Christmas present – I hung a stocking on the end of the bed and got an apple and an orange and a little book. I was well chuffed, because that's the first time I'd ever seen anything like it. Being with Mr Duffield and his wife was probably the best time I had when I was young. I got on well with him and her, so well that he brought me and Ronnie up to London to visit my mother. While we were there, Mr Duffield asked my mother if he could adopt me – not Ronnie, just me. My mother was really ill by this time and going in and out of hospital, but she said it would have to be my decision. I didn't want to leave my mother again, so I said no.

Mr Duffield left without me.

4

THE CARE HOME AND MY
MOTHER'S DEATH

After that, the only thing Gracie could sort out was a care home. Now, I don't want you to think I'm whinging or anything, if me and Ronnie had to go away for a bit every now and then, then that's just the way it was in them days. I accepted it as a fact of life after a while. No use fucking bawling about it – just get on with it. One thing I didn't accept, though, was people trying to push me around and take fucking liberties – nobody did that!

So, me and Ronnie were taken 'in care of a home', which meant we weren't orphans, but the home was caring for us. There were loads of children actually in the home, because their parents had died or been killed and they had it far worse than we did. They were under the sole control of the home and the home could do anything they wanted to them. But they knew we would be going back to our family eventually and they had to be a bit more careful with us.

We were sent to a place called The Norwood Home in Hertfordshire and it was run by a geezer called Mr Simons. Mr Simons was a big bloke with black hair and bulging eyes and a red boat race, and he was a horrible, malicious bastard. When he was angry, he'd puff up his cheeks and you could see the blood rushing to his face – and he was always fucking angry. Everyone was terrified of him, because he was a right sadistic cunt and he used to beat the children unmercifully. We had to attend lessons and there would be about fifty of us kids in the main hall for that. We also had to wear the clothes from the home, like a kind of shabby uniform, grey and black and raggedy. After being with Mrs Plum, I got a taste for nice dresses and stuff and I used to see the local girls walking past in their lovely little frocks with bright colours and me having to wear the rotten old home clothes. We got teased endlessly by the village children because of this – we were from London, so they thought we were all pickpockets or chimney sweeps, like in Oliver fucking Twist. I think this is when my violent side really started coming out, because I started fighting a lot. I couldn't be bothered with slanging matches, I just wanted to hit them. So I did!

Mr Simons would give everyone lessons, like sums and stuff, and he'd wave his cane around in the air in a threatening way to put the fear of God into us. One day, he dragged Ronnie up to the front of the hall for some reason and I knew Ronnie was in for it. Mr Simons didn't have to have a reason, he'd just pick someone at random and now it was Ronnie's turn. I don't know what happened, some-thing just snapped in my head – I wasn't about to sit there and see my little brother get beaten up by this cunt. No fucking way! So I pushed my way up to the top of the class and grabbed the cane from his hand and hit him across the shins so hard, the stick broke in two. He wasn't expecting that and he blew up like a fucking puffer fish. It went deathly silent in the hall, the kids couldn't believe their eyes and all their little mouths were wide open, like they'd been struck dumb. Then Mr Simons grabbed another stick from his desk and I realised he was going to get me good for that. So I grabbed Ronnie and we legged it out of the fucking place.

We jumped a train at the station and wagged it back to London. I remember we were starving, because I broke the cane just before we were due to go for dinner. The train was packed with Yank soldiers and there was no place to sit down, so me and Ronnie just stood in the corridor and watched out the window, in case that cunt Simons was coming after us. The soldiers gave us some chocolate and that kept us going – we must've looked like half-starved urchins to them. I remember hearing them talk to each other and their accents were really strange and they didn't seem to wonder why we were the only children on the train – they were laughing a lot, like they were on holiday and not in a fucking war.

By the time we got to London, we were really hungry. The first thing I noticed was the smog and smoke. The sky looked dirty and there was noise everywhere, but I was reassured and relieved to be 'home'. London was what I knew and everyone I loved was here and, for some reason, I didn't experience the same fear I felt before, at the start of the war. I was older and stronger and I'd seen a bit of the world and all I kept thinking about was I hoped there was some food at home. We got off at Liverpool Street and we were getting some funny looks by this time and I thought we'd better get out of there sharpish before some nosey cunt started asking questions about where we'd come from. So me and Ronnie jumped a tram to Camberwell Gate.

It was in the afternoon sometime, but you wouldn't think it, because there was loads of dust and ash in the air and it was dark. I could hear fighting going on in the sky and the sound of doodlebugs. Sirens were going off everywhere and we couldn't find a shelter, so I dragged Ronnie into a shop doorway and we lay down there with our fingers in our ears until things quieted down. Then we got up and went home. I just wanted to see my mother.

When we got back, there was nobody in the house to take us in, so we climbed in through a window. Then Jimmy came back from the hospital, where my mother was still very ill. Tommy arrived and he and Jimmy had a big fight over fish and chips or something – Tommy was drunk, as usual, and he always started a fight when he was on the ale. It ended up with Tommy beating Jimmy up with a webbing belt. Me and Ronnie ran to Mrs Moyes for help and she came back to the house with me to try and get Jimmy out. But she was afraid to go in, so I ran back in on my own. It was terrible inside, Tommy was so drunk and raving like a madman and flinging his belt around and smashing everything. Jimmy had blood all over him, his shirt was ripped from his back and I could see the marks across his skin where the belt had hit him.

I grabbed Jimmy's hand and tried to pull him out of the house, but he wouldn't budge, he stood his ground against

Tommy. But Tommy was going fucking crazy and, in the end, Jimmy was worried that I'd get hurt, so he came out of the house with me. We went back to Mrs Moyes's house and left Tommy smashing the place up. Mrs Moyes helped to clean Jimmy up and gave him one of her husband's shirts to wear. Then she phoned Gracie from a public telephone box.

We stayed with Mrs Moyes until Gracie arrived from the Land Army, a few days later. Gracie wasn't happy that we'd run away and she decided we had to go back to The Norwood Home and Mr Simons. She took us to Liverpool Street station and handed us over to a fat geezer in a tweed coat called Mr Kemp. He took us back to The Norwood Home.

Mr Simons had it right in for us when we got back. He was afraid to hit me with his stick, because he knew I'd hit him back. He did threaten me, but I fucking told him I'd put his fucking cane right across his head if he came near me with it, so he kept his distance. But he invented new ways to punish me, like making me stand outside in the yard in the rain all afternoon because I got my sums wrong. It didn't break me, just made me hate him all the more. Ronnie was a different thing though. I remember playing with some girls at break time once and I didn't realise that Ronnie had got into a fight with an older boy on the other side of the yard. Mr Simons came over and whacked him across the side of the head really hard and perforated his eardrum.

Mr Simons kept up the abuse all the time we were at The Norwood Home. The way I saw it, if they were going to treat me bad, then I was going to act bad. They didn't give me any respect, they just treated me like I was dirt, like I had some incurable disease or something. I saw farm animals being treated better than me and Ronnie was at The Norwood Home so, if they were going to act that way to me, then by fuck I was going to make them pay for it. They tried their best to break me, but they couldn't, no matter what they fucking did. They set the other kids on me and then blamed me for the bullying and they'd keep me back for extra lessons when the others had gone and I'd have to do extra work while everyone else was eating – by the time I got out, I'd missed dinner. Mr Simons and the carers would have to make reports about me to Gracie and they kept telling her what a little monster I was, but she knew what I was like already, so it came as no surprise to her.

I wrote to Gracie and told her what they were doing to us, so she took some leave from the Land Army to sort us out. When she found out how we were being treated, she decided she couldn't leave us there. But she had to get married to get us out, because she had to become our legal guardian and it wasn't thought proper for a single woman to do that. She married this geezer from Wiltshire real fast – his name was Ale and I don't think she loved him or anything, she just did it to get me and Ronnie out of the fucking Norwood Home. She would write to me saying: 'I'll come and get you soon, Eileen. You'll be out of there soon.'

But it dragged on from weeks into months and I was losing hope. But Gracie was as good as her word – she come and got me in the end.

But she wasn't allowed to take Ronnie. Ronnie was three years younger than me, and Gracie got married so fast, the authorities wanted to see if she could manage one of us before they let her take the other. It was like they put her on probation and tested her with me. I had a reputation for being difficult and they didn't think she could control me. So Ronnie had to stay there on his own and it really upset me because I knew there would be no one to protect him from Mr Simons and the bullies and the rest of the cunts. Ronnie was beaten regularly by Mr Simons after I left, and he wasn't allowed out of the home. All I could do was behave for Gracie and not do anything to jeopardise Ronnie's release. It took a whole year of going against the grain – but I did it, for Ronnie's sake.

We went to live in Wiltshire with Gracie where, like I said, she'd married this geezer called Ale Rudman. I think she always wanted to marry Mark from Sheffield, who I told you about, but he was a Desert Rat in the 8th Army and was reported missing in action. It broke her heart, but she settled for Ale to get me and Ronnie out of The Norwood Home. After the war, Mark came home from a POW camp to marry Gracie, but it was too late, she was already married to Ale.

I missed London and my mother so much that, after Ronnie got out, I made Gracie's life a misery and kept running off and jumping trains to get back home. They always sent me back to Wiltshire, because my mam and dad couldn't look after me. I remember, on one of these runaways, being sent back with a little case under my arm. I was walking down the street when I saw a little terrier dog wandering about. I knew he belonged to a woman in our road whose bitch had a litter of them, but she didn't look after them properly and they looked skinny and starved. So I decided to give this one a good home in the country.

I punched some holes in my case and put the little dog inside, then I took it on the train with me to Wiltshire. The fucker was sick on the few clothes I had in the case, but I gave the dog to my brother Ronnie and he loved it, and he looked after it too. I never told Gracie it was nicked, she was like my mam and wouldn't stand for stealing. So I told her I bought it for a couple of bob and what she didn't know didn't hurt her.

Anyway, someone must have seen me lifting the dog because, when I ran away again, the woman came up to me and accused me of stealing it. But she couldn't prove anything and I told her if she didn't leave me alone, I'd get my brothers to come round and see to her. I never heard no more about it.

But, in the end, Gracie couldn't put up with me no longer and she ended up taking me and Ronnie back to London for good. We left the little dog in Wiltshire.

When we got back, I found out my mother was dying. All the family were told and Johnny was even brought back from Burma. Even now, with my mother dying and all, there was still fighting in the house. Johnny had his arm in a sling, where he'd been wounded, but that didn't stop Tommy fighting with him. Johnny couldn't defend himself properly, so he called to Jimmy for help. It all spilled out into the street and Jimmy ended up doing Tommy over the head with a bottle. Then Tommy ran into the house and came back out with a gun – we'd hidden it under the floorboards, because we knew what a mad fucker Tommy was and we were afraid he'd kill someone with it. He chased

Jimmy all over the street, trying to get close enough to shoot him. My brothers thought they'd taken all the bullets out, but one was left in there and Tommy kept pulling the trigger until it fired – luckily, the bullet missed.

My mother was so ill by now, she couldn't even eat, but I really wanted to see her. Jimmy used to go see her every day, come wind, rain or shine, and take her a bottle of Guinness. I kept asking Dad if I could go up too, so one day he took me with him to Greenwich Hospital where they were keeping her. I had old shoes on that had holes in them and, by the time I walked all the way from Camberwell Gate to Greenwich, I had fucking blisters on my feet. I took my shoes off when I got there because it was raining and my socks were soaked. But I didn't want to complain because I knew Mam was so ill and Dad was so upset, I didn't want to make things worse. We had to wait outside until we were allowed in – they were very strict about visiting times. Dad called a nurse to look at my feet and she washed them and put some kind of antiseptic liquid on them that stunk. She gave me a little bandage thing to cover the sores, so I could walk back again, but I had to leave my socks off, they were so wet.

The nurses were nice at Greenwich, but the hospital was fucking horrible. It was dark and dismal, there wasn't much light because of the brown tape they covered the windows with in case of bombing and the heavy black curtains they used for the blackout. A matron sat at a large desk at the top of the ward in her big white hat and she controlled everything and what she said was law. But the place looked so dilapidated, even to me, who wasn't used to much. The nurses were doing their best, but it looked like a place where people just went to die. As we walked up the aisle between the beds to reach my mother, I saw loads of people who'd been injured in the bombings. There were people on both sides of us who'd lost arms and legs and some had bandages all round their whole heads because of the horrible facial injuries they'd suffered. They were just people who'd been hurt bad, but they didn't look human to me; the bandages made them look like mummies out of the old black-and-white Boris Karloff films. They were moaning because they were in pain and that frightened me and I clung on to my dad for dear fucking life.

When we got to Mam's bed, it was surrounded by a blind on wheels, like a frame that had curtains on, and my dad moved it back so I could see her. She was wasting away and the sight of her shocked me – she was nothing but skin and bone and she'd lost some of her teeth. I mean, I was thin myself, but Mam looked like a fucking skeleton. I'll never forget the look on her face, it was like she'd lost all her life and energy, like there was nothing left for her. She was giving up, what with the war and the disease and the constant sirens and running in the middle of the night to the shelters – I don't think she could take any more, I don't think she wanted it any more.

The nurses told Dad she wouldn't eat and he begged and pleaded with her to try. I remember Dad saying to her: 'Grace, you have to eat . . . you have to eat, Grace.'

But she just couldn't. He even tried to feed her himself by hand, tried to open her mouth for her while she was lying there, and I remember seeing tears in his eyes when he was doing it. But Mam was too weak. All she kept saying was she wanted to come home and I can't say I blamed her

– the whole place reeked of death. I think she must have known she was coming to the end and wanted to die at home, with the people she loved. I wanted her out of there too, away from all the suffering and dying. I would have cried my eyes out, if it wasn't for being so petrified and for the stink of the antiseptic that made it hard to breathe.

We only had half an hour with her and then the matron came and told us to go. So we started the long walk home again. Me and Dad didn't talk much on the way home, but he knew like I knew that she was dying. He was crying, but he tried not to let me see. It was raining anyway and I pretended I didn't notice. I don't remember the pain in my feet walking back, I was too upset about Mam. On the way, the sirens went off again and we had to run for the nearest shelter. It was a normal thing by now and we did it automatically.

They let my mother come home to die and, one night shortly after, we were all in bed when the sirens went off. We ran to the shelter but, by the time we got there, it was full and we couldn't get in. So we had to take shelter in a crypt under a local church. By now the exertion was too much for my mother and she was coughing up blood so badly, in the end we decided to bring her back to the house and take our chances. My brothers were carrying her and, as we made our way down the road, I heard the loudest bang I've ever experienced and I looked back – the church had taken a direct hit, everyone inside was killed, including one of my best friends. They were all blown to bits and, if we'd been in there, we would've been too.

After that, my mother just got worse and worse, until there was absolutely nothing left of her and she was coughing up blood all the time. We never told her she was dying, but she must've known and she was probably wishing the end would come, so she wouldn't be such a burden to us. I know this because, late one day, Gracie went upstairs and found her trying to drink bleach – she just didn't want to go on. Shortly after that, she fell down the stairs, because she kept fainting all the time. It was getting very close to the end and we would try to bring her round by putting vinegar on her lips. We had to leave her downstairs on the sofa and I remember looking at her and saying to myself: 'Her freckles are all gone.'

I was sitting on the step at the back door about a week later, when my father came out and said: 'Can you get my shoes from the menders, Eileen? By the way, your mother's dead.'

It was like being hit with a lump of concrete. I still don't know why he said it like that, so cold and matter-of-fact. Maybe he couldn't deal with it himself – maybe it was just a front, to hide his grief. All I know is, I'll never forget it and I don't think I ever got over it either.

She was forty-eight. I was fourteen. They waked her in the house before the funeral. I remember going into the room and seeing the coffin there. I remember looking in over the edge and seeing her – she looked like she was sleeping, but all the colour was gone from her and she was pale as a ghost. My mother was gone.

It was the winter of 1945 when my mother died and the war was over at last. It was foggy on the day of the funeral and I was up early and we all stood round my mother's coffin in the front room. My brothers carried her out when the hearse came – it was a large black carriage, pulled by eight black horses. We didn't have the money for such a big funeral, but my mother was so well liked, she'd help everyone she could and she had lots of friends, that everyone chipped in and they all turned out to pay their last respects and there was the most beautiful bouquet of flowers.

It was so hard for me, even though I'd known for a long time that she was dying from tuberculosis. I was so cold I was shaking, but I think it was more emotion than anything else. Ronnie took it real bad and refused to come to the cemetery, but when she was placed on the carriage and driven down the road, he came running after us crying. It was awful. We couldn't afford to get Mam her own plot in Streatham Cemetery, so she was laid to rest in a communal grave. During the war they dug very large holes for multiple burials because so many people were dying and mass graves were the only way they could cope with the number of decaying bodies. My mother was one of twenty people in that particular hole and we weren't allowed to have a gravestone because of that. So Gracie had cards made to send to everyone and on them she wrote:

> We saw her fading like a flower,
> But could not make her stay.
> We tended her with greatest care,
> Till the angels took her away.

5

RAGPICKING AND OTHER JOBS

The war had ended and my sister Gracie came to live in London with her new husband, Ale, to help look after the family. They lived in our house for a while, but Ale didn't like it, because there was too much rucking between my brothers. Gracie got me a job in Woolworths, but it was really fucking boring. They put me on the till, but I was useless at it – I didn't pay attention when they told me what to do and I was always making mistakes. As well as that, I had a soft heart and I wouldn't report people for stealing stuff – in fact I fucking encouraged them. But you should have seen these poor cunts, they looked like they hadn't had a decent meal in months, so how could I grass them? So the fuckers sacked me.

Ale got a job as a foreman, making Victorian fireplaces in a factory on the Walworth Road and he employed my brothers to work under him for a while. But they didn't like Ale, he was a bit quiet and didn't really understand Londoners. They wouldn't do what he told them and they ended up knocking the fucker out. Gracie couldn't take no more of the violence, so she packed her things and moved back to Wiltshire with Ale and let us fend for our fucking selves.

By this time I was hardened to a tough life, full of fights. Nothing scared me any more. I smoked Woodbine cigarettes to look big – the huckster shops would break open the packets and sell them to children in ones and twos, because they never had enough money for a full pack. I ran with gangs of teenagers in the bombed-out streets and derelict buildings and I have to tell you this, 'feisty' is a modern word and it don't go far enough to describe what I was like. I was a fucking hellraiser, and that's the up and down of it!

When I was fifteen, I went to work in a sausage factory. The factory was on Stanford Street, Bermondsey, and my job was to link the sausages as they came out of the machine – that means I had to put the skin onto the sausage machine, then the filling would be pumped into the skin from the machine. Once enough filling was inside the skin, I'd twist it to make individual sausages. I hated the fucking place, it was dark and greasy and you couldn't have a laugh nor a chat or the fucking gaffer would come round and shout at you. A couple of times I nearly belted the cunt, even though I was only young.

Anyway, I decided to earn a little on the side, because the wages were shit, so I started nicking the sausages. Now, the guv'nors were a suspicious shower and they searched our bags when we left the factory at the end of our shift. So I took to tying long chains of sausages round my waist, under my clothes. I had to make sure I wore something loose, because I got braver and braver the more I got away with. It got to the point I was stealing so many sausages they were tied from my waist all the way up to my fucking armpits. I dunno how they missed it, because I looked like I'd put on ten stone in two fucking weeks and it could get a bit messy if the skins broke.

At first, I used to take them home for the family so we had loads to eat. Then, as I nicked more and more, I took the surplus over to the Elephant and Castle to sell. It was a good little number while it lasted, but some narky little cunt went and tipped off the gaffer. I was in the toilet, wrapping the sausages round my waist, when I heard all this shouting from outside. I looked out and saw security heading my way, searching all the girls as they went. I wasn't the only one nicking and sausages were being thrown out through windows all over the place. I could imagine the people passing by in the street outside, getting hit by a shower of fucking sausages and wondering what the fuck was going on.

I was fully loaded by now and the scabby security guards were coming closer. I panicked and ripped the sausage strings from around me and stuffed them down the toilet, but the fuckers blocked up the bog when I flushed it and the water welled up and poured out all over the fucking floor. They came in and caught me red-handed. I tried to talk my way out of it, saying it must have been someone else and I only came in for a pee, but it was no use. They sacked me.

The factory closed down shortly after that.

I then went to work in a pickled onion factory. It was under the old arch at Camberwell and it was a lousy fucking job. I hated it! I had to peel the onions and pickle them in vinegar. My eyes were streaming and red all the time and I absolutely reeked by the end of the day. I stank of vinegar and onions everywhere I went and, as resourceful as I was in them days, I couldn't find a way to make some money on the side. Nobody wanted to buy the pickled fucking onions. So I left.

After that, I went to work in a brewery, smelling bottle tops. In them days, the pubs would get tuppence a bottle if they were sent back to the brewery to be reused. They never knew what had been kept in the bottles, so they had to wash them out thoroughly. But I had to smell the bottle tops to see if there was any pong of chemicals off them. If there was, that top couldn't be used again. They were ceramic things with a screw thread and a rubber bung type thing, so it was airtight in the bottle. God help anyone who got my bottle tops, because half the time I never bothered to william tell the things and, anyway, they all smelled the fucking same to me. I didn't stay long at that job, about three days – it was so fucking boring. I just walked into the manager's office one day and said: 'That's it, I've had enough! Can I have my wages?'

I also worked making sandwiches at Waterloo train station. I really loved this job – probably the first and only fucking legitimate job I ever wanted to stay in. They had a big loudspeaker on the station and it would always be playing the latest music – stuff like 'Zip-a-Dee-Doo-Dah' and 'The Anniversary Song' and the 'One O'Clock Jump' and 'I'm Looking Over a Four Leaf Clover' and 'Now Is the Hour'. I loved meeting all the different customers, most of them were smart and suited and booted – men dressed like men back then and women dressed like women – and I'd be there with my Jane Russell blouse and a twinkle in my eye while I served tea to the businessmen. I made more money from tips than I did from actual wages, so it paid to be nice and polite.

The place was like a big cafe on the station, with two sides to it – one side serving tea and sandwiches and the other side serving beer, with a large seating area in the middle. I did try serving the beer, but I wasn't very good at it and ended up spilling it onto some geezer's new suit. He could have chopped straws with his arse and I thought for a minute I was going to have to belt him. That's why they only let me do it the once, then they kept me on the tea and sandwich side. I've always loved to chat with people and all my friends used to come round to chinwag. It was where I first met Shirley Pitts and Mad Frances and Johnny Bradbury – mates I was to have dodgy dealings with later on. It goes without saying that I always gave them free food and drinks and if they gave me a shilling, I'd give them two bob back in change.

But it couldn't fucking last, could it? I got into an argument with this posh woman who brought her tea back and said it wasn't made right and told me I didn't know what I was doing. She was giving it all the mouth and making me look stupid in front of the other customers and I think she expected me to just stand there and take her insults. But she must have caught me on a bad day, so I went round the counter and belted her one. She wasn't expecting that!

My next job was a rag-sorter, under the arch at Camberwell Gate – this is where rags that were collected by rag-and-bone men got sorted into good and bad, the good got sold and the bad got thrown away. I would sit there and have to go through the bits of cloth, to see what could be used and what couldn't. During the bombings of London, lots of people were killed and, after the clean-up, there was tons of excess clothing. Some of it was useless, because it was all burnt and torn to shreds, but some was OK, just a bit dirty and bloodstained. Because the country was still poor and struggling after the war, rag-sorters were used to try to recycle as much as possible.

It wasn't a good place to work, because the piles of rags were running alive with rats and the sorters used to come down with all sorts of infections. As well as that, the guv'nors made me make the fucking tea all the time and I soon got fed up with that lark. I complained to my brothers about it and they told me, if I didn't like it, to do something about it. So, the next time they asked me, I threw the fucking tea all over them and scarpered. I didn't know that one of them was a semi-professional boxer, and this geezer came round our house with some men, to have a go. They were outside in the street, shouting up at my window. My brothers wouldn't stand for that and they went out and beat the shit out of the lot of them.

It was like violence was a part of everyday life, something that was around me all the time, and I didn't think it was different anywhere else. All right, some of it might've been in me from the very day I was born, but the rest came from growing up with four tough brothers. We were 'The Killicks' and everyone knew you didn't fuck with us, unless you wanted to get hurt.

For instance, one day we were sitting down having dinner in our house in Camberwell Gate, when we heard a load of shouting and hollering in the street outside: 'Where do the fucking Killicks live?'

It was a geezer called Rocky, from Brixton. He had some grievance with my brothers and he'd brought a crew up with him. They were all tooled up with flick knives and cut-throats and ready to kill some fucker. Next thing I knew, the table got thrown over and my brothers all ran out into the street. I ran after them and a massive fucking ruck kicked off. Rocky went down on the ground and, while he was down there, I was kicking him in the head. He got beaten so bad, he ended up in the hospital and the rest of his crew didn't want no more, so they scarpered – and that was the end of that. They never came back.

Another time, my brother Johnny was coming home to Camberwell Gate on his own, when he was attacked by a gang and a geezer named Router slashed his face with a cut-throat razor. Johnny and my other brothers went out after Router and his mates and ended up in a big ruck over on Camberwell Green. Router had to be taken to hospital when Johnny was finished with him. A gang war erupted after that and it was always kicking off all over the place, whenever Router's crew and my family crossed paths.

My brothers were in fights like that all the time. Like after the war, when my brother Jimmy got a job in a place called 'the spike'. It was an old disused factory with rows and rows of old second-hand beds and it was a dosshouse for all the homeless men. Lots of houses had been bombed and lots of others were in a dangerous state, so there were loads of homeless people about. The women went to the workhouse and the men went to the spike. It was Jimmy's job to patrol the spike at night and make sure there was no fighting or rough stuff going on. A lot of the men in there would be drunk and, because everyone was so poor, mugging and stealing was commonplace.

Jimmy'd had it rough growing up, just like me, so he knew well how to handle himself and could have a fight with anyone. He needed to as well, working in the spike, and I remember him coming home one morning covered in blood. I saw him over the kitchen sink and I thought he'd been hurt bad, but he was actually washing other geezers' blood off his hands, from the fighting the night before. It was so bad, the claret had splashed all up his clothes and his face, but it wasn't his, it belonged to the muppets who'd tried it on with him.

They also knew lots of the London villains and characters who were about then, like Mickey Progle, who was a well-known prostitute and famous for escaping from Holloway. She was a fighter and a shoplifter like me and Ronnie lived with her for a while when he got older. She was always up for a dodgy earner and she was attracted to the 'glamour' of the big villains like the Richardsons. Bunny Bridges was another one, he introduced Ronnie to Mickey Progle and was later electrocuted by one of the south London gangs. I remember a geezer called Taffy, who used to go nicking the lead off the roofs – Taffy, Bunny and Ronnie were all part of the same gang who knocked off everything they could to make money.

Ronnie met Derek Bentley in borstal, who was epileptic from falling off a lorry when he was young. Bentley was buried in his house when it was bombed during the war and he suffered severe head injuries. He teamed up with a boy called Chris Craig and broke into a warehouse on the

Tamworth Road, down in Croydon, but they were spotted and the police turned up. The rest is history. Craig had a gun and killed a copper called Sidney Miles after Bentley supposedly shouted: 'Let him have it, Chris!' Craig served ten years in prison and Bentley was hanged, even though he didn't fire the gun and he was never the full shilling.

When he got older, Ronnie and Charlie Richardson used to go totting together. They started off with a little hard cart like a wheelbarrow and, after six months, they bought a horse and cart and made good money out of it for a while. They used to take the scrap to a yard that was run by a Jewish geezer and they used to weigh the metal before they took it in, so they didn't get ripped off. One day the weight didn't come out right and Ronnie knocked over the scales and saw they were using dodgy weights. The Jew started mouthing off, so Ronnie clumped him, then loads of geezers started coming down the chains with meat hooks. So Ronnie and Charlie picked up a couple of metal pipes and took them on. The cunts never got near them, but they took their scrap elsewhere after that, until Ronnie had a bust-up with Charlie over something and they went their separate ways.

Ronnie then went totting with another mate of his and they were down in Surrey one time and nicked a load of copper. But the police must've been watching, because they stopped them and asked them to get out of the lorry. Ronnie swung the door into one of the Old Bill and knocked the bugger out, then he jumped over a fence and legged it to the railway station, where he jumped a train for London. But when he got back, the London coppers were waiting for him – the other fucker had grassed him.

Ronnie got probation and, a couple of weeks later, he and Jimmy saw the geezer in the street. Jimmy held him, while Ronnie kicked the shit out of him. And that's the way it was, we never went crying to the cops, we sorted things out our own fucking way.

On another occasion, when he was about sixteen, a local geezer and his mates insulted Ronnie. There was about six of them and they were all built, so he knew he couldn't do nothing about it then. He just came home and tooled himself up with an iron bar and went back. He found the geezer sitting on his steps and he done him right over the head with the bar and he was laid up in Lewisham Hospital for three weeks and it was touch and go whether he'd survive or not. Ronnie was shitting himself, because the death penalty hadn't been abolished then. Thankfully, the geezer pulled through, but it taught Ronnie a lesson, about how hard to hit people in the future.

By the time he was twenty-five, Ronnie had forty-two convictions for grievous bodily harm and went to prison three times. He went to four different borstals for fighting. He escaped from the Grange Borstal in Dudley with a couple of geezers from the Elephant, but was picked up again in Stratford-upon-Avon and kept in Wormwood Scrubs until a place came available in Hull. But he got involved in a riot there and was moved to a place they called 'the nut house', especially for boys who couldn't be controlled. They used to make them exercise in the yard till they were fucking exhausted, then hose them down with freezing cold water, just to try and break them. Ronnie told them he took fits and actually faked a fit in front of them. But all the fuckers done was put him in a padded cell and he could hear the cunts laughing about it outside.

Jimmy had a fruit stall in Camberwell Green and Charlie Richardson used to work for him for a while, before going totting with Ronnie. He knew this geezer called Danny Irving, who was a well-known fence – if you wanted something, he could get it and, if you wanted to get rid of something, he could do that too. This meant a lot of people got to know him and didn't like to cross him, because he had some powerful friends. That didn't stop my brothers from striping him across the face with a razor. He came to our house a week or so later with a gang of his mates and they tried to kick the fucking door in. So me and my brothers boiled up loads of water and chucked it out of the upstairs windows on top of them. All you could hear was their screams as they legged it down the street. We were all pissing ourselves laughing.

It was just a life of fucking violence all the time, and when Jimmy and Ronnie were working on their fruit and veg stall on Gordon Road in Peckham, they were in at least six fights a week because of the gang culture of the time. Our family had a reputation for trouble and they had to prove how hard they were no matter where they went. There was always some crew who thought they were harder, but Jimmy could handle himself proper, because of all the shit he had to take from Tommy, and Ronnie was well able to have a tussle too.

My brothers always hung round with their gangs back then and they took on any other gangs that thought they could try it on with them, or came onto their turf. I remember a gang called the 'dumb-dumbs', who came from

Brixton and they got that name because there was three brothers who couldn't speak. My brothers used to go there regularly to kick off with them.

So, you can see how fighting was nothing uncommon to me, and you can also see that I did at least try to work at an honest job – it just didn't suit me, that's all. In the end, I gave up trying and started stealing lead off the roofs. I didn't get up on the roofs because I was afraid of heights, but I'd bag it as it was thrown down and take it to the break- ers who'd weigh it and pay us with no questions asked. Scrap metal was big business back then, because there wasn't much metal about – the government had used it all up to make weaponry. There were lots of burned-out and derelict buildings and it was really easy. Whole streets had been bombed out and all you had to do was go through the rubble and you could find loads of stuff. You had to be careful, of course, because everything that was damaged became government property and you could get arrested for scavenging. Lead was worth a lot of money and it was a brilliant way to earn – much better than fucking working in a horrible factory, where you had to graft for pennies and some other cunt took all the profits.

Westmoreland Road Market was the place you could get rid of any dodgy gear you wanted to flog. There were no supermarkets back in those days and you could buy anything on the market. It was in an alley off Westmoreland Road, and a dirty one at that and it was always heaving. The whole place was lined with stalls selling everything from fruit to fabric and, if you knew the right people and knew the right questions to ask, you could get your hands on knocked-off gear at a good price. I always went there to flog stuff that I'd lifted – it was a fucking free-for-all, where they'd literally sell you any fucking thing you wanted.

There was a pie-and-mash shop at the top of the road where I'd meet my mates. It had wooden benches and you could get jellied eels and pie and mash and liquor, the famous green parsley gravy. Next to that was a local bakers' called Leatherdales; it was an old-fashioned shop with little wooden racks for the bread, fresh out of the oven, and rows of cake stands with all different kinds of lovely pastries on them and you could smell the place halfway down the street. I used to go in there and get doughnuts for me and my mates and charge them to Fat Mike's account – 'Fat Mike' was an Italian barber from the Walworth Road, who was a bit sweet on me and he was loaded and he used to take care of the bills. He only pulled me about it once, when I really took the piss and his bill was about five times what it should have been. He liked to think he came over all hard and tough, but he was just a big softie and I could wrap him round my little finger.

6

THE LAND ARMY

I was a right fucking rebel, no mistake. Always fiery and quick-tempered – and a very sore loser. I said exactly what I thought and didn't hold back, because that would've been a sign of weakness. I had too much pride to ever admit defeat and I was well able to fight any fucker – man or woman.

At that age, I was really coming into my own as a fucking tearaway. I had no ties nor responsibilities and my mother dying really sent me off the rails. I was getting into trouble left, right and centre and I hung round with the toughest in the area, nicking and fighting. My dad couldn't control me no more, so my sister Gracie decided to take me under her wing again, as I was going completely fucking wild in London. Gracie was a straight as a die kind of person, who believed that hard work was a great fucking thing altogether. She'd become a forelady over a group of girls in the Land Army and she wanted me to join, so she could keep an eye on me. I was only sixteen, so Gracie lied about my age on the forms and they took me in. It was 1947 and the Land Army lasted until it was disbanded in 1950.

I remember a big parcel coming for me and I was really excited to see what it was. It was only a fucking uniform, consisting of a brown cowboy hat, a beige shirt, a green jumper, a three-quarter-length brown coat with 'Land Army' written on it, tan corduroy britches and long socks that met the end of the britches and a pair of heavy brown shoes. I hated the fucking thing as soon as I saw it.

But I was kind of glad in a way to be getting out of London for a while. The country was recovering from the war, but London was in ruins, so it felt like I was going on a big adventure. Gracie met me at the train station in Melksham, Wiltshire, in a big army-type lorry. Like I said, she was a forewoman and controlled the lorries and the rotas and could do what she liked. Gracie loved that kind of thing, being in charge and having responsibility and stuff like that; it made her feel like she'd achieved something in life and got out of the ghetto. I thought it just substituted for her not being able to have any kids, after the accident in the factory.

She took me to a large, Victorian building called Wolfe House that had been converted into dormitories and she introduced me to all the girls. They were all older than me, eighteen and nineteen and over and they came from all sorts of backgrounds, rich as well as poor. But I wasn't fazed by that, because I got a room to myself because Gracie was my sister. But that's as far as the favours went – the rest of it was like being in the foreign fucking legion – Land 'Army' was the right fucking name for it, because the cunts were all the time trying to break you down – at least, that's what it felt like to me.

I was woken up at six o'clock in the morning, before it was even fucking light. Then I had to go and make my own breakfast and sandwiches for the day, which I'd take with me to the fields in a little tin box. Then I had to wash and dress and be out of the place by seven. We'd get in the back of an open-top lorry, even when it was raining, and sit on the wooden benches on either side. Five girls would fit on each seat and we would go out in groups of ten to pick vegetables in the fields.

When I first started, I was put picking potatoes with German prisoners of war. Now, the way I looked at it, these were the same cunts who blew up my mam's piano and made us live for three months in a house with no roof. The same fuckers who bombed half of London and who killed all those kids I used to go to school with and who took me away from my mother and put me in a care home when I was younger. So I hated them and refused to work with them. Gracie was called and me and her ended up having a right fucking barney in the middle of the field and I ended up throwing the sandwich tin at her. In the end, Gracie moved me away from the Germans, but the leary fuckers always gave me dirty looks whenever they saw me after that.

Funny enough, I didn't have many fights with the Land Army girls. I think they might have been a bit wary of me, because Gracie was my sister and they didn't want to get into trouble. Needless to say, I took full advantage of my status as the forelady's sister and fucked off to the RAF camps in the evenings to dance with the MPs in their white hats and belts and gaiters.

I remember sneaking off once with a couple of other girls to meet up with some Yanks that we were talking to earlier when they pulled up in a Jeep. We were supposed to be digging a ditch, but sod that. So we ran across some ploughed fields until we came to a high fence. The girls I was with got cold feet at that stage and wanted to go back, but I said: 'Fuck that, I'm going on.'

So I jumped the fence and was going through the field on the other side, when I heard this grunting noise behind me. I looked round and, oh my fucking God, there was these four giant bulls in the field and they were coming at me. Now, I didn't even like milking the fucking cows when I was evacuated, but these were different things altogether, and massive – I'd never seen anything like them in my life. I started to run and the bulls started to run and it was a good job they were so far away from me. I ran faster than I ever ran in my life, with the bulls at full fucking gallop behind me, until I came to a hedge and just took off through the air like I was on springs. I landed in a pile of cow-shit, right in front of a farmer who was burning stuff on the other side.

Gracie used to cover for me. She didn't like doing it because she was so strait-laced and prim and proper, but I suppose she reckoned it was better than me running amok in London. She tried to get me to better myself, like she'd done – she got them to put me on the tractors, instead of picking. Now, I had no fucking idea how to drive a tractor. They gave me some instructions, but I had a short concentration span in them days and didn't listen much to what anyone told me. In any case, I said to myself, there can't be much to it if the fucking yokels could do it. Anyway, the field ended up having criss-cross drills running through it and I didn't know if I was even in the right field, because I went through a hedgerow that shouldn't have been where it was and then I couldn't stop the fucking tractor, so they had to run after me and jump up on it, before I ploughed into the fucking Germans. I'm sure the bastards believed I done it deliberately.

Gracie then got me onto the threshing machines. We were in a big field of corn and it was my job to feed hay into the machine constantly, as we moved up and down the field. I would feed it in one side and then go round the other side to collect it in bags when it came out the other side all chopped up. I had to wear a pair of heavy goggles, because I was usually at the front and bits and dust would be flying everywhere and could blind you. It was dangerous as well, because I had to stand very close to the machine and, if I tripped or fell into it, I'd be fucking done for. The other girls didn't like the threshing machines and that's why I ended up doing it. I didn't get on too well with the animals.

We had to do everything in the Land Army, not just picking potatoes, but carrots and cabbages and lettuces and other vegetables as well. This always hurt my back because we had to do it all by hand. I remember once, while I was digging up carrots, I put the fucking fork straight through my boot. It was my own fault, because I was chin-wagging to the other girls instead of watching what I was doing. Part of the fork went through my foot and I had to go get a tetanus injection. But I was lucky, it could have been worse. This all used to be men's work before the war and we had to use a lot of dangerous equipment that we weren't used to. I had a few near misses, like one time I was using a large blade thing on a stick, like a scythe, to cut grass and I ended up catching my right leg and slicing it down one side. I had to have fourteen stitches. They took me to some remote hospital in Devizes and I was given light work for a week after it, which was cushti enough, as far as I was concerned.

We also had to milk the cows and cut down trees. I never liked milking and only done it the once. The fucking cow tried to kick me and, after the incident with the bulls, I had a phobia about big animals, like some people have about spiders. Probably my favourite work was cutting down trees. Two of us would use a big saw, one each side of the tree. We had to get a rhythm going and we'd sing songs or whistle to do this. I loved to see the tree fall after we'd sawn it through. Then we'd have to cut up the trunk for firewood and that always took a lot longer and wasn't so much fun.

It was very demanding work and the hours were long – six o'clock in the morning until it got dark – and it began to change my appearance. Because I was out in the open all the time, I had the best tan of my life, but the air dried out my skin and completely destroyed my hair. You couldn't do this work and look dainty as well – I started to develop muscles on my arms and legs and became as strong as a fucking man.

I always liked going out to different places and meeting different people. I remember at Christmas one of the girls asked me to come and stay with her family in Birmingham. I must have been accident prone or something because, when we arrived at New Street train station, I was still wearing my Land Army uniform and I was looking around so much I wasn't watching where I was going and slipped and ended up on my back on the platform. People were laughing and I was furious and almost got up and laid into them. But I didn't want to embarrass the girl I was with, who'd invited me. Then, going down the street, I leaned against a shopfront window and the fucking glass gave way and the whole fucking thing collapsed, causing a hell of a commotion. That got me and Birmingham off to a bad fucking start. Little did I know then that I'd end up living there, many years later.

I remember the rows of houses down her street. They looked different from London – newer, and the place wasn't as busy, and the people looked at me funny. I think because I had blonde hair, that I used to dye with peroxide, ammonia and soap flakes and I was five feet eleven inches tall even then, when I was sixteen, and I towered above most other girls my age. Everywhere I went, people would say: 'Ain't you tall!'

And they gave me the nickname 'Lofty'. I didn't like that and was glad to get back to Wiltshire after the holiday.

But the Land Army was nothing but work, work, work and no play, so I soon got fed up with it and told Gracie to go pick the fucking potatoes her fucking self. Later, me and this religious girl was stopped by a couple of Yank soldiers and they asked us if we'd sell them some bread. I nicked the bread from the hostel where I was staying and this caused another big bull-and-cow because the religious cunt grassed me. Gracie had me transferred to another hostel after that, because she said I was a bad influence on the other girls. I was sent to Chippenham, but that didn't work neither. I point-blank refused to work on the land any more because I was sick and tired of having chapped hands and messy hair, so they put me to work in the kitchen instead. They were a cliquey lot at Chippenham and I think they must have heard about me at Wolfe House and they weren't keen on me one little fucking bit.

They were all Northerners and all a couple of years older than me, so I suppose they thought they could take liberties, because I didn't have Gracie behind me. This one bird thought it would be funny to take the piss out of my cockney accent. Now, I didn't take kindly to this, because when I was little I had to take a lot of teasing about the way I talked. Anyway, we had these large heavy tins for packing sandwiches in, so I put one straight into the bird's mush. She went down, spouting blood all over the fucking floor and didn't get back up. You see, she wasn't a fighter, just mouthy. I was brought up with brothers who knew how to fight and I knew that some girls will give it the big un and slag and shout, but won't be able to back it up.

They sent me back to Gracie at Wolfe House after that.

What I didn't know at the time was, there was this Welsh cunt who was always telling tales on me to my sister. If I'd known at the time, I'd have done her good and proper, but she was a go-lightly sort and kept her head down. She took great enjoyment out of grassing me up and, eventually, I made it so hard for Gracie that she couldn't cover for me any more. Things were beginning to get fucking difficult.

I wouldn't mind, but I was getting all the stick and the lazy POWs were sitting around in the sun, laughing at me while I was slaving my arse off, picking fucking potatoes like a hunchback. I'd hear them laughing and I'd look round and see them sitting on upturned galvanised buckets smoking. I couldn't even stop for a fag and they were able to smoke their fucking heads off. They knew I didn't like them and they looked so fucking smug, knowing they were pissing me off and they knew I wanted to go for them. But I couldn't, because I'd only get in more trouble than I was in already. It came to a head one day when I tripped over something and ended up flat on my face in the muddy fucking field. I could hear this fucker laughing, so I got up and started throwing potatoes at him. One of them hit him on the head and he started throwing them back. So I rushed at him and knocked him off his fucking bucket and he landed right in the mud. He got up and I was right in the bastard's face, shouting at him in English and him shouting back at me in German. I'd have hit him too, if the other girls hadn't pulled me away and if Gracie hadn't come to sort it out.

We'd go down to the fields in the early mornings to pick the potatoes and we'd be walking upright, with straight backs. In the evening, coming home, we'd be walking like fucking cripples, bent over and leaning on fucking sticks. To me it wasn't fucking fair, the POWs, who were all men, didn't have to do that kind of work and it looked to me like they were having an easy life and laughing at us girls. So I rounded up the others and we all demanded that the POWs be made to do proper work. It was going well too, until Gracie came and tried to exert her authority over me. I almost caused a mutiny and it made Gracie look bad. After covering for me for so long, she wasn't on my side no more after that.

We were based on the farm in Wiltshire, but we'd often have to go help out on other farms and hospitals. The final straw came when we were told to go to this big hospital to pick up carrots. I didn't know it was a mental hospital and all the cunts there were as mad as fuck. It was a horrible fucking place and, when I sat down to have a cup of tea, one of the fucking patients came along and hit me on the back of the head for no fucking reason. Well, I wasn't standing for that, so I chased the fucker with a rake.

Gracie was talking to one of the farmhands at the time and didn't see what was going on. The mad bastard was running round, shrieking like a fucking banshee, until I hit him with the rake and knocked him into a big hole. I don't know what they were digging, but the hole was so big the hospital orderlies couldn't find him for a couple of days. They thought he'd escaped and the geezer was nearly fucking brown bread by the time they came across him.

I just went back to my work and never told nobody, but they eventually found out and Gracie went fucking mad at me, screaming about how much she'd done for me and how I done nothing since I got there but abuse her trust.

It was time to go.

7

PETTY CRIME

I was going on seventeen when I got kicked out of the Land Army for attacking that mental patient. It was more that I ran off than got kicked out, because the buggers were going on about bringing charges, even though the cunt hit me first, and I didn't want to hang about until they made up their minds. By this time, I'd had enough of the fucking country and just wanted to go back to Camberwell. I had to make my own way back to London from fucking Wiltshire and I had to sleep in the scullery when I got back to Dad's house, which was like a basement room with a tiny little window in the far wall. I liked it down there, at least I didn't have to share with anyone else, and I was glad to be out of the Land Army and back where I belonged.

Back in London, I thought I was the bee's fucking knees – I thought I could do whatever I wanted. Dad couldn't control me any more and l think he just gave up. I was back getting into trouble again, living in Camberwell Gate and hanging round with all my dodgy mates. My family lived in one big house – it was really two houses, but it wasn't, if you get my meaning. My brother Tommy lived upstairs with his wife and kids and I lived downstairs with my dad. My brother Jimmy had moved down to Dartford and Johnny and Ronnie lived upstairs next door and an old man lived downstairs from them.

I didn't have no worries back then. But, there wasn't any benefits like today, so I had to go to work, at least for some of the time. The first job I had, when I got back from the Land Army, was an usherette in a picture house at the Elephant and Castle. I wore a burgundy coat thing that went over my clothes and there would be queues round the block to see the films – especially the American ones, like *Fighter Squadron* with Edmond O'Brien, *Key Largo* with Humphrey Bogart, *Yellow Sky* with Gregory Peck and *Easter Parade* with Judy Garland – I remembered her from *The Wizard of Oz*. I worked from 3.00 p.m. till 10.00 p.m. and it was my job to show people to their seats. I liked working there, because I got to see the films and eat loads of snacks, but we used to get drunks in too, who got a bit too friendly sometimes. Once, some dirty old git tried to put his hand up my skirt while I was showing him to his seat, but I turned round and hit him so fast I knocked him off his fucking feet and he went rolling down the central aisle between the seats. I also had to try to stop people from bunking in for free, but they were mostly my mates or people I knew, so I let them in without paying.

When I came out at 10.00 p.m., I'd hang round the coffee stalls on the corners in the Elephant and Castle. There weren't any fast-food places then, so teenagers hung round

the stalls that used to be on the corners of the streets, selling tea and coffee and hot dogs and stuff. All the spivs
were there, young geezers in striped suits and hats made of
rabbit-hair felt. Their barnets used to be slicked down with
hair oil and boot polish and they had little thin moustaches
like Arthur fucking English, who was the 'Prince of the
Wide Boys'. Some of them wore black shirts and white ties
and they all carried shivs or cut-throats in their top pockets. I knew every one of them. I liked jobs that had perks,
not just money. I could get money by lifting stuff and the
spivs were a perk of the cinema job. I liked the excitement
and I seen loads of bust-ups between the spivs and geezers
from other areas. There was a lot of hatred between the
gangs and it often spilled over into mob-handed rumbles,
with loads of blood all over the streets.

I fitted in well with this crowd and I got to know the
other girls who hung round the spivs too and one of them
was Shirley Pitts, who I had first met when I worked in
the sandwich bar at Waterloo station. Now, I loved good
clothes. I loved the latest fashions, but I couldn't afford
them on the wages I was earning at the picture house.
Shirley was a professional shoplifter; later she even wrote
a book about it called *Gone Shopping*. She was the best in
the business and she started to take me with her.

Shirley was about the same age as me and she was a
slim girl and a very likeable sort. I got on well with her
mother too; she was called Nell and she was rumoured
to have been part of a gang called 'The Forty Elephants',
who were professional shoplifters at the beginning of the
twentieth century. They were called that because of 'The
Forty Thieves' and the 'Elephant and Castle', where they

operated out of. Nell was always smartly dressed, because
of her connections, but she was a heavy drinker too, which
I didn't like – I never liked drinking because of my brother
Tommy and the violence it brought to our house. Anyway,
Shirley took me with her when she went up West and I was
soon learning all the tricks of the trade. I always nicked
the best and the newest styles and was soon looking like a
million dollars, as the Yanks used to say. I became so good
at it, I soon packed in my job in the picture house and went
nicking full-time. I fucking loved it!

My first trip up West with Shirley was to a big furrier
shop. I never seen so many fucking fur coats in my life and
I didn't know what I was supposed to do. It was lunchtime, so there was only two shop assistants in the store. I
was a good-looking teenager at the time and Shirley told
me to go chat up the geezer – the other one was a hard-
looking woman. The geezer was young and me and him
were chatting away, when Shirley started putting on loads
of coats, one over the other. He never noticed, because he
was too busy looking at me. The hard-faced woman did,
though, and she started making a move on Shirley. Next
thing I know, Shirley's hit her across the fucking shins
with a loose clothes-rail pole and legged it out of the shop.
The woman's hopping up and down and shouting to the
geezer to go after Shirley, which he does. Then she goes
into the office to phone the police and I'm on my jack jones
in the shop. So I throws on a couple of fur coats and casu-
ally walk out the door.

Me and Shirley had cased the place before we went in
and we knew how to duck down the many alleys and back-
streets in the West End and where to come out so we could

jump on a tram back to the Elephant and Castle. The geezer had no chance of catching Shirley and nobody followed me – I don't think they even noticed me nicking the coats. Now, girls like us never wore fur coats on our own manor – to do that would be to bring the Old Bill round asking questions even more than they did already, so we had to sell them for a fraction of what they were really worth. It broke my heart to do it, but that was the game.

My dad used to go to work for 7.30 every morning. I never told him I'd packed up work as he'd only have wanted to know how it was I had so much money. What he didn't know didn't hurt him, did it? After he was gone, Shirley and some other mates called Tanis and Mad Frances would come round and we'd go to 'work' together. We'd go everywhere and anywhere – Croydon, West End, Hammersmith, Hampstead – anywhere they had nice shops. We had a few favourite ones that we'd visit regularly, ones that were 'easy', but we still had to be careful and not get too lazy.

We'd take it in turns to get what we wanted. One girl would be doing the lifting, while the others would be creating enough of a disturbance to distract the shop assistants and floorwalkers. A favourite trick was to take in a couple of large, wicked, Alsatian dogs. Dogs wasn't allowed in the shops, so all the staff would be trying to get rid of them and the other customers would be shitting themselves and the dogs would be barking and growling and running about all over the place and we'd be lifting stuff all around us. Once we left, Shirley would let out a loud whistle and the dogs would run out after us and make their own way back home.

We'd always be smartly dressed when we went into a store to shoplift, so we wouldn't arouse suspicion. I'd always only wear a light, flimsy top or jacket, even in winter. That way, I could slip on loads of clothes and just walk out wearing them. Don't forget, they didn't have no CCTV cameras back then.

Other times we'd go into the really posh shops up West in Oxford Street and I'd make out like I'd fainted. All the assistants would come running in case I was someone special, like a celebrity or something and everybody would be rubbernecking to see what was going on. Meanwhile, the other girls would be over at the jewellery counter, filling up their bags with whatever they could half-inch.

Another good trick was, one of us would pretend to be pregnant, with pillows or cushions stuffed into our blouses and pretend to take a funny turn. That worked a treat too, but a couple of times we nearly got caught, because they wouldn't let us go until they sent for a doctor. If that happened, one of the other girls would break something that made a loud crash and whoever was doing the pregnant act would run out the door. It was comical to see sometimes, these girls running down the street, holding on to a pillow stuffed up their blouse.

The people we had to be careful of most were the floor-walkers. That's what they were called in them days – they're store detectives or security now. But we could spot them a fucking mile off because they were always smartly dressed and they'd be walking round looking all important and serious – like they owned the fucking place. Sometimes we'd just crowd them to confuse them and they wouldn't be able to work out where to look or who to watch or who to follow. We all went into the shops separately and never spoke to each other when we were inside, so they didn't know we were working together.

On a really good day, we'd stash the gear with one of the local newspaper sellers and then go back for more. We wouldn't be able to carry it all about with us from shop to shop, so we'd pay the news-sellers to stash the stuff under their paper stands until we were finished. They were mostly old geezers who we could trust and they'd hold the stuff for us and wouldn't grass us if things went bad. If we had to make a run for it, we'd come back the next day and pick up the gear from them.

We'd take all the stuff we nicked over to Deacon Street and flog it to a regular buyer we had there. He owned a cafe and he always took whatever we had at a knock-down price. Deacon Street was in the Elephant and Castle, along the Old Kent Road – there was loads of little roads that came off the Old Kent Road back then, but it was all demolished. The only part of the Elephant that's left the same is the picture house and the Underground. We always kept back a few things for ourselves, stuff that was right fashionable and classy. But we had to sell the rest as fast as we could, because we were getting so much of it by now. As well as that, we were beginning to get known and we didn't want any of the stolen stuff stashed in our houses, in case someone grassed us and the coppers came round to search, which they done quite regular.

We had lots of tricks in the shoplifting game, some were simple and some were more elaborate. Like, sometimes I'd just load up with stuff and ask one of the shop assistants to help me get it 'out to the car'. Not many people had cars back then, so the stupid shop assistant would think I was a toff, because I'd be all dressed up to kill and I'd flash my eyelashes at him and he'd take it through for me, not knowing that it hadn't been paid for. Once outside, I'd say I was waiting for my husband to come with the motor and that would cool him down a bit and he'd fuck off back into the shop.

Sometimes we'd take the stolen clothes back into the shop we'd nicked them from and ask for a refund. They never asked for a receipt and it was better than flogging them at a discount.

When I went out shoplifting, I used to stay out all day, unless things got too hot and I had to pack it in early. One day I came home at lunchtime, which was unusual, and I found my brother Johnny's wife, Lil, and her two sisters trying on all my clothes. They were jealous because I had so much top-of-the-range clobber because of the nicking. I told her she had five fucking seconds to get them off, but she faced up to me, so I ended up kicking all three of them down the stairs and dragging them out into the street by the hair. When I got them out there, I paid them proper. I pulled all Lil's hair out and beat the shit out of her sisters. I don't think she ever forgave me for that.

I think I got addicted to shoplifting, because it was so fucking easy. The more I got away with, the more brazen I became. I'd choose shops where there was a sit-down cafe on site, then I'd fill up my basket right to the brim with everything I wanted or knew I could sell. I'd take the basket into the cafe area and have a cup of tea, while scoping out where the floorwalkers were. When I thought the time was right, I'd just get up and walk out with the gear. There was always loads of people shopping and I had ways of blending into the background and not making myself conspicuous, unless I was supposed to and I got away with loads. It was so easy, I did it over and over again – I couldn't stop, it was like taking a fucking lollipop from a chavvy.

One of my shoplifting mates was called Mad Frances, because she was always popping pills. I don't know what she took, blues or bombers or something, because drugs wasn't such a big thing with teenagers then as it is now. But whatever they were, they knocked all the fucking sense out of her. We'd load up with gear and then just walk out without paying. It took some bottle and you had to look all casual-like and not suspicious. We had some close shaves, because she was always high as a fucking kite, the mad bitch, and didn't know what she was doing half the time. She'd be staggering about and banging into other shoppers, like she was drunk or something – talk about keeping a low fucking profile! Half the time I think the shop assistants were so glad to see her leave, they didn't even think about her not having paid for nothing. I dumped her in the end and started going it alone.

Like I said before, my youngest brother, Ronnie, got into the totting game with Charlie Richardson, collecting scrap metal and old iron which they could sell for good money in them days. Ronnie knew this neighbour of ours who lived two doors away; his name was Johnny West. Johnny later changed his name to Johnny Bradbury and ended up working for the Richardsons' gang, who controlled parts of south-east London at the time. They were also known as 'the torture gang', because they used to nail people to the floor and cut their toes off with bolt-cutters.

The Richardsons sent Johnny out to South Africa to shoot a diamond merchant, but he didn't do the job for some reason and grassed up the gang instead. So he could never come back to London because he knew what was waiting for him if he did. He ended up selling televisions or something out there in Cape fucking Town or somewhere.

Anyway, Johnny was a right fucking crook and I was coming home from 'work' one day with another mate of mine from back then called Johnny Kellard – there was a lot of Johnnys about then, they liked that name because of the films, lots of the crooks in the movies were called 'Johnny' – Kellard was later shot and killed in a pub called the World Turned Upside Down in the Old Kent Road. Anyway, Johnny West told us about this car he'd just seen, full of really expensive clothes. So me and Kellard went and broke the lock off the car and done away with the gear sharpish and brought it straight back to my house. We stashed it in a suitcase, then jumped a tram to the Elephant and flogged it.

What we didn't know was the car we just broke into was an unmarked police car and it was part of a sting some plain-clothes CID had set up to catch some big-time crooks. They were watching the car and they thought me and Kellard were just a couple of nosey kids. But then we had the gear away so fast, we'd scarpered before they could get to us and they lost us in the maze of back alleys on the way to my house. When I was coming back from the Elephant, I got tapped on the shoulder by one of the CID blokes. He knew I looked like the kid who broke into the car and he searched my suitcase. Luckily enough, I'd got rid of the gear by then and he let me go. I had loads of near misses and close calls like that and it was only a matter of time before my luck ran out.

And it did. One night, me and my mate Tanis were walking home along Walworth Road, when we see all these lovely clothes on display in a shop called Gamodes, right on the corner where Westmoreland Road cuts into Walworth Road. It was a double-fronted shop that sold gabardine drapes and skirts, hopsack coats, petrol-blue suits and black guards coats. This was a real upmarket store and the clothes were very expensive and the very latest styles. I could never afford anything displayed on the mannequins in the window, not in a million fucking years. We thought, why should the toffs have all that lovely gear and we couldn't? It would be a fucking sin to just leave it there going to waste.

So I threw a brick through the glass door and we got in and climbed into the display window. Walworth Road wasn't the West End and the stores there didn't have burglar alarms back then, or maybe they just didn't think anyone would have the nerve to do what we did. Anyway, we were taking all the clothes off the models when we heard footsteps plodding our way along the street. It was a couple of policemen and me and Tanis couldn't get out of the window in time. So we just stood still as statues, posing like mannequins and hoping the Bill wouldn't notice the smashed door. The coppers came level and looked in the window for a moment, then moved on down the road. We put our hands up to our mouths to stop ourselves from laughing, then we nicked all the gear out of the window and took it back to my house and stuffed it under a sofa.

That was a mistake. Tanis dropped a belt on the steps outside and when the police came, like they always came to our house when something happened in the neighbourhood, they found it. They broke in while everybody was sleeping and caused fucking mayhem. My brothers went mad and there was a big fight and the house got broke up and police helmets flying every fucking where. In the end, I was arrested and brought to Camberwell police station. I spent two weeks on remand in Holloway women's prison in north London, before I was taken before a judge in Lambeth and sentenced to two years' probation. The judge said I was out of control and was hanging round with the wrong kind of people, like Shirley Pitts and Johnny Kellard and the Richardsons and the like. So I was sent to live with my aunt and uncle to keep me out of trouble. But I didn't get on with them cunts neither, so I soon ran home to live with my dad again.

The thing about it was, it made me a bit windy doing the shoplifting. I knew the cunts were watching me now, so I had to think of something else. While I was thinking, I got a job in the Black and White Milk Bar in Tottenham Court Road. They were stool-and-counter milkshake bars and they had black-and-white chequered floors and chrome steel stools. There was six of them in London and they were places where teenagers hung about and played the jukebox and stuff like that. I was hired to serve the knickerbocker glories and cakes and sandwiches. They didn't pay very good wages and I used to give my mates back more money in change than they paid and free food and drinks and I never got caught doing it. But it wasn't long before Tanis and me had to come up with another money-making scheme. So, we started to sell dates – not the fruit, but dates for men with the girls we knew. Like if someone said: 'I really fancy your mate' I'd tell him I could fix him up. 'But it'll cost you.'

The geezer'd pay me and whoever he fancied would go out with him on a date. But, after a few minutes, she'd make some excuse and fuck off. The geezer'd be so embarrassed he'd never mention it to his mates and he wouldn't ask for his money back neither, because he knew I'd cause a scene if he did.

We made so much money that way. I think I already told you about this Italian barber called 'Fat Mike' who had loads of money, well he fancied Tanis like fuck and I said I'd set him up if he paid me thirty quid. I can't believe he fell for it, but he did and he paid up. Now, thirty quid was a lot of money in them days, so me and the girls all went up West to the Black and White Milk Bar to celebrate. Anyway, this villain called Harry Neil and his crew came in while we were there and Harry started proper showing off in front of a girl that my brother Johnny was having a fling with, even though he was married to Lil. Johnny came in while this was happening and went fucking mad, because Harry was trying it on with his bird. Johnny told me to go get Tommy – Tommy came round and a full-scale fight kicked off. Tommy ended up biting this Harry Neil geezer's fucking ear off – he took it clean off – then he went to get his gun. But the police had been called by then and we all had to scarper sharpish. The manager of the Milk Bar didn't grass us, he didn't dare, because he knew what Tommy would do to him – but I lost my job over the ruck.

I spent some time after that flogging TV sets with my cousin Louise. We found a way of getting the sets on HP, by giving different dodgy names and addresses. In the good old days before computers, they never checked nothing and you didn't even have to put down a deposit; a tallyman would come round and collect the payments from you. We'd collect the television sets from the shop and, when the fucking tallyman came round the dodgy address, it was either empty and derelict, or the people there knew nothing about it. I had to laugh to myself a few times, imagining the tallyman trying to get money out of people for fucking nothing – I bet the cunt got his nose broken a few fucking times.

Anyway, we got loads of stuff like that and I started selling them to the black people in the area. It was a fucking joke! I had to stand there in some geezer's house, holding the fucking aerial above my head, trying desperately to get a good picture – because the buggers wouldn't buy the TVs unless they saw a good picture, which was difficult to get sometimes if you wasn't near a television mast. I'd be posing all over the fucking front room until they'd say 'stop'. Then they'd have to find a way of keeping the aerial in that position, which took some of the cunts for ever. By the end of the day, my fucking arms would be killing me, so I gave it up as a bad fucking job, even though we were making good money out of it.

It was round about this time when I caught on to 'rolling the toffs'. We'd go up West to the posh hotels and pretend to be prostitutes. We'd try to pick up rich geezers by giving them the impression they'd get something by the end of the night. Usually, this would end up with me and my mates legging it out the back door, once we got the money off them. Otherwise, I'd do the git over and take all his money and run. We only picked rich geezers, because we knew they'd be carrying a lot of cash. Sometimes, if the geezer looked a bit handy I'd get one of my brothers to lay in wait and I'd lead him into a trap, so my brothers could do him over and get his money – only then I'd have to split the money with my brothers.

It was foolproof because they couldn't even call the coppers or they'd get done for picking up girls. But you had to be careful they didn't see you again or, at least, not recognise you. You see, in the beginning, I used to pick geezers up from the same sort of places and sometimes I'd get recognised and the geezers wouldn't be pleased to see me a second time. Once, I walked into the Haymarket Hotel up West with a few girls and started schmoozing some old git near the hotel bar, when I noticed another bloke standing across the room, giving me daggers. I immediately recognised him as someone I'd made a fool of before. He looked bloody menacing and I got worried, because you never knew – not all the rich geezers were toffs, some of them were villains who'd made money and they were right rough cunts.

I decided to get out of there, but he blocked my way and then tried to grab me. The other girls saw what was happening and got between him and the ladies room as I made a dash there. They didn't pretend to know me or nothing, just made like innocent partygoers and, by the time he got through them, I'd jumped out the back window. The alley at the back of the hotel was stinking with the smell of rotting food and I couldn't believe how fucking posh it was at the front and how rotten it was at the back. I never went back there again.

Anyway, this experience led me to start changing my hairstyles regularly. I had every hair colour under the sun – blonde, brown, red, black – but I came a cropper when I dyed it brown and then back to blonde again. It turned green and I had to smother it in tomato sauce to fix it. After that, I resorted to wearing wigs. This wasn't too bad, because it actually made me feel quite glamorous, like a movie star or something. It was a fucking art in itself. I would dress to kill and act like the lady of the manor – proper dignified and mysterious. If you wanted to reel in a rich upper-class geezer, you had to act the part. These were hard times and a girl had to do what a girl had to do.

Another time, in the Savoy Hotel on the Strand, a few of us picked up this well-known Member of Parliament. He was a right toff, suited and booted and wearing a bowler bloody hat and all. I played up to him and he asked how much for me and my mates to 'play' with him later. I can't remember what price we asked, but it was a load of money in them days. We knew we'd have to be careful with this one, because he was well connected and we'd get into a right shitload of trouble if it went wrong. But, if we did it right, we'd be well in the money.

Anyway, this fucking old git wouldn't come across with the gravy until we went to a room in the hotel with him – so we had to play along. We goes to the room and this fucker is proper kinky, he has all sorts stashed around the gaff – ropes and whips and stuff and he's locked the door and put the key in his pocket. Well, we didn't know what we'd let ourselves in for this time – I mean, it ain't like it is today, where any fucking thing goes. We'd never seen a set-up like this before and we were well out of our depth. If we started screaming, he'd say we broke in to rob him and if we didn't – well!

I was just getting ready to do him in and run the risk of getting done for assaulting a Member of Her Majesty's Parliament, when the geezer takes off all his clothes and then asks us to tie him up and hit him with one of the whips. I'm telling you, we were trying our best not to fucking laugh out loud. Anyway, we tied him up and got the keys out of his pocket, then we took all his money and fucked off, leaving the door wide open behind us. He looked a right silly bollocks, naked and tied to the bed, but it was a close shave and I thought I'd better give the game a miss for a while, in case he came back and recognised me.

There was a bombed-out church just across the road from our house in Camberwell Gate and pewter was worth a lot of money at the time. So, me and my mate Vicky Nicholson got in and started to break up all the organ pipes. There was so much of the stuff, we were taking it out a bit at a time. Now, there was this woman called Mrs Toogood – by name and fucking nature – who lived next door to the church and she was watching us coming and going with the pewter pipes. She had two CID men lodging with her and she grassed us up, the fucking nark. One night, when we were coming out of the church, the Old Bill was waiting for us and we were arrested.

As I was still on probation, it didn't look too good for me. But, to make things worse, while I was at the police station, this female copper comes towards me with something in her hand. I thought she was coming to do me over, so I went at her like a fucking madwoman. I think she was only coming to give me a cup of tea or something, but I never hesitated when someone was making a move on me. That's why I got sent down for so long. Vicky got probation in Crown Court – the judge said I was unpredictable and aggressive and gave me three years.

8

PRISON AND BORSTAL

I was eighteen when I got sentenced in 1949 and I wouldn't be back on the outside again until I was twenty-one. I was sent to Holloway women's prison again, this time for three months, because all the borstals were full up. This was the old Holloway prison, not the new one, and it was a fucking shit-hole. I'd spent two weeks on remand there for the smash and grab at Gamodes and I thought I could tough it out. But two weeks on remand is a lot different than three months on one of the main wings.

Now let me make this clear, I ain't pretending that I'm some kind of Mother fucking Teresa; I deserved a lot of what happened to me, but there's a lot I didn't deserve neither! I thought I'd be sent to an open prison, where I could swing the lead, but the judge slag said I was unpredictable and aggressive, so I got sent to a hard nick instead. For the first time I was all alone; no hard-as-nails brothers to take my side when things got really rough. I knew I'd have to fight to survive.

There was a group of us in the meat wagon on the way to Holloway and someone gave me a Marmite sandwich to eat – I hated fucking Marmite! It was a bad omen. On that first day in Holloway I thought I was in a fucking madhouse. It was like the place time forgot – out of the dark fucking ages, like Newgate or something. There was screaming and shouting all over the place and the screws were trying to get some woman into a straitjacket. They took all my clothes and possessions away and I was thrown into a horse-trough and made to sit in it for a fucking hour. It was in a cubical without a door and every nosey fucking parker passing by could see in.

They issued me with the standard Holloway uniform – a shabby grey dress that felt like it was made out of barbed wire, a black cape and hobnail boots. After I got dressed, I was led up an iron staircase, past rows of cells with VD written all over them, to the landing where my cell was. You couldn't even call it a cell, it looked more like a fucking torture chamber – you wouldn't put a dog in there today. The walls were grey and dirty and made with that old stone they used back then. There was graffiti everywhere and some other residue stuff on the walls that God only knew what it fucking was. They must have tried to clean it after the previous prisoner, though, because the whole place reeked of disinfectant. It had a small window with little panes of thick glass that you couldn't see through for the grime. If you needed more air, you could open two of them slightly, but not enough to get your arm through.

There was an old iron bed with a thin mattress and two coarse blankets – they were dark brown and really rough and smelled of something fucking horrible and unrecognisable. There was also a very old, used, stained chamber pot in the corner and a bell to pull on if you needed the screws for anything. That was all. I remember trying to write a letter home to my dad and the shock of it all finally hitting me – as tears fell onto the paper I remember telling myself I had to be tough and I had to survive this. I kept repeating it: 'I have to survive this! I ain't taking no shit from no one!'

When I came out of the cell the next morning carrying the horrible chamber pot to slop out, I could see there was six landings. There was big nets to catch people who threw themselves over the side or who got thrown over the side. I followed the others along the landing and down to the communal recess where I emptied the chamber pot and washed, then I joined the queue for porridge. There was a big wooden table with massive vats of the stuff. The prisoners serving it up slopped a ladleful into my bowl and I went back to my cell to eat it.

After breakfast, I had to go do whatever jobs the screws wanted me to do. They were a fucking sadistic bunch at Holloway and you could tell they loved their fucking jobs, always swinging and rattling their keys at us and telling us how lovely it was on the outside. My job was to wash down the landing. One day some fucking screw came up and said I wasn't doing it right, because it was too wet and some bird had slipped on it. The bitch kept picking at me, goading me. There was only so much I could take of that because I wasn't used to being told what to do all the time. So I just went for her and we had a scrap up and down the landing, with her trying to hit me with her truncheon and me whacking the fucking daylights out of her. A load of others came running and blowing fucking whistles and pulled me off her, but not before I gave her as good as I got.

They threw me into solitary confinement for three weeks after that, which suited me down to the ground, because I didn't have to do any work nor talk to any fucker. The determination made me stronger – and I never did take no shit from no one. You see, Holloway at that time was there for one reason only – punishment! There was no attempts at rehabilitation nor re-education, nor nothing like that. It was a punishment, inflicted by total sadists, for being a bad girl and bucking the system and, if you accepted that and didn't bother feeling sorry for yourself, then you got your mind right!

Pigeons must love prison. Every one I've been in had flocks of the fucking things all over the place. They used to sit on my window ledge cooing the whole fucking time, it was enough to send a sane person doolally. They made us queue out in the yard for dinner – it was always some unrecognisable slop and tinned potatoes – and the pigeons would be all over us. They didn't seem to care that we were humans and bigger than them, they swooped on us and shit on us and tried to steal our fucking dinner before we could get back inside with it. Bastards!

The food was complete fucking shit anyway – horrible stew concoctions and I never knew what was in it. We also got some kind of sponge pudding with runny custard all over it which was made with water. The food was always sloppy stuff, so you couldn't tell what it was, sometimes burnt sausages, sometimes a cob of bread and cabbage, sometimes a little bit of cheese and a small knob of margarine and a mug of cocoa – the mug didn't even have a handle, so you couldn't hold it proper without burning your fucking hand.

There was a mixed bag of villains in Holloway, mostly older women and a few young girls for petty crimes, who shouldn't have been there at all, waiting for a place in borstal, like me. They wouldn't be there nowadays, they'd be doing community service or have ASBOs or something. But it was different then, the beaks put you in nick if you were poor, you didn't have to be guilty of anything except that. There was murderers and serious offenders there too, but they were segregated from the rest of the prison and I never saw much of them. The place was a little world of its own, away from reality, and I left people alone as long as they left me alone – apart from the screws. I hated them cunts and they hated me – and I had three years to go.

But somebody must have pulled some strings somewhere because, when a place came open at Aylesbury Borstal in Buckinghamshire, I was sent there. They were glad to see the back of me after the three months I spent in Holloway. I gave the cunts something to think about if they tried to fuck me about and I made it as hard as I could for them. I rang the bell in my cell so much one of the screws said: 'When you get out, Killick, you should become a fucking bell-ringer.'

I thought Aylesbury would be easier than Holloway, even though I was still hoping for an open prison and, even though I could be quite violent, I was convicted of non-violent offences. Normally that's what would have happened, but I suspect the cunts at Holloway made sure I'd pay for giving them a hard time because, on the way from Holloway to borstal, the screws kept winding me up, saying how good it was at borstal and how I'd be putting on weight and having a good time. The lying cunts!

As soon as I came through the gate, I could smell the disinfectant. The place looked like hell, it wasn't made for comfort, that's for fucking sure, and I knew I certainly wouldn't be putting on any fucking weight there. On my very first day, I was brought before the governor and told I would be doing six weeks in solitary confinement. The cunt never said why and I didn't ask. It was like being in a fucking dungeon, so far underneath the ground, no matter how you screamed or shouted, nobody would hear you. It was a tiny little cell with no window and a thin mattress on the floor and a chamber pot. Solitary was run by the real sadistic screws and they'd do you over good and proper – you know, to teach you manners. They didn't try it for long with me, though, because they got to know I wouldn't stop, even when I got out of solitary, they knew I'd be still up for whatever they wanted to try with me.

I never let them see weakness. I just couldn't – it was a pride thing that wouldn't allow me to lose, no matter how bad I got hurt. I ate my stinking meals in that solitary cell and was only let out for half an hour once a day to 'exercise' by walking round the filthy fucking yard. That place was reserved for girls who used to smash up their cells and smash windows and deface the walls and go berserk and stuff – I never seen no point in doing stupid things like that, because I got into enough trouble for fighting. But on my first day they threw me in there for nothing, just because the screws at Holloway told them I'd need it, to make me toe the fucking line.

After the six weeks were up, I was sent to the 'special' side of the nick. This meant hard labour. When they found out I'd been in the Land Army, I was put on making roads. There was a large cart with two wooden handles, one on each side. It was full of stones and had to be pulled along by me and a girl called Rita Burns. We had to dig up all the old roads with pickaxes, then shovel what we'd dug up into the cart, then put down new stones and finish it over with hot tar. We had to wear big heavy boots that got stuck in the tar, with the screws watching us all the time. By the time I left borstal, I think I must have made all the fucking roads in Buckinghamshire.

That's how we got the nickname 'bootie girls'.

When we were on the roads, if the screws weren't watching, some girls would do a runner. They wouldn't be gone far when the bastards would let off the hunting hounds after them. Them fucking dogs could run; no matter where you went, they found you. You could be up a tree and the bastards would stand underneath and howl until the screws got there. I seen lots of girls do it and none of them escaped, so I didn't see no point in trying it for myself.

One day, while I was pulling the cart, this tall screw with a mousey barnet came along and stuck a sharp key into my back to make me move faster. There was a watering can full of hot tar on the side of the cart and I grabbed it and threw it all over the horrible cunt. But some of it splashed back on me and stuck to me and burned all down the side of my neck – I still have the scar. I was bandaged up and bunged back into solitary after that, but the screw got the message – don't fuck about with Killick! When I came back onto the 'special' side, they put me on shovelling coal, away from the hot tar.

The screws always kept us working, I think they just wanted to keep us busy and wear us out, so we wouldn't be too much trouble to them. We had to do lots of different types of work: if it wasn't making fucking roads or shovelling coke for the furnaces, it was building walls or feeding pigs on the farm or sewing mailbags or shovelling snow in the freezing fucking winter or cleaning out the baths. I only got put on the real shit jobs like that, never in the kitchens or the laundry or nothing easy like. In winter, when I'd be shovelling the snow, the screws would tell the other girls to throw snowballs at me. This was guaranteed to start a fight and it broke the monotony for the fucking screws.

Then they put me on farm duty – it was fucking horrible, they had me mucking out the pigs and they were great fat bastards. I remember being in the sties one day and I used to keep the letters from my dad with me all the time, in my pocket, in case any of the cunts went in my cell and found them. Anyway, the letters fell out of my pocket and one of the greedy fuckers started to eat them. Now, those letters were very important to me, because they were the only link I had with home and this fucking great pig was chewing on them. So I got the broom, that had hard stiff bristles on it, and I stuffed it right up his nose. Well, he dropped the letters and went squealing round the place like he'd been castrated. That didn't go down well with the animal-loving screws and I got a warning.

The screws knew I didn't know much about animals, coming from inner London, and they would send me across this field to collect eggs from the chickens. The field had horses in it and I had this phobia of large animals that I told you about, after them fucking bulls in the Land Army.

The horses scared the living daylights out of me, because they'd run towards me and I didn't want to get kicked or trampled on. I used to run across the field as fast as I could and run back with the eggs. One day, this big black horse came running at me as I was on my way back – the faster I ran, the faster the fucker came after me. I was running for my life and the fucking horse was galloping. So I started throwing the eggs at him to get him to stop. It didn't work and the eggs hitting him only seemed to make him angry and I just barely made it to the edge of the field before he caught up with me. When I got there, all the screws were laughing their fucking heads off and saying: 'What, no eggs today, Killick?'

There was this right dyke screw called Mimi, who really enjoyed her job. She liked to get troublemakers like me cleaning out the baths whenever she could. It was no easy job, like you'd think; they were huge baths, where twenty girls at a time would wash. You'd be on your hands and knees scrubbing, while she'd be standing over you laughing and jeering. Well, I wouldn't fucking have that so once, while I was down scrubbing, I pulled her feet from under her and she went straight back over the edge of the bath. She didn't half smack her head – we could hear the fucking thud. It nearly knocked her clean out and she was seeing fucking stars for an hour and a half afterwards. It got me back in solitary, but it was fucking worth it!

The food was a bit better than in prison, at least the potatoes were fresh, but the regular meal was always fucking stew. I got so sick of it that I never wanted to see another bowl of fucking stew in my life. Even to this day, stew reminds me of when I was banged up. The governor was always trying to make good girls of us; she introduced country dancing and sewing classes and cooking classes and flower gardens and stuff like that. It worked with some, but I wasn't interested in none of it. I knew they couldn't care less about us and they were only trying to make things easier for themselves. So I deliberately fucked up the dancing steps and sewed the pieces of cloth onto the clothes of the girl next to me and poisoned the cooking and killed all the flowers. So they didn't want me doing none of that stuff after a while and just told me to go away.

Borstal was different to Holloway – I think it was because all the girls in borstal were young and full of it, while in Holloway there were fully grown women who'd had the spirit knocked out of them. The atmosphere was more tense, like it was always ready to kick off. Borstal was tougher, but it suited me better, most of the girls were on my level, they had the same mentality as me and I understood where they were coming from. I could see the look in their eyes when they passed me – it was menacing, like they wanted to challenge me.

My first fight was with this black girl. I'd never seen a girl so big before – she was as big as a fucking man and she knew it. We were in the queue for dinner and she came pushing past the girls to get to the front. She shoved me as she went by and I wasn't expecting it and got sent flying. When I got back up, I went after her and laid into her. We were still fighting as the screws were trying to drag us apart. All the other girls were shouting and cheering and goading and I must have done some damage to her, because I whacked her with my steel plate and booted her in the face and they ended up taking her away for medical attention. I was thrown back into solitary again and I thought the screws were going to come and do me over and just leave me there to die. They didn't, and when I came back up I found out they'd transferred the black girl to an open prison.

The screws would always try and incite trouble between the girls, so they could have a laugh and get to throw someone in solitary. Especially with me, because I would always take the bait – I was just that way, I couldn't help it. So they'd tell one of the other prisoners to piss me off, like start a rumour, or call me a name, or throw a snowball at me – anything, it was that easy. They wouldn't want to do it, the others, but the screws would promise them some privilege or threaten them with solitary, and they'd get them to do it somehow. I'd always get the cunt responsible and have them there and then. So, really, they were between a rock and a hard place, as they say, the poor girls.

I just fought with everybody! Well, everybody who wanted to try it on with me. But I wasn't a bully. In fact, if I seen a weaker girl getting picked on, I'd make it my business to protect her. It was easy, because I'd made a name for myself and most of the girls were afraid to cross me. I wasn't interested in fighting with weak people – I liked a challenge. And, besides, I ended up having the weak girls queuing up to sew the mailbags for me.

Thing is, I could never back down from nobody, no matter who they were. It went against everything I knew, so I was intent on kicking seven colours of shit out of anyone who tried it on, even if it meant tearing up the whole fucking place to do it. Because of this, I began to get a right reputation for fighting in borstal. I couldn't help it. Being a new girl, I got tested. The ones who ruled on the inside were quick to feel me out, to see if I was a soft touch. But I wasn't going to let anyone get one up on me, and I wouldn't stop fighting until I won. The name 'Killick' soon got shortened to the nickname 'Kill' – I was making my fucking mark! I didn't know it then, but this aggression, fighting spirit and fucking contempt of the 'guv'nors' would stand me in good stead later on, when I really needed it.

There was certain codes in borstal and one of them was called 'book for the doctor'. If someone said that to you, it meant they wanted to fight you, usually in a quiet place later on. By that time they'd be tooled up with a glass or knife and someone would be cut up good and proper. This never happened with me, I wasn't interested in going somewhere private to fight it out. If they wanted me, they had to take me there and fucking then. I didn't care who was around, screws or not; if they said 'book for the doctor' to me, I downed them where they fucking stood.

One day an inmate called Eileen Burtles called out to me: 'Killick . . . book for the doctor!'

She was surrounded by screws, so she thought she was safe. But I didn't give a fuck about the screws and I shouted back at her: 'Come on then, cunt!' – and lunged right at her, knocking her to the ground.

By the time the screws pulled me off, I'd banged her head and blacked her eyes so bad she had to be taken to the hospital. I got solitary again and when I came back up there was fifty mailbags waiting in my cell to be sewn up. But that didn't matter much, because I was able to palm them off on the divvy girls, who knew my reputation and were shit scared of me by now.

Another time, the screws brought this big lesbian bitch called Diane Richardson back from Holloway. I was sitting eating with a group of girls when she came for me. Now, this sort was built like the black girl and she could fight better. I knew that, because I'd seen her go at it before. I heard my name being called behind my back, so I just stood up and tipped the whole table over. I turned to her and shouted: 'What're you calling my fucking name for?'

She sneered at me: 'What're you going to do about it?'

So I headbutted her straight in her ugly mush. I remember seeing the blood coming down her face, but she didn't fall over. Next thing, we'd launched into a full-scale ruck, with both of us rolling round the floor. The screws came and dragged us off each other and we were thrown into separate cells that had a thousand mailbags to be sewn. But I just got the idiot girls to do them for me again. And as for Diane Richardson, she was tough all right, but she didn't try it on with me again.

Jack Spot was a notorious London gangster and psychopath who liked to be called 'King of the Underworld' in those days. His stepdaughter, Thelma Davis, was in Aylesbury borstal at the same time as me and she thought she was untouchable, because of who she was. She came up to me in the recess area of the nick and said – 'You think you rule this place? Well, you don't . . . I do!'

She was right in my face, shouting at me. So I hit her straight in the mush and she fell to the ground. I kept on hitting her, just to make sure she knew who did rule the fucking place. The screws eventually broke it up and took her away to the hospital wing. She didn't bother me again after that.

It got so bad in borstal that, at one point, I spent six months straight in solitary, but they couldn't break me. I would never give in – I enjoyed the challenge too much. In the end, the screws didn't bother throwing me into solitary no more – they knew it wouldn't make any fucking difference.

The governor called me in every month and made me sit on the floor, and every month she offered me the same thing: 'One clear month without fighting and we can release you.'

I think they wanted to get rid of me and I did try. Once, I almost got through the month and I was waiting in a cell close to the governor's office, to be seen about early release. Then a couple of leary prats called Jessie Ervine and Jean Smith came past and shouted in through the hatch: 'Killick, you're a cunt!'

As soon as the screws opened the door, instead of turning left to the governor's office, I turned right and went after them and beat the shit out of them. I didn't bother trying again after that, I knew it'd be impossible to get past a few fucking days without fighting, never mind a full fucking month and the governor categorised me as 'uncontrollable'.

But not everyone was as tough as me in Borstal. Some girls went crazy and some harmed themselves and some even died there. Don't forget, some of them were only kids and never should have been in a place like that. They got sent there in them days by the fucking shit-don't-stink judges for nothing – for stealing a bit of this or a bit of that, to help feed their families who were fucking starving. I remember a girl called Elsie Hughes, one night she rang her bell over and over, all night long. But the screws thought she was just making work for them, so they ignored her. When they opened up her cell the next morning, they found her dead. They said she had a heart attack.

The thing about me was, I'd seen so much shit and violence and hardship before I went in there, I never let it get to me that way. I never even went for medical treatment while I was inside – except for the time the tar stuck to me – no matter how many fights I had.

There was a system in borstal, whereby inmates were awarded little bow ties for good behaviour, which they pinned to their shirts. There was brown, green, red and white bow ties, each for a different level of arse-kissing. If a girl had three months clear of reports, she got a brown bow tie, six months for a green one, nine months for a red one and a year for a white one. These bow ties entitled the snitches and grasses and brown-noses to different degrees of privileges and 'luxuries'.

I never earned a single fucking one.

But the strange thing is, when I look back now, I realise just how much I actually liked being inside. I ruled the place and sometimes I think I'd go back and do it all over again. I looked on those years as being as good as any in my life, because I had respect. I had to earn that respect the hard way, beating down any and every fucker who tried it on with me, but I got it and, inside nick, that's the kind of thing that matters. It's different on the outside; you can get away from it if you don't like it. But on the inside it's there all the time, or it was in them days, the violence, just waiting to kick off. Those were lessons well learned, because things were going to get a whole lot fucking harder as the years went by.

They eventually threw me out when I got to twenty-one. When I was walking away, I overheard one of the inmates saying: 'Thank God, we can breathe easy now Kill's leaving.'

As I was going through the gate, they were bringing in a new mad lesbian called Barbara Allen. I still regret not having had a chance to take a swing at her!

I was on licence when I got out, so I was made to go live with Gracie in Wiltshire again. But we didn't get on any better than when we were in the Land Army, so I fucked off back to London. And that's when I met Harry 'Big H' Mackenney. I was walking up the road where we lived and he was sitting on some steps with my brother Jimmy. He said: 'Cor, I like the look of her. Who is she?'

Jimmy turned to him and said: 'I wouldn't have anything to do with that one, Harry. She's fucking mad!'

But it wasn't long before he asked me out for egg and chips.

I accepted.

9

'BIG H' AND ME

I had to adjust to having my freedom again, after I came out of borstal. Don't get me wrong, I kind of enjoyed my time in there – it was like a test of character, and I passed the test. But now I was out and free to do whatever I wanted, whenever I wanted. So I did! I was only a day or two out when I went with my brothers Tommy and Ronnie to celebrate my freedom. They took me to The Rock pub on the Walworth Road, which was a popular local place. Now, I don't really take much to drinking, but I do like the odd egg-flip or the occasional Guinness. On this particular night, I got completely elephant's trunk, not being used to the alcohol. I was staggering all over the place and Tommy kept trying to get me up to sing on the microphone. I can't remember exactly what it was I sang, but the whole pub started roaring and clapping, so I sang some more songs for them. What I didn't know was, Tommy had tugged enough people in the place and told them they better be nice to me and, because most people in the area were afraid of Tommy, I could have sounded like a strangled fucking cat for all I knew.

Thelma Davis, Jack Spot's stepdaughter, even came round to see me after I got out, even though I'd done her over inside. We got to be friends and Ronnie even dated her for a while. But it didn't last, because she was knockout gorgeous, and he couldn't compete with all the attention she was getting from other blokes everywhere she went. Thelma was good friends with Ruth Ellis, the last woman to be executed in England. Ruth was a nightclub hostess in the West End and, because I used to go over there loads to roll the toffs, we sort of moved in similar circles. I knew her, but I didn't really get in with her. She was very glamorous and attractive and she could have had her pick of the men, they all liked her. She was no fool neither; she was smart and strong-willed. After borstal, some of my friends whispered things in my ear about the men around her and that she was having problems, but I was too busy making money and looking out for myself to worry about what was going on with other people.

Anyway, I accepted Harry Mackenney's offer to go out for egg and chips and that's how our relationship started. Me and him had some mutual friends, so I knew he was all right and not a nark or anything like that. Harry came from fuck-all and had fuck-all, just like me. We were in the same boat, me and him, like two fucking stray cats. I got a job in a cafe where the old dossers who slept rough under the Embankment would come in for a cup of tea. And Harry'd come in to see me at night and I'd give him free grub and, if there wasn't many people around, as much cash as I could nick from the till. But I should have known we were doomed to failure – we went and got married too quick without testing it out for a few years, like they do nowadays.

Harry was born in Camberwell in 1931, same year as me. There was only him and his sister, and her name was Eileen too. Ain't that a coincidence? His mother was Irish, she came from Cork and her name was Jean. Harry's dad found her running round with no fucking shoes on her feet when he was over there with the army. She was a right bit of a Gypsy, with black curly hair and brown eyes, and she was also a very strict fucking bitch. I had plenty of run-ins with her! I'm not saying she was evil or anything; she was good to me in ways and knitted clothes for my kids, Harry Junior and Loveinia, after they were born. But she was a nosy cow, my brothers didn't like her at all – and she hated me.

Harry's dad was a lovely man in the beginning, when I first knew him; he was so tall and a proper gent. I got on very well with him, unlike my mother-in-law – until he refused to recognise his grandchildren in a prison waiting room, many years later. Just like me, Harry had been banged up in borstal before I met him. He was very young at the time and when he came out he got involved in one kind of criminal activity or another. His mother didn't agree with the way he was living, so she kicked him out and he went and joined the army and served in Germany after the war.

Harry loved vehicles of all kinds – planes, cars, motorbikes and anything else that moved, sailed or flew. He learned to fly while he was in the army – at least I think he did – he told me he was self-taught, but he must've got some training in the military. Anyway, when he came out, he was a fully qualified and licensed pilot. He was also a driving instructor and, later on, before he was fitted up for murder, he was only hours away from becoming a flying instructor. He could handle large aeroplanes and he planned to fly a Boeing, before he went to prison. That was Harry, he was a really intelligent man – more than anyone I'd ever known. That added to his attraction, but also to my fucking insecurity when I married him.

Harry went to live with my brother Jimmy in Dartford, after he came out of the army. He was discharged because they said he was 'indifferent' and I can believe that, because they all probably bored the fuck out of him in there. That's how I first met him, as I said, sitting on those steps of our house with Jimmy. I remember thinking how handsome he looked. He was six foot five inches tall, with lovely wavy hair and big brown eyes. He had a beautiful smile and I thought he was the nicest bloke I'd ever seen. You have to remember that no one from the area had ever asked me out before; all the geezers were scared of my brothers and steered clear of me. So, Harry was brave as well as beautiful – and that impressed me no end.

I remember one night my eldest brother, Tommy, put his arm through the glass panel in the front door during a fight and sliced himself so bad we thought he was going to fucking bleed to death. But, even though he didn't get on all that well with Tommy, Harry carried him on his back, all the way to King's College Hospital. He saved my brother's life, there's no doubt about that – that's how brave and considerate he was when I first met him. But people change all the time, don't they? I didn't know it then, but Harry was going to change, and I was going to be the reason he changed.

We went out together over the following few months, before he asked me to marry him. One of the jobs I took after leaving borstal was as a cleaner at Guy's Hospital. I didn't want to go thieving again so soon after getting out, because the coppers might have been keeping an eye on me and I didn't want to go back to fucking Holloway. So I tried to go straight, but I swear I only lasted four fucking days. They had me scrubbing floors and corridors on my hands and fucking knees with a scrubbing brush – a fucking scrubbing brush! You can imagine how long that fucking took, I'd just peroxided my hair and it looked lovely, until I had to get down on my hands and knees like an old fucking washerwoman, and then it looked a right fucking mess. No fucking way was the straight life for me!

So I reckoned my future was with Harry, and it wasn't as if he didn't know what he was letting himself in for. I mean, we argued all the fucking time – I think I was a bit fucked-up in the head after coming out of borstal and I just couldn't seem to stop fighting. But we must've had something special between us, because we got through it and he did propose to me.

'If you don't marry me now, then we're finished!'

That's what he said. I've heard more romantic lines over the years, but it was good enough for me then. I said yes. It was 1953.

We got married soon after, in a registry office on Walworth Road. It wasn't a big affair, we went down to the registry office in the morning with a couple of my sisters-in-law for witnesses and I wore the uniform I had for working in a snack bar on the Buckingham Palace Road. We went to a pub afterwards for a drink, then I went back to work. We never had no honeymoon or nothing, and I came home after work and told my father I was married. Shortly after that, Dad left London. He'd had enough of struggle and stress in his life, so he went off to live with Gracie in Wiltshire. He gave me the whole downstairs of the house, which didn't please Tommy, because he only had two rooms upstairs for him and his family.

Harry moved into our house with me. He was working as a driver at the time, delivering frozen foods in a van – this was when frozen food was a very new thing and I remember he went round to see my brother Johnny one day, who'd moved to a house in the Elephant and Castle. He sneaked up on Johnny while he was asleep in bed and threw a load of frozen strawberries all over him – Johnny didn't know what the fuck they were for a few seconds, he thought someone had shot him. That was Harry's sense of humour, that was his style – you never knew what he was going to do next. But, like I said, he never got on with my brother Tommy, because there was so much fighting going on and, while Harry could hold his own in a tear-up, inside he wasn't really a violent man.

We eventually had to move out because of the rucking and we got a couple of rooms in a house down the road, at 16 Camberwell Gate, that didn't have no electricity. Only one woman down Camberwell Gate had electricity at the time and Harry ended up running a cable across the roofs from our place to hers and hooked it up to the power supply. He was real clever like that, he knew about electricity and engineering and could make anything. He kitted out our place with all kinds of modern things – even made two little bears that sat on the television and they'd light up when someone was at the front door – but I smashed them up during one of our rows.

Harry got bored with the frozen-food job and turned it in but, before he left, him and his mate Sixer nicked a lorryload of the stuff. This was before the shops had freezers, so they had to sell it fast, because it was all defrosting – they were practically giving it away in the end, rather than waste it.

My brother Johnny got Harry a job scaffolding, but he didn't like that kind of work, all he wanted to do was drive. He got another trucking job locally, but his big ambition was to drive long distance – and this was to be the root cause of all our problems. I didn't mind that much when he first told me he wanted to drive long distance, but I went fucking mad when he actually started doing it. Harry and I were both jealous of each other when we first married. He was so handsome and I was so wild, we just didn't trust each other.

One evening, my brother Ronnie brought his mate Teddy Broadie round to our place. When Harry came home, he went fucking crazy, because he thought Teddy was trying to chat me up while he was away. He kicked Teddy's teeth in and Ronnie had to put a kettle over his head to try and stop him. Harry had found himself a long-distance driving job by then and he had a massive lorry full of tea outside. The next night, Ronnie came back with a few mates – one of them was Bunny Bridges, who I told you was later electrocuted by the Richardson gang – to get revenge on Harry for doing in Teddy Broadie. The buggers only nicked the lorry full of tea and Harry had to go to Carter Street police station to report it missing, so he wouldn't lose his job. Even though he knew who nicked the lorry, Harry never told the coppers. But they tried to make out he'd staged the whole thing himself and they beat the shit out of him in the cells.

They couldn't prove anything against him, but Harry got the sack from that job because of the fucking peelers. He soon got another long-distance driving job, though, this time trucking up north. This drove me fucking mad. I knew what these lorry drivers were supposed to be like for picking up girls wherever they stopped overnight. You see, Harry was fucking gorgeous – everyone fancied him, even the men and the fucking lesbians! I ended up having to fight off every admirer and it was driving me insane. He used to be all dressed up in his American flying jackets and it was an endless battle trying to keep the dolly birds away from him.

We didn't have a telephone and, one New Year's Eve, Harry rang the woman next door and asked her to tell me he'd broken down on the road. I didn't believe that story, so I went looking for him with my brothers. It turned out there was this party going on in John Ruskin Street, not far away. I kicked the door in and found him surrounded by birds. I went fucking mad! My brothers tore up the place, while I sorted out the tarts. We had another blazing bull-and-cow when we got home – I threw stuff at him and tore up all his clothes. He said he'd had enough of my family and stormed off to get his lorry, which he'd hid over by Tower Bridge. So I got one of my mates to come with me and we followed him. We were sneaking along behind him, trying not to be seen, when we got stopped by the coppers, who thought we were a couple of prostitutes. They let us go after questioning us for a while, but we were lucky not to get nicked for soliciting.

Harry had two false teeth on one side of his mouth and I demanded that, every time he went on the road, he left the teeth behind with me. My mate told me: 'The teeth don't drive the fucking lorry, Eileen!'

She was right; it didn't put my mind at rest at all. He was roaming all over the country and I was convinced he was cheating on me everywhere he went. I was in a permanent fucking state of paranoia – and I was wild enough already without that! I never did catch Harry cheating on me, and he swore he never did. He was always good to me while we were together and gave me his money, but I just couldn't cope with him being away so much because I couldn't control what was going on.

Flying was also in Harry's blood, as well as driving. One time, him and his mate Doddsy took me and Doddsy's wife out for the day to Biggin Hill airport in Kent. He'd hired a small aeroplane and wanted us all to go for a spin in it. But I'd never been in a plane and I was scared to get into it. So he flew off with the others and came back an hour or two later. I thought to myself: 'This is great! If he ain't driving, he's fucking flying. How the fuck am I going to keep up with what he's doing now?'

After the flight, we all went for something to eat at a local restaurant. But I was wound up and ended up wrecking the place, because I thought he knew the waitresses and they were chatting him up. I challenged one of the whores and she admitted she knew him from a few years ago. That was enough for me! I done her and her mate right there and then, and we had to scarper before we all got arrested. Doddsy and his wife never came out with us again after that.

It was only because I loved him. I mean, I really, really loved him. But he was too good-looking and I never felt like I could relax, in case someone else would catch his eye. You can imagine how I felt when he got a job trucking from Scotland to London. Fucking Scotland to London! 'Fuck that!' I thought. 'I'll never fucking see him.'

So I put a stop to it. I rang up the company and told them he was a criminal and he didn't have a driving licence. He got the sack even before he started – and never found out why!

I already mentioned Harry's mate, Patrick Connolly, who was nicknamed Sixer because six girls grabbed him and kissed him one time. Sixer was a good-looking fella, with a lovely smile and dark hair. He was a real sweet-talker and full of charisma, different to Harry, who could be quite standoffish and quiet when he wanted to be. Harry and Sixer were great mates and used to do jobs together – when I say 'jobs', I mean jump-ups and stuff like that. One morning I woke up and found this Sixer geezer asleep in my front room. Harry never told me he'd asked his mate to stay over, so I completely done my nut and threw Sixer out onto the street. My brothers were outside and seen this happen and a big fucking ruck started. Harry ran out of the house to try to help Sixer, but my brothers had already knocked all his teeth out.

It was such a shame – he had such lovely teeth.

Thinking back now, I realise I was a complete fucking nutter. Harry was always good to me when he was with me and provided for me and loved me in his own way for as long as he could, and I think I must've drove him fucking distracted. It's like I wanted to know where he was every fucking minute of the day and, if there'd been mobile phones back then, I'd have tracked him everywhere he went! No one wants that – no one wants to be under constant surveillance and having to account for every minute of their fucking day. If Harry was up to nothing and I was still accusing him, then he probably thought: 'I might as well do it, seeing as I'm going to be blamed for it.'

My first son, Harry Junior, was born at Camberwell Gate in 1954 and it wasn't like it is today, I didn't have any scans or tests or anything like that. I could've gone to the doctor if I'd had complications, but the pregnancy was straightforward enough. My biggest problem was loneliness. I was still very much in love with Big H and he was away a lot of the time, trucking up and down the roads. We didn't even have electricity and I hated sitting around on my own all day, but I knew I couldn't go doing anything stupid, because I had to protect the little child who was growing inside me. That made me feel vulnerable, because I was used to standing up for myself and holding my own in a fight, but now I was weaker and I felt lost. I didn't have any mother to go to for advice and Gracie couldn't have children, so I felt really fucking isolated.

Luckily enough, Harry was at home when I went into labour. I remember the terrible pains across my back coming, so he called an ambulance and they took me to St Thomas' Hospital in Lambeth. The hospital was clean and the nurses and midwives were brilliant; they had a matron in charge who kept up very high standards on the wards. I wasn't given any pain relief, like women are today, and I was in labour for about five hours, which isn't that long for a first chavvy, I suppose. But I had a delayed afterbirth, because the placenta was still inside me and wouldn't come out. They didn't have any special tools like forceps, so the doctor was called and he had to put his hand up inside me to pull the placenta out. It was fucking awful!

Harry Junior was a big baby, nine pounds, and Big H stayed there the whole time I was having him. He wasn't allowed to come into the delivery room like nowadays, but he stayed in the hospital and he seemed delighted to have a little son, who looked just like him. I was kept in the hospital for five days for observation, but I was healthy and feeling positive and looking forward to the future when I left.

I have to say that this was probably one of the happiest times of my life. Oh, it wasn't easy being a new mother – we lived in one room with a small kitchen and everything was hard work – washing, cleaning, using those poxy towel nappies that had to be steeped in a big bucket of disinfectant. Harry Junior used to sleep in a drawer and I had to get up every night to see to him, Big H didn't help out, as it wasn't his place. But he was a good baby, never sick or anything. I can't remember ever having to take him to a doctor. He was big and strong, like his father. I was with the man I loved and I had my baby boy. Things were good for a while.

Camberwell was being demolished to make way for new developments and the council asked all the tenants where they wanted to go. I wanted to move to the country,

Eileen's parents with young Tommy

Teenage Eileen, before Borstal

Young Eileen and Jimmy

Eileen's mother when she was quite ill

Eileen and Ronnie with Doris Duffield

Eileen (front), Gracie (middle right) and Ronnie, with little dog in Wiltshire

Ronnie and the dog that tore the trousers

The Brotherhood of Bad Boys

Gracie

Eileen (back row, 2nd right) and the Land Army Girls

Eileen in the late 50s, with 'Italian look'

Big H, when Eileen first met him

John and Daniel at 49 Crutchley Road

Harry Jnr, with the Miami Vice look

Benny the Bull, just before he died

Eileen and the kids, just before her divorce
from Big H

Eileen and Shelley in 1985

Sixer in his later years

Eileen and Shelley at 49 Crutchley

Harry Jnr in his favourite pose

Find Hit Man Harry

BIG names BIG news

DAILY EXPRESS

THE VOICE OF B

No. 24,599   Thursday July 26, 1979   Weather: Dry, Sunny

FIND HIT MAN HARRY!

Dragnet for underworld mastermind with a gun

A HIT MAN known as Harry the Bandit was being hunted last night over the disappearance of a dozen or more people "fingered" by London gangs.

He is 6ft 4in, a plane pilot, a skilled sub-aqua diver, and a small-arms expert who carries a .38 revolver.

Scotland Yard believes he may have slipped the net and be hiding in South...

By OWEN SUMMERS and COLIN PRATT

With him is a blonde wife of a missing short-hostage...

NAMES

New supergrass sparks off massive police hunt

Yard warn: Beware of this dangerous man

SCOTLAND YARD yesterday named Henry MacKenny as Britain's most-wanted man. They appealed for public help in tracing him but warned that he could be armed and very dangerous.

MacKenny, 47, is the central figure in a massive investigation by 50 detectives, sparked off by a man who wants to be the underworld's biggest-ever squealer.

By PETER BURDEN
Chief Crime Reporter

The supergrass has told of huge armed robberies and of how cash totalling £300,000 was buried ready for share-out.

He has also given details of four executions carried out by a hit-man in recent years.

For weeks, the crack team of detectives led by Det. Chief Supt. Frank Cater have been following up leads.

Yesterday, after a conference with the head of the Yard's CID, Assistant Commissioner Gilbert Kelland and the Chief of the Flying Squad, MacKenny's picture was made public.

Initials

A statement issued said: 'On no account should he be approached because there is reason to believe he may be armed and extremely dangerous.'

The advice was: 'Don't go near him. Dial 999 or contact any police station or officer.'

MacKenny was born in Clapton, London. He is 6ft 4in, well-built, and has brown eyes and dark brown, greying hair.

He should be identifiable by the tattoos on his hands. On his right hand there are two birds, a heart, crab and diamond, with the initials LTSC on the fingers.

On his left hand, there is a dragon and blindi, a brown and anchor and dice, with the initials ESUK on his fingers.

MacKenny is known to have holidayed abroad this year. He is believed to have visited the Spanish airports, accompanied on some trips by a woman.

It is not known whether he is in Britain at present.

The files on missing people being studied in the inquiry include those of George Brett and his young son Terry, who vanished from their farmhouse in Upminster, Essex, five years ago.

MacKenny ... tall and tattooed

Yard Warn: Beware

Big H is arrested in raid on London house

By ROBERT STRANGE and BARRY GARDNER

HENRY MacKENNEY, known as Big H, was arrested today in East London by armed police.

The 47-year-old man known as Big H was held in chains of silence and handcuffs at Marne Close, Plaistow.

MacKenny will be questioned about the disappearance of several underworld figures and a £300,000 robbery.

Detective Lan Gimson, 44, who saw the arrest from his bedroom window said: "I saw a man with red hair on the house with his hands in the air."

I'LL SHOOT

As he was walking out of the police station Strange's man shouted to him: "One false move and I'll shoot you."

He was then told to point up the ground and slam to him with his arms outstretched.

MacKenny was handcuffed and led away escorted by armed policemen. He was taken to a local police station.

Detective Chief Superintendent Frank Cater of Southend Yard's C11 Serious Crimes Squad said: "When we knew the house was surrounded by policemen armed with guns he came quietly.

Police made the arrest early in the morning, the description, photograph and copies and warrant seven days of the public out to try and apprehend him.

The man, robbery charge is connected to be the by-product of a gangster raid in Manchester where nearly £200,000 was spirited away. Then stacked away almost £300,000.

The raiders put up the cover of a Security Express uniform before culminating an five-man raid...

Mrs. Sida: "Like an invasion"

Big H ... he came quietly

Story of Barack when the police arrived.

Ben John, 12, was in his bed up-right, sleeping.

Mrs Sida said : "Our big began hacking and then a police inspector knocked on the door.

He asked if it would be all right if he and his men came inside.

We looked out and then armed police everywhere. They were something along the garden fence and behind cars.

When I saw all these men with their helmets and rifles I thought we were being invaded. It was just as if the army had surrounded the house.

The inspector told us to be in the kitchen floor except my husband who went upstairs with some of the armed policemen.

They asked him to draw a plan of the house next door. They were both terribly as they crept their room through the walls to look when we were in.

We were all petrified. We could only whisper to each other and inside the minutes tick by.

DON'T MOVE

Eventually a policeman with a riot helmet and an earring a rifle went out at the back and told me heard someone shout 'This is the police. Don't move'.

The police eventually left about 1.15 in the morning after coming army an old Ford Anglia which was parked just across the road.

It was all unbelievable. I have never seen so many policemen. Int takes several minutes with everything it was like something out of a film.'

Before the police left the inspector told beaming engineer Mr Sida : 'Thank you very much for your help. We have been after Big H for months.'

Another neighbour said: 'There were plainclothes police with what-ever thing everywhere around the...

Annette Ellison: "Glad he's all right."

Big H arrested

Mass killer quizzed about gossip at a prison

CHAMBER OF HORRORS BOAST IS ALL LIES...

'I don't want to end up beside the body-snatchers'

PROFESSIONAL killer John Childs denied yesterday that it was ever his ambition to be included in the Chamber of Horrors.

Childs was asked at the Old Bailey if he had told a fellow prisoner that "it would be great" if his wax effigy was exhibited at Madame Tussaud's next to body snatchers Burke and Hare.

He told counsel: "I am afraid that you are making that up."

Childs, who had confessed to murdering six people, is the chief prosecution witness in the trial of his alleged accomplice Henry Mac-Kenny.

Cross-examined by Mr. Michael Mansfield, defending MacKenny, Childs said that he had never contemplated killing anybody on his own. But he had often considered handing out punishment—"like most normal people."

Childs admitted: "I have thought of shooting them, I have thought of stabbing them."

By GEORGE GLENTON

And he recalled one instance where he had thought of "chopping a body into pieces, setting it in concrete blocks and dropping it into the sea."

Life

Asked if he regarded himself as a normal person, Childs replied that he never certainly did.

Mr Mansfield: "I put it to you that you would not, at the end of your evi-

dence, be willing to see a psychiatrist?"

Childs: "Most certainly not. There is no need."

Childs, 47, said that he had thought of writing a book about the murders for which he is serving a life sentence.

He told the court: "I have most certainly thought of writing about what has happened. My ultimate situation should not arise again."

"That was not the only reason, he admitted.

He told the jury, "If I

was to write a book and any publisher was to accept, it would be most certainly for money so that I could eventually escape from this country and prevent myself being murdered."

Title

Childs said that he had been approached by other prisoners with suggestions for a title. But he said one was "East End Butchers."

"I find no amusement

in being described as a butcher," he said.

"If I had to think of a title there would be only one and that would be 'I Confess.'"

He added as an afterthought: "Or, 'Thou Shalt Not Kill'."

Burned

Answering further questions from Mr. Mansfield, Childs denied saying that he would like to see his East End flat—where bodies were allegedly cut up and burned—turned into a museum.

But he agreed that he thought of killing Mr. Mansfield read out Childs's evidence in the lower court, in which he said: "It would have walked until he had gone through his front gate.

"As he walked down his garden path, silhouetted in the lamplight, I would have shot him in the back."

Mr. Mansfield questions from Mr. Mansfield, der victim Ginger Marks in talks with fellow prisoners.

He said: "It is quite possible K mentioned Marks in the context of MacKenny. Pinfold and myself intending to kill one of the people who had in fact killed Marks."

CHILDS: He said he got no pleasure from killing.

"That man is now dead."

MacKenny, 48, denies having been a partner in six killings.

Another accused man, 47-year-old Terence Pin-

fold, denies three murders.

Two more, Leonard Thompson, 41, and Paul Morton-Thirtle, 34, each deny one murder.

The trial continues.

All Lies

THE PEOPLE 7/8/1988

WHAT'S HAPPENING TO OUR POLICE + WHAT'S HAPPENING TO OUR POLICE + WHAT'S HAPPENING

50 RIOT COPS AND A HELICOPTER TO DELIVER BREATH-TEST SUMMONS

By SUE BISHOP

FIFTY police in flak jackets and brandishing pick-axe handles appeared from nowhere, shattering the summer calm.

Screaming and cursing, they swarmed over back gardens, breaking fences and setting loose giant dogs.

It was chaos. Innocent people were turned and pushed aside and one house was turned upside down without a warrant.

The purpose of the raid — to pick up a man who'd allegedly failed to answer a drink-drive charge!

People investigates

Butchered

HOUNDED Innocent granny Eileen MacKenny

CLEARED OF ASSAULT Harry's sister, Loveena

HARASSED Harry MacKenny and (inset) his mass killer father, Big H

Riot cops and 'copter deliver breath-test summons

because I'd had Harry Junior and I was pregnant again and I thought it might be best for us to get out of London. I was secretly hoping Big H would find a job where he didn't have to travel and we'd all settle down and be a normal family. But Harry wanted to stay in London, where he could pull the odd caper and he made us move to New Cross – and that was where all the big trouble with the police began.

But before we went, I hit on a foolproof scheme to make an earner. All I had to do was to get all my mates to sign up for new cookers on the hire purchase. The tallymen were always knocking on the doors, trying to get us to sign up for something, so I thought we should sign up for something that would be easy to sell. Anyway, we all got new cookers and I bought them cheap and sold them for a good profit anywhere I could. When the tallymen came round looking for their money a week or two later, everyone had been relocated and the houses were being torn down.

The happy feelings I had after my first baby was born didn't last. I gradually began to feel even more paranoid than before. Harry was trucking up to Manchester and I was convinced he was seeing other women. He'd go on a Monday and he wouldn't come back till fucking Friday. Looking back now, I suppose it was more than just jealousy – like I said, I was lonely. I grew up in a house full of people and then I spent years in borstal, surrounded by other girls and screws and everything. This was the first time I'd ever been truly alone and it was a shock to me. I couldn't stand the solitude – so I decided to go with him. It wasn't easy, for either of us. They had no disposable nappies then and the baby had to use terry towels. And Harry didn't like stopping, because he was on a strict delivery timetable and we had to sleep in the lorry. He didn't want me there, I knew that. I was cramping his style. He wasn't able to do whatever it was he got up to while he was away. This caused more tension between us, but I didn't care.

We moved to a maisonette in Kender Street, New Cross in 1955. I was none too pleased about this, because I used to live in a house and I saw it as a move in the wrong direction. But it's what Harry wanted, so it was what we settled for. The block of maisonettes was called Hayden House and it was brand new. We were on the first floor, but we had three bedrooms and a garden, so that was cushti enough, but it was murder pulling the big Silver Cross pram with my new son in it, especially as I'd fallen pregnant again very quickly after he was born, because birth control wasn't as readily available back then as it is today. Harry Junior was nicknamed 'Harry-Boy', and that nickname has stuck with him till this day. His sister, Loveinia, was born eleven months after him. The second pregnancy was easier than the first, in the sense that I knew what to expect this time round. But the loneliness was worse than ever and it felt like Big H was never at home any more, even though he was.

I never had any physical problems during pregnancy, but my insecurity was coming out more and more. I never got to dress up and put on make-up and my body wasn't like it used to be. Big H wasn't the attentive type and he never really tried to understand how I was feeling or the effect the hormonal changes were having on my moods; men didn't in them days, did they? So it led to more rows and Harry spent longer and longer away from me. He wasn't at home when I went into labour with Loveinia, but I was visiting my family and my sister-in-law Lil called the ambulance and I was taken to St Giles' Hospital in Camberwell.

This time I was all alone and I was in labour for fifteen hours, with no pain relief. Big H turned up after a couple of days and he seemed genuinely sorry for not being there. He told me his lorry had broken down up north and he held Loveinia and said how beautiful she was. I called my daughter Loveinia because my brother Jimmy had married into Gypsies – there were loads of them in Dartford at the time and the woman he married was named Loveinia and everyone called her 'Luvvy'. They had a big massive wedding for her and Jimmy and loads of them turned up and it was a great fucking party. Anyway, I thought it was the most gorgeous name I'd ever heard for a girl and that's why I chose it – it was unusual and special, just like my daughter.

Loveinia was beautiful, but I'd lost a lot of weight and didn't feel attractive any more and I wondered if I'd be able to cope with two kids and everything else as well. They kept me in the hospital for a few days, then sent me back to Kender Street.

Everything in Hayden House was white, because it was new-built, and I wanted it to stay that way. But Harry decided to jazz it up, so he used a car-spraying machine to spray-paint the walls red and gold and silver. It looked like a fucking nightclub! It's probably still there today – I wallpapered over it, but the spray-paint is probably still underneath, as I can't see anyone being able to get it off without knocking the fucking walls down.

We didn't have anything like central heating, we had a coke fire, which we would light in the front room and it was connected up to heat the water too and I had to carry the bags of coke up the road on my back, to light the fire. We didn't have carpets, we had Marley tiles that I used to mop daily. The one thing we did have was electricity and that was something new to me because, although Harry had connected us up at Camberwell Gate, it was just a makeshift thing. At Hayden House it was all built in and all mod-con. The place had a good community spirit, the neighbours were all like us, ducking and diving to make ends meet and everyone looked out for each other.

I've always loved dogs. I've had boxers, Great Danes, Alsatians and Dobermanns and, when I moved to Hayden House, I bought a pup from *Exchange and Mart*, and he got sent to me by courier in a little box. He was the cutest pup I'd ever seen and I called him 'Boy-Boy'. When he got bigger he used to stand up at the front door and knock the knocker to get in and I used to leave the kids asleep in their pram outside in the sunshine with him, while I went upstairs to clean the house – I knew they'd be safe. One day, however, someone tried to kill Boy-Boy. They slashed him across the throat and I knew it wasn't no animal attack, it was some cunt done it to get back at me for some grievance or other, I didn't know what. There was blood everywhere and I couldn't afford a vet, so I filled the wound with black molasses and this cleaned it out and helped it to heal up as well. To this day I swear by black molasses, I use it for everything and it always does the trick.

This is where I met a woman called Millie, who was to become a good friend. Millie was married to a local villain who used to beat her badly, then she'd turn up at my door with all her children in a right two-and-eight and I'd take her in until the bastard calmed down. He'd come round and beg her forgiveness and she always went back to him, then she'd be back at my door again a few days later. Millie was a lovely looking girl; her first child, Eugene, was born in Holloway while she was in there for stealing. She became one of my partners in crime, always game to earn a bit of money on the side. I loved Millie, she was absolutely beautiful, with waist-length red curly hair. It was rumoured that Danny Kaye asked her to marry him when he was over here performing at the London Palladium, before she went and got pregnant by her violent husband. Her son, Eugene, later became infamous for being 'the biggest drug-smuggler in London' and one of the SLGs – the South London Gangsters. He was found hanged in his Chislehurst mansion.

Nobody had their own washing machines back then so, at Hayden House, there was a system called 'the bag wash'. I'd put all my washing into big bags and seal them – one bag for whites, one for coloureds and one for darks. They'd all be taken away by a big lorry to the wash-house to be cleaned and they'd be brought back the next afternoon. They never took the clothes out of the sealed bags, they just plopped them all in together into big vats, like a giant washing machine – that's how they kept all the clothes separate and never mixed them up. There was also a little nursery in the road called St Mary's and my kids were allowed to go there for half the day free of charge. This allowed me to go out to work, or to go out and make money in other ways.

The isolation I felt when I was having the kids faded and me and Big H seemed to get back close again after they were born. While we were living in New Cross, we got involved with people like the cop-killer Harry Roberts and the family of Michael McAvoy, who would later go on to be leader of the Brinks Mat gold-bullion robbers, and the safe-cracker Alfred Hinds. There were all sorts in south London back then, some went on to be famous as stars of the stage and screen and others went on to be infamous and ended up as prison fodder. It was the time of Elvis Presley and rock and roll and the hand jive and all that stuff. It was also the time of the Teddy boys with their drapes and brothel creepers and duck's-arse haircuts and flick knives. My brother Ronnie and Johnny West were into the Teddy boy fashions, but Big H preferred the American flyer look. There was lots of action happening and me and Harry fitted in well and you could say we were like the Bonnie and Clyde of south-east London, but we still had a lot of personal tension between us.

I fell pregnant again, after having Loveinia. I didn't want to, it was an accident, but abortion wasn't an option back then and I had to carry it. Everything was all right until I was gone about five months and there were no difficulties. Then, one day, I felt an excruciating pain in my stomach so bad I couldn't move, and then I started bleeding. Harry was driving long distance, so there was nobody there to help me. I miscarried on the floor and all I could see was masses and masses of blood. I didn't have time to be upset, or to feel any sense of loss; that hit me later. I just wouldn't stop bleeding and I had to make my way down the street to a public phone box to call an ambulance. I was swaying and feeling light-headed and I could feel myself starting to pass out, but I knew I had to get back to my two young children. By the time the ambulance came, I'd lost so much blood I just didn't know where I was. They rushed me to St Thomas' Hospital, while I was going in and out of consciousness, and they got Johnny's wife to take care of the children for me.

In hospital I wasn't able to walk and barely had enough energy to talk, but I was alive and that's all that mattered. I remember the papers were all full of my mate Ruth Ellis at the time – they were getting ready to hang the poor cow and I felt sorry for her. When it all came out about her shooting that racing driver, Blakely, I could understand how she felt, me being like I was over Harry and all, and 'there but for the grace of God go I', as they say. She wasn't a bad woman, she was provoked. I knew what jealousy was like and if I'd caught Harry with anyone, I'd probably have shot him too. That's another thing, I was also thinking about Big H, while I was lying there – thinking that, if I died, all the fucking birds would be round him and I wasn't fucking standing for that – so I kept that thought in my mind and I'm sure it's what made me pull through. I was kept in hospital for five days and, when I got out, I was still very ill.

There was a billboard advert back then that said: 'Keep death off the roads!' It had a grim reaper figure and that's exactly how I looked. I was drawn and I'd turned yellow and lost about four stone. I was nothing more than skin and bone and I had to attend hospital every day for about a month as an outpatient. Then I remembered the black molasses, it worked for Boy-Boy and I started taking it for the iron. I got better.

But my body changed after that and I could never get my weight back again. It wasn't like nowadays, where everyone wants to be thin, I just wanted to be the woman I was before. Big H took the piss and called me 'rabbit-arse' because I hadn't an ounce of fat on me. But he didn't do himself any favours, because I felt more insecure than ever and that made me even more suspicious of him. Harry was 'pirating', which meant going anywhere for a job, driving long distance all over the country. Like I said, I hated him being away, so I constantly nagged him to get back home, rather than stay somewhere overnight. To tell the truth, because of the pressure I put on him, he did try to make it back whenever he could.

But, one night, the police came to tell me he'd had an accident in his lorry at Hitchin, in Hertfordshire. He'd fallen asleep at the wheel while trying to get home after a long drive – the lorry crashed and turned over, then caught alight. Harry was rescued by the fire service, but it was a near thing and he'd broken both of his arms. Nobody knows this, because he didn't want people to take the piss, as they do, but he had to have metal plates and pins put into both his arms to fix them properly. It was a big operation in those days, not as easy as it is now, and I'll never forget the way he looked when I went to see him in hospital. I thought he was going to die! He had to stay in hospital for a month and it taught us both a lesson – Harry had to get out of long-distance driving and I had to stop nagging at him to be home all the time.

The area of New Cross where we lived was a rough place in those days. There was a pub called the Montague Arms in Kender Street, where all the local villains used to hang out. It used to have a skeleton in the window and a pack of Alsatian dogs on the flat roof, but it was a lively dive, with jazz bands and cockney singers and the pearly king and queen and all that kind of stuff going on. I got a job cleaning the pub, and I was vacuuming a carpet one day when CID walked in. They were looking for stolen Persian carpets – just like the ones I was vacuuming at the time. The guv'nor was worried that he'd lose his licence for having stolen goods on the premises, so he asked me if I'd say I brought the carpets with me when I came to work there and sold them to him and he had nothing to do with where they came from. After I thought about it, I agreed, because I knew I'd have the fucker over a barrel from then on. He'd owe me for taking the rap and he'd have to pay. So, I bought loads of knocked-off silver from a mate called 'Benny the Bull' and the guv'nor let me sell the stuff in his pub for a good profit. He didn't like it, but he knew he had to keep me sweet.

The CID turned up again shortly after, and now they had their fucking mincers on me. But they weren't interested in the carpets or the dodgy silver this time, they wanted a bird I was hanging around with called 'Peg the Leg' – she was called that because she had a beautiful set of pins under her. They pulled me one day in their car and tried to intimidate me, saying Peg was a big-time criminal and they knew I had inside information, because I hung around with her and they threatened to put me away if I didn't give them what they wanted. I knew Peg was doing fraud big time and was earning a lot of money out of it. She was forging pension and benefit books, anything that could be cashed at the post office, where security wasn't all that tight. But the coppers got suspicious, because she kept getting seen with new stuff, like clothes and cars and she might as well have put a sign on her fucking head, because she wasn't even working. I knew about it, but I wasn't involved – it carried too much time for my liking, if you got caught, and I had kids to look after. But I wasn't about to turn grass neither and I never told them fuck-all – so I got done for the carpets and the dodgy silver and I received a heavy fine and a suspended sentence.

I don't know if the rozzers ever did manage to get Peg; I stopped hanging around with her shortly after that.

Because I'd taken the rap for the carpets, I decided to get some payback from the Montague Arms. While I was cleaning the gaff, I used to throw bottles of single-malt whisky over the wall onto the grass behind the pub. Then I'd run round and collect them on my way out. I was thieving about half a dozen bottles a day and flogging them to Benny the Bull. I don't know where the guv'nor thought all his single-malt Scotch was going, but he never said nothing to me about it.

Benny was a district nurse in a large London hospital and him and me were like partners in crime back then. And Benny knew how to keep his mouth shut. So me and him went on our travels, to see what we could pick up and we ended up over in Croydon and lifted a load of fur coats and sheepskins from the shops down that way. We couldn't carry all of them, so we'd bag them up and leave some with the bloke who sold newspapers on the corner.

But we overdid it and eventually got caught – I think the shops in Croydon were on the lookout for us, because they were losing so much gear. We'd already got some stuff the paper-seller was holding for us, but we went back again for more. Benny was lifting the coats, while I was having a row with the owner of the shop, to get everyone's attention focused on me. I was complaining about how I was treated the last time I came in and screaming and shouting abuse, so Benny could get on with the business. But we made the mistake of walking out together and we got stopped, but Benny was carrying the coats and I never had nothing on me. Benny took the collar for me and went off to the police station, while I went down the road to the paper man and collected my coats and took them to the Elephant and Castle to sell. He took the fall for me because I was on a suspended and would have went down for sure and I owed him big time after that. When he got bailed, he came round and I gave him half the money I'd earned. That's the way it was.

Benny was always up to something and one day he came to me with a load of gold rings. They were real quality, all inlaid with diamonds and tagged up and everything, and he said the manager of the Crown and Anchor pub down the Old Kent Road gave them to him, because he was shit scared for some reason and wanted to get rid of them. Benny asked me to hold them for him and I was more than happy to take them, not thinking twice about the implications. I tried to sell them everywhere, but nobody was interested, which was strange – so I buried them in the garden, just to be on the safe side. Well it turned out they were part of a big heist that was done by the Kray twins' gang, who were trying to find out what had happened to them. The gang got hold of this geezer called Scouser and they put the frighteners on him good and proper. Scouser grassed up the pub manager and they went round there and smashed the place up and done the manager over. He said he'd sold the rings to a geezer known locally as Benny the Bull.

I found out about this and told Benny and Sixer, because Harry wasn't around at the time and I was a fucking nervous wreck. I was tough, but these cunts had a fucking reputation, if you know what I mean, even then, in the fifties, before they got their celebrity status during the sixties. The gang didn't know where we lived, but I knew it would only be a matter of time before they found out. Sixer went out and got hold of a German Luger gun – we were expecting trouble, and I mean big fucking trouble. I stashed the gun upstairs, for when it would be needed. Anyway, next thing I know the fucking Kray twins are at my door, wanting to know where the rings were and how come I had them. It turns out some silly cunt had half-inched them and passed them on to Scouser, who tried to flog them in the Crown and Anchor. I gave the rings back to them sharpish, but I never told them I got the stuff from Benny – if I had, he'd have been a dead man. I told them some geezer on the market sold them to me and I never knew his name. I said he looked foreign and they believed me for some reason – maybe they knew someone like that and maybe some poor innocent sod got done in, I don't know. On the way out, Reggie Kray gave one of them to Harry-Boy as a little present. I'd saved Benny the Bull's neck. We were even.

My brothers heard about the visit and went fucking mad. They wanted to know who these geezers were who came round my place threatening me. I said I didn't know who they were, but my brothers got the gun from me and put a crew together and went round all the pubs trying to find out. Nobody told them anything, so then they made me get into a car and they drove me round to all these different houses to try to find the geezers who came to me – that was how things were done. I knew who they were, of course, but I didn't say anything, otherwise it would have ended up in fucking murder. That was too heavy for me, so I kept my mouth shut. So did Benny! But it had to come out eventually and ended up in a full-scale battle between my brothers and their crew and the Kray gang. The confrontation happened in the Montague Arms, of all places, and the pub was smashed to pieces and the guv'nor was badly beaten up.

That ended my fucking cleaning job, along with all the perks it brought with it!

I told you about my mate, Millie, who lived on the Old Kent Road and had four sons and two daughters and her husband used to beat her. Well, she came to me one day and told me these two geezers she knew were having to scarper abroad because things had come on top for them and they had a shed full of blue spots, which is what we called record players where you could lift the lid and play LPs and 45s and there were radios built into the front – they were state-of-the-art gear at the time. We called them 'blue spots' because that was the maker, some German company that used a blue spot in front of its name. Anyway, I got all the gear shifted to my maisonette and used Benny the Bull to fence it for me. I'll never forget the living room in that place, which already looked like a fucking nightclub, full to the ceiling with blue spots – but it turned out to be a nice little earner and I was doing all right.

10

HIJACKINGS, HOLD-UPS
AND SMASH-AND-GRAB

Harry gave up the long-distance driving after his near-fatal accident, which pleased me no end, because I didn't have to worry about him getting chatted up by sorts and tarts. Instead of the odd little caper, he got me involved in hijacking lorries, or 'jump-ups', as we called them, to make up for his loss of driving wages. Harry and his mate Sixer would do the job and I'd follow them in a motor, in case anything went wrong. If it did, Harry and Sixer would abandon the hijacked lorry and jump in the car with me and we'd be off.

Harry and Sixer were partners in crime and they used me as back-up whenever they could. My connections could suss out if the loads were expensive enough to be worth the risk and if the gear would be easy to get rid of or not. We were soon hijacking lorries all over London. Harry was meticulous; he planned everything down to the last detail. He'd never just jump-up any old lorry, he always had to know what it was carrying and he had the stuff sold before it was even nicked – stolen to order, you might say.

Before each job, he used to investigate what lorry was going where. He knew all the stops and when the drivers would take a break to rest and eat. Sometimes they would be inside jobs, Harry would meet the drivers beforehand and pay them off. They'd arrange a place to stop, where the keys would be handed over. The drivers would tell their guv'nors that the robbers were armed, so what could they do? Sometimes they'd take a clout on the head to make it look authentic – nothing serious, more visible than vindictive like.

Once, when Harry did a jump-up with my brothers, the lorry ended up in the fucking Thames. It slid backwards down a slope near Woolwich and the load ended up floating down the river towards Barking Reach. I don't know how the fuck Harry got out, but he said he'd never do a caper with my brothers again – they weren't professional enough for him. But, no matter how good he thought he was, the coppers were always close behind. They blamed him for every fucking hijacking and they were always at my door – no evidence, no proof, just because it was Harry Mackenney.

I remember one night we planned to knock off this load of expensive gear that was strapped to the back of a lorry up north of the river near Stoke Newington. It was late when Harry and Sixer got into the truck and my job was to tail behind them in a souped-up Austin Princess. That way, if the coppers got wind of the hijack and came onto them, they could abandon the lorry and jump in with me and we could make our getaway. But it was very foggy on this particular night and I lost sight of the lorry when it went over London Bridge. As well as that, the load came loose and ended up all over fucking Bermondsey Street in the Borough. The coppers chased Harry and Sixer in the load-shedding lorry, but when they jumped out to make their getaway, I wasn't there. They were nicked and they went down for eighteen months apiece.

How long does it take to make a cup of fucking tea? Harry and Sixer were in and out of prison all the time back then, either on remand on doing the time. But, as soon as they got out, they were back into blagging again. Now they were doing smash-and-grab as well as hijackings. There was this massive jewellery shop on Rye Lane, in Peckham. Harry and Sixer took me with them and hooked a cable to the steel security grille over the window, with the other end hooked up to a tow bar on their motor. Then they drove off slowly and pulled the fucking grille, window and front of the shop out into the fucking street – there was glass and metal and masonry all over the fucking place and alarms were going off like fucking wailing banshees. But we kept our cool – my job was to listen to a scanner to see when the coppers were on their way, while Harry and Sixer ransacked the jewellers. It wasn't so much a scanner, more like an old radio that Harry had adapted so we could tune into the police frequency. We could tell what they were doing and where they were going and I'd listen to it and warn him and Sixer if the coppers got too close. That's how we always got away with it.

In them days, we were into everything and earning plenty of money. We were doing really well and the maisonette was kitted out with everything anyone could need. I never knew what it was to travel on a bus and Harry made sure I had everything I wanted. But, even when he was in prison, I kept on doing the dodgy stuff, either with my mates or with Sixer, on the times he didn't get banged up with Harry. I didn't see any reason to stop thieving, just because Harry was inside.

Sixer's nephew worked in a butter factory and we used to get away with loads of the stuff – until one day the stupid fucker tried to do a scam with some sewing machines and got caught. The cunt sung like a canary to the coppers and told them all about the butter, even though that had nothing to do with why he was nicked. End result was the police came and arrested me. I was banged up in Peckham police cells and Harry-Boy and Loveinia were put into a detention room, because I wouldn't let them be taken to any relatives. The bastards grilled me for hours about the fucking butter, trying to pin a 'receiving stolen goods' rap on me, and knowing I knew the kids were on their own and probably upset. But I wouldn't admit to nothing, so they eventually had to throw me out, along with the kids.

It was all right living like a queen, except I don't know of any queen who got arrested as many times as me.

Harry had three big customised Yankee cars at the time and, while he was inside, they were nicked from outside Hayden House and I saw one of the geezers who took them. Well, I knew Harry would go fucking mad, so I reported it to the police and said I could identify one of the car thieves, if they could get the motors back. Like I said before, I ain't no grass, but I couldn't just let them take the piss while Harry was inside – it was a cheap shot, and they knew it. The police showed me mugshots of a lot of people and there was this one face who had dark staring eyes and I recognised him immediately. Anyway, a couple of days later, this geezer with the staring eyes turns up at my door with an offer I couldn't afford to refuse. Apparently, the coppers gave him a tug and told him he'd been fingered by me, so he knew where to come. He had some heavies with him and they asked me, nicely like, to change my statement to the police. The geezer was later to become one of the Great Train Robbers. What could I do? At least, Harry got his cars back!

Harry wasn't long out of prison on one occasion, when one of my mates asked me how my trip out in the car with him was. I didn't know what the fuck she was on about, because I hadn't been out with him in the car recently.

'Sorry, Eileen, I thought it was you sitting in the car with Harry.'

'Well, it wasn't fucking me, was it?'

'I'm sure it was perfectly innocent.'

I'm sure it was too, but I didn't give him the benefit of the doubt. I went fucking berserk. When he came through the door a couple of hours later, that was it! I couldn't help it, I stabbed him in the face! We had a full-on fight in the kitchen, which ended with me chasing him out of the maisonette with blood pouring down his chin.

'I'm gonna get my fucking brothers after you, you cunt!'

He was so angry he jumped in the car and tried to run me over. He still has the scar above his lip where I had him with the knife.

But that's what it was like between us. To say we had a volatile relationship is an understatement. I ripped up all his photos, even the ones of him in the army. I broke loads of his stuff and tore up all his nice clothes. I was such a bitch to him. Whenever I bought clothes for him, I made sure they were horrible and cheap-looking. I'll never forget seeing a picture of him years later, holding Loveinia when she was a baby – he looked like a fucking tramp.

Whenever Harry was caught and put away for hijacking – and it happened more than a few times – I would be out lifting the stuff I was accustomed to having. And, I shouldn't say this, but I never felt all that bad about it, because I knew there wasn't any birds in the nick for me to worry about.

Fuck me, I *was* crazy – just like they all said.

It was like I was married to two men at the same time. If Harry was in and Sixer was out, or vice versa, me and the one who was out would carry on the 'family business'. I also did some blags with the Great Train Robber who I got to know when he stole Harry's cars – and also some people related to Mad Micky McAvoy, who went on to pull the Brinks Mat bullion job in 1983. We started doing more smash-and-grab as well as the jump-ups, because the scanner made it safer than it would normally have been.

It was Sixer who got us involved in armed robbery in the first place. In the beginning, it was small-time, doing over pubs and clubs that were outside our manor. Going up north of the river and turning over gaffs for a few grand. We didn't used to have any ammunition in the guns to begin with, but that got too hairy, so we tooled up proper to protect ourselves, in case someone started fucking shooting back.

We also graduated to sticking up jewellery shops in Hatton Garden, which came out of Harry running stolen cars from the docks for Alfred Hinds. The cars were always brand spanking new and the latest top-of-the-range models. They were sent over from Ireland and Harry would collect them and drive them to wherever they had to go. I never saw so many fucking cars in my life and we used to drive everywhere in them and all the heads would turn when we passed. But Hinds had ambitions to be a big-time crook and we went along – he was a master safe-cracker and liked to do over jewellery stores. That was before they had all that modern security stuff and self-locking doors installed. They'd break in and do the safe, or sometimes just walk in with a couple of sawn-offs and help themselves to the sparklers. I'd be waiting outside with the engine running and keeping an eye out for peelers.

Harry ended up going inside for three years and, later on, for a seven stretch. They tried to get him for the armed robberies, but they couldn't pin nothing on him, so they done him for ringing cars. It was inside, during one of his stretches, that Harry met John Childs and Terry Pinfold, two of the men who would later be involved in the big frame-up that would ruin Big H's life. When he came out, he tried to bring them round our house, but I banned them, because I didn't like them and didn't trust them. If I'd only known at the time what was going to happen I might have treated Harry better than I did and tried not to be so jealous of him and not drive him away from me.

I was very dedicated to Harry while we were together, and when he went away for the stretches he did I used to travel all over the place to visit him. I'd go with either Sixer or Benny, come wind, rain or shine, and I'd go out and do an earner to get the money for the trip. I wrote to him all the time and I took care of any business he needed doing on the outside. It was 1957 and I thought then that everything would turn out all right for us, that we'd make a big score and be able to retire from the game and have a nice little life together in a nice little normal house and the kids in a good school and the future looking all bright and rosy. That's what I thought, but I was naive and didn't know what I was up against.

I once went with Benny to visit Harry in prison, on the Isle of Portland, near Weymouth. We had no money to get there that day, so we jumped a train and got out at the other end without a fucking penny in our pockets. The prison was a long way from the train station, so me and Benny went to look for ways to get some money to get out there. Benny ended up lifting some jewellery from a shop, while I chatted up the assistant, then we went about trying to find a pawnshop where we could hock it. But do you think we could find a fucking pawnshop in fucking Weymouth? I thought to myself, 'What kind of fucking people live in a place without a hockshop?'

In the end, me and Benny ended up walking all the way to the prison and back, because I'd never let Harry down – but we sold the jewellery when we got back to London and went and bought pie and mash.

But things were changing for me and Harry – our rollercoaster relationship was coming to an end. The first sign I saw of this was when I went to Brixton Prison to visit him and I took the children with me. When I got there I had to stay in the waiting room till I got called. In Brixton, they didn't call you by your own name, but by the name of the prisoner. So, when they called out 'Wife of Harry Mackenney', I got up with the kids to go see him. But this other bird stood up at the same time and came from behind me, with Harry's dad. She was tall, with dark hair and she actually looked a bit like me. I couldn't believe what I was seeing and I was confused for a minute, as I watched her on her way up to see Harry. But I soon recovered my senses and I grabbed her and pushed her flying into the nearest screw. There was such a fucking commotion – I started shouting that I was the wife of Harry Mackenney, but the lying bitch said she was. The kids were crying and the screws were getting agitated. Harry was standing at the back with a look of horror on his face – he must've sent out two Visiting Orders for the same day by mistake – and his dad just stood there saying nothing.

Anyway, the visit was cancelled, because they couldn't work out who was Harry's real wife and we were all told to leave. I was fucking livid as I walked to the bus stop to go home. The kids were upset and Harry's fucking dad hadn't even the common decency to say hello to his grandchildren. I was working myself up into a fucking state. When I got to the bus stop, who was there? Only the fucking cunt from the prison with Harry's dad. I heard her say to him: 'How do I get back to Dagenham?'

I stayed back out of sight and tried to restrain myself for the sake of the children. But the fuckers got on the same bus as me and I watched them go to the upper deck, while me and the kids stayed on the lower one. But my temper was brewing and then something just snapped in me and I went after her.

It was the fact that Harry's dad was with her that made it so bad. I liked the man and I felt betrayed. He didn't expect me to be there visiting his son, while he was there with his son's fancy bird, so his way of dealing with it was to pretend me and his grandchildren didn't exist, like he condoned his son cheating and deserting his family. Big H's parents didn't get involved when things went wrong with us. His mother never liked me to start with and she tried to shut the door in my face once, but I stuck my foot in the door and told her what I thought of her, the old cunt. But I didn't expect this from the old man and it kept going round in my head, winding me up.

In the end, I couldn't help it. I ran up the steps to the top deck, with the kids after me and I fucking laid into her proper and she never knew what fucking hit her. I pounded her with every ounce of rage inside me. She was covered in blood and she collapsed onto Harry's dad and sort of fell against the window and passed out. I could have done more to her – I wanted to kill her, but the kids were crying. So I walked away. I found out later that the bitch was called Edna and Harry had met her on some kind of blind date. I never found out the exact details, so I let it go.

That was the beginning of the end for Big H and me.

One time in 1958, when Harry came out of prison, he got a job as a bus driver, trying to go straight and do things right. But I didn't like it. I mean, how the fuck could I trust him any more? All the birds would chat to him when they were getting on and off. As bad as things were before they were a damn sight fucking worse now. I remember getting on his bus one day and seeing a female conductor talking to him. I knocked the slag right off the bus and me and Harry ended up having an almighty row, right in the middle of the bus. Then some fucking idiot passenger tried to do the Good Samaritan and step in to stop the argument, so Harry knocked him the fuck out!

Harry soon had enough of my jealousy about his bus-driving job, so he went back to the dodgy stuff with Alfred Hinds, after the infamous safe-cracker's third escape from Chelmsford Prison, when he was living in Ireland as a used car dealer, under the name William Herbert Bishop. Like I said before, Hinds was sending in the stolen cars from Ireland and Harry was collecting them and driving them from the docks to New Cross, or wherever else their final destination happened to be. That's the way it was, if you couldn't or wouldn't hold down a legitimate job, then there was always a scam or a con or some other sort of crookery to be had.

The criminal fraternity in London used to be a closed society and you couldn't help rubbing shoulders with all sorts of villains, if you were involved in that kind of thing. Harry was involved with Alfred Hinds and others and I was mates with Michael McAvoy's mother-in-law and people who saw thieving as a legitimate way of life. In fact, the solicitor who defended the Brinks Mat robbers also defended me, years later, when I was charged with fraud at the Old Bailey for forging post-office savings books – but that's another story. Maureen Gator was also a dodgy mate of mine and she went out with my brother Ronnie for a while, before going on to marry Eddie Richardson. Some of my family worked on the doors of clubs in Catford that was owned by the Richardson gang. It was a small world.

You might know what was going on, but you kept your nose out of other people's business and didn't step on anyone's toes.

Another mate of mine at New Cross was a woman called Sissy. Me and Sissy got on real well; she liked a bit of ducking and diving and we pulled some strokes together. Her granddaughter, Jackie, went out with Mad Micky McAvoy and settled down with him and they had two kids. As I already said, McAvoy went on to do the Brinks Mat bullion robbery in 1983 and you can see how it was such a small world, where everybody knew everybody else, from the Krays to Bruce Reynolds and Ronnie Biggs and Buster Edwards. We were all made in the same mould. We were all at it, one way or another – including the police. In fact people used to say, 'There *is* organised crime in Britain – it's called the police force.'

We might have been villains to some people, but we never saw ourselves as anything other than ordinary people. As I said, everyone was at it – the rich were stealing from the poor and the poor were stealing it back from the rich. The villains were stealing from the banks and the banks were stealing from the public. The police were stealing from the villains and the government was stealing from the police. So, it was all swings and fucking roundabouts to us.

Some were killers and some weren't. Harry wasn't, and neither was I. But the coppers couldn't get Harry for anything big, so they decided to bide their time. The way they looked at it was, he deserved to go down for a long stretch, and he was as good as anyone else to take the fall. They even told me so when they raided my house after me and Harry split up. They bragged about it and laughed about it, but I had no contact with him then and he was mixing with the people who would bring him down good and proper. Even if I had managed to contact him and tell him, I doubt if he would have believed me.

The irony of it all is that Harry was a really nice bloke. He loved life and he loved everything – even animals. He hated seeing anyone ill-treating anything and wouldn't fucking stand for it. He was doing a delivery to a farm once, when he was driving, and saw the farmer kicking some pigs to move them into a pen. He went mad and took on three of them, the farmer and two farmhands and beat the shit out of them. But he didn't like violence and wasn't a man who resorted to violence without a fucking good reason. He never even wanted to do the jump-ups or the rest of the crime stuff. It was because I didn't want him driving long-distance – so, in a way, I suppose it was all my fault!

11

THE SIXTIES AND SIXER

Things were changing; we had the war in the forties and rationing in the fifties because the country was trying to recover, but then the sixties came round and it was like the world suddenly discovered it could have fun again. There were so many new things to see and do and nothing to worry about. Huge supermarkets were popping up everywhere – I'll never forget when I first saw one, there was food everywhere, readily available to be nicked. Nobody would ever be hungry again! In the forties and fifties the shops were small and you were always being watched by the staff. But these massive supermarkets and department stores were like Aladdin's caves to someone as light-fingered as me. It was a fucking bonanza – if you knew what you were doing!

I nicked my first television in the sixties and my first fridge-freezer after that. I was going up in the world. Clothes were becoming more colourful and daring, all sorts of fashions – you could wear what you liked, anything went. And I loved it. The latest fashions were being advertised everywhere and people wanted to keep up with the trends – so did I, so I went out and stole them. I always loved clothes, even when I had none. Now I made regular trips to Oxford Street and Carnaby Street and High Street Kensington, wherever the trendy stores were. I kitted the kids out in the best designer gear and I'm sure the neighbours must have thought I was on the game, because we never had nothing but we dressed like film stars.

But the good times didn't last.

At the end of the 1950s, Harry had started going missing for long periods of time. He'd be gone for a while, then he'd come back again. Our relationship was volcanic and he couldn't always stand the constant fighting and violence from me. Well, Big H got a load of furniture on HP when we were at Hayden House; it was all from Harrison & Gibson down in Bromley – only the best of gear. A three-piece suite, beds, new kitchen, all the stuff I needed for the house. It was all right when we were together, but when he went on his missing sprees, he forgot to pay the HP instalments and, in 1960 after he left, the fucking bailiffs turned up at my door.

They were right fucking bully-boys too. One of them tried to push his way in past me, so I hit him and sent him sprawling back through the door. I had my kids standing behind me, watching all this and I was distracted when they rushed me and grabbed me and dragged me back into the house. They locked me in a room and I was screaming at Harry Junior to run and get help. The boy was only six and, by the time he ran down the road and brought help back to get me out, the fucking bailiffs were gone and had taken everything in the fucking house – and I mean everything. They cleaned the whole place out. We had to sit on orange boxes and sleep on the fucking floor, until I could go out and steal some more stuff – which is what Harry should have done in the first place, instead of bothering with fucking HP. But then, Harry was always trying to go straight and do things the proper way – he never fucking succeeded.

There were a lot of self-righteous cunts about then, just as there are now, I suppose. Like when Harry-Boy was going to Samuel Pepys School in New Cross, but he got very ill with an infection and he had to stay home for about two weeks. Back then, if kids didn't attend school, the school-board man would come looking for you, and he came to my house every other fucking day. I told him time and again that Harry-Boy was ill and he'd be back to school when he got better. Maybe I was a bit abrasive with him, I don't know, but these sanctimonious civil servants had a way of looking down their noses at poor people and they were always looking for some excuse to 'bring us to book'. So, the fucker went back and made a bad report about me and I was sent a summons to attend the magistrates' court. Harry-Boy had to come with me and I remember he was wearing a little Robin Hood hat and didn't really know what was going on. I thought they'd call me, but they didn't – little Harry got called before the magistrate and the self-opinionated cunt demanded that he take off his hat in front of his fucking lordship. Then the boy was made to repeat after him that, if he didn't go back to Samuel Pepys, he'd be taken away and sent to a remand school. The bastard frightened the life out of my six-year-old son and it was all I could do to hold myself back from running up there and sticking one of his pencils into his fucking eye.

Harry-Boy was so shaken, he ended up leaving his little Robin Hood hat behind him and he cried his eyes out over it.

Another time, I was making a cup of tea and these two birds turned up at my house, giving it all the big 'un about how they were going to teach Harry-Boy some manners and give him a slap. Before they had a chance to say another word, I knocked the first one out and, before she even hit the floor, I was on to the second one. They were both out cold before the kettle had a chance to boil. I was just heaving them out the door, when Jimmy turned up. He used his boot to shift the bodies over the threshold and we shut the door and left them there and went and had a cup of tea.

But other things were happening too. I always had a soft spot for Sixer, ever since that time my brothers knocked his fucking teeth out. Harry was coming and going non-stop – he never told me where he went and he'd be gone for days on end. When he got back, we'd have a mad row because he refused to tell me anything. I heard he was off with his mates that he met in prison, Terry Pinfold and Bruce Childs and the like, people I never took to. He was very distant all the time and it seemed like he didn't want to talk to me any more. Then, one time he said he had to go out on business and he wouldn't be back till the next day. I knew something wasn't right, so I followed him all the way to the train station. He knew I was following him and he even waved me goodbye as he got on the train. He shouted: 'Keep my dinner in the oven!'

And I was left standing on the platform.

Years later, when I went to visit him in Parkhurst Prison on the Isle of Wight, the first thing I said was: 'I still got your dinner in the oven.'

Harry never came back. We'd finally parted company for good, and it was as much my fault as it was his. I was too jealous for him to live with and I made his life a misery – he swore he never had no affairs, but I never believed him – and still don't. It was 1960.

Years later, when Harry was being slagged off in the newspapers and accused of murder, I defended him. I know I was insecure and jealous and impossible to live with, but I loved him with all my heart and would have done anything for him. But he walked away from me and his children and left us with nothing. I could forgive him leaving me like that, but not the innocent kids. The fact that he never had anything to do with Harry-Boy and Loveinia after that cut me to the bone. He could have come to see them and I wouldn't have stopped him. He could have sent them a birthday card or a Christmas card or a present or a bit of money, but he never did – not once. It was like he walked away and, all of a sudden, they didn't exist no more. Even when he saw them later on, when he was in trouble, he showed no emotion, no love, no regard for them. I defended him because I knew he didn't kill those people, like they said he did. But I still had anger inside me for the way he walked out and left his little family.

That was my introduction to the Swinging Sixties! It might have been swinging for some people, but not for everyone. I remember going to the market on Walworth

Road and, as I crossed the street, I bumped into June Bush, a mate of mine who'd been in borstal with me. She was pushing a pram and I asked her where she was staying and what she was doing these days. She said she was staying in the workhouse down on Westmoreland Road and I was stunned, because I didn't think they still had places like that. Apparently, she took up with a Polish bloke and had a chavvy for him and he scarpered, so she had to go into the workhouse. I felt so sorry for her and promised I'd come see her.

So I started to go see her in the workhouse – it was like something out of a fucking Dickens novel. It was a horrible-looking Victorian building that was all run-down and dark and dingy and dirty. The walls were covered in old grey and brown distemper and the floors were bare, except where they were covered by dirty, stained oilcloth. The windows were small and high up in the walls, so you couldn't look out through them and the whole place had a nasty, musty smell to it. It was so overpowering that it made me feel like throwing up when I first went in there. There wasn't any individual bedrooms or anything and June had a bed in a dormitory for her and her baby. The beds were old iron things and the blankets were made of itchy sacking, like army blankets. When I went in there for the first time, I was shocked to see how many women were in there. There wasn't even enough beds and some of them had to sleep on the floor on makeshift mattresses. It was a place for poor people, for runaways and for women who had a child out of wedlock. It was called a workhouse, but they didn't have to work, just keep the area round them clean and tidy. But it was still the lowest of the low and

June told me all they got to eat was porridge, like in *Oliver Twist*.

I couldn't bear to see her stuck in there, so I introduced her to a mate of my brother Jimmy, a man called Pat. Him and June hit it off and they got married and he took her out of that fucking place. I lost track of her after that.

I was very poor after Harry left. I tried everything I knew to make money and eventually had to get a cash-in-hand job doing night work in the cafeteria at the *Daily Mirror*, over in Holborn. My mate Millie was looking after Harry-Boy and Loveinia for me and I hated leaving them, even though she was a very good friend – but I had no choice. My hours were 7.00 p.m. till 5.00 a.m. and I had to get a bus over there every night in the middle of winter. I had holes in my shoes again, just like when I was a young girl and I could feel the cold and the snow getting through to my feet as I walked along. My clothes were second-hand, given to me by friends, because all the money went on the kids and running the house. It was frowned on to be a single parent back then, even more than it is now and everybody assumed it was the woman's fault if she was left alone and she deserved whatever she got. I wasn't sleeping properly either and I didn't go out socialising any more.

It was just me, on my own, and I couldn't afford to be ill. So when I got a cough I ignored it and carried on working. It got worse and worse, until I'd be walking along coughing up my fucking guts every five fucking minutes. I lost more weight and, when I wasn't working, I had no energy to do anything. I thought it was just the night work that was doing it, but it came to a head when I started having severe pains across my back and I couldn't breathe. I went to the doctor and he sent me for an emergency X-ray that showed I had pneumonia. I'd had it for a while and had been walking around with it. The doctor gave me a tonic and some tablets to fight the infection and told me I was run down and should rest. I went back to work.

My father came to visit me in Hayden House round about that time, when I was really down and out. He just turned up at the door one day and I let him in, then I left him looking after the kids, while I rushed out to try to nick something to give him to eat. When I got back, he was trying to cook a couple of fish he'd brought with him but he couldn't get the cooker to work. I told him the gas had been cut off because I had no money, so he taught me how to use a little oil burner safely – like a little camping stove thing and you could buy refills from the oil shop across the road. He taught me how to ignite it and how to use a little pan and pot to cook one thing at a time on it. I did this for about two months, until I could get the money to pay for the gas to go on again. Dad stayed a couple of days, then he went back to Wiltshire. Next time I saw him, he was ill with pneumonia.

I was fed up being on my own and I was still doing some stuff with Sixer, so it was only natural like that we struck up a relationship. Sixer was a lovely man, quiet and well spoken, always a gentleman and he loved children. He moved in with me at Hayden House when Big H left. His mother didn't like me at all; she was a schoolteacher and very old-fashioned, even though it was the sixties. She looked down on the likes of me and thought I wasn't good enough for her son and he was wasting his time with me. Remember, I was still married to Big H and had two children, and she didn't approve of unmarried couples living together. But Sixer went against her to be with me. He was a very affectionate man, something Big H wasn't, and I was very happy with him to begin with. I wanted to marry Sixer, but I could never find Harry to divorce him, so I was stuck. I wanted to do the decent thing, but I couldn't without Harry's signature.

You'd think I'd have learned my lesson with Harry, wouldn't you, but all that did was make me worse, because now I didn't trust any man. The old green-eyed monster came back and I was convinced that Sixer was going to leave me too. Our relationship was volatile, just like mine and Harry's, and I used to go spying on him. We had gas meters in those days, a bit like pay-as-you-go cards now. We'd put a shilling in the meter and turn the handle when the gas ran out and that would top it up again. We used to raid the gas meter regularly, by forcing the padlock and taking all the money out, then we'd put a shilling back in about twenty times, so we had a good supply of gas and replace the lock. When the gas man came round to collect the money, he couldn't understand how we'd used so much gas and there was only a shilling in the fucking meter.

Anyway, I did it this time and used the money to pay for a taxi to follow Sixer. He was doing night work for the *Evening Standard* over on Fleet Street and I made the taxi driver park up while I watched. The geezer thought I was mad and said: 'Who the fuck d'you think you are, Perry fucking Mason?'

I was so fucking stupid, the taxi cost me a packet and he'd never given me any reason to suspect him, but I never trusted nobody, that's just how I was. I followed him again when he got a job on a building site, just because I'd heard there was a bit of a slag making the tea over there. When I got there I saw some fucking blonde tart serving rosie from a poxy little stall. Sixer wasn't even near her, but I just saw red and I went for her. I pulled her out from behind her tea stall, in front of everyone, and pulled a few bunches of her blonde barnet out. Sixer was embarrassed as fuck for me showing him up like that, so I told him to clear off, he wasn't wanted any more. Then I went back over to the blonde bird and told her if I ever seen her near him, I'd kill her stone dead. She was fucking petrified.

Every time I chucked Sixer out, he'd go live with his mother for a few days then come back to me. No wonder the old cunt hated me! We'd be all right for a while, until I'd get it into my head he was knocking off some bird in Hayden House or down the street or somewhere else. I'd pretend to be asleep at night and wait to see if he tried to sneak out – this was because I woke up one night when I was with Harry and he was gone. I looked everywhere for him and then went back to sleep. When I woke again in the morning, he was back in the bed and when I asked him where he went, he said he never went anywhere and I must have been dreaming. I wasn't going to make the same mistakes with Sixer as I'd done with Harry, so I put flour down on the floor and the stairs after we went to bed, without him knowing. I thought, if he sneaks out during the night, he'll leave footprints – I never found any.

Sixer didn't like me doing my criminal stuff when we got together. It was all right before, when we was, like, associates, but now we were lovers, he didn't want me taking chances – especially when I fell pregnant again. I had two kids for Big H in the fifties and now I was doing it all over again with Sixer in the sixties. But I felt better about it this time. Sixer was different to Harry; he wanted to be at home with me and I didn't feel the terrible loneliness I felt before. Sixer loved Harry-Boy and Loveinia, and I knew he'd be a good father to his own kids. He didn't go out drinking or anything and, for the first time in years, I felt some kind of contentment. So I didn't mind giving up the thieving, for a while, because I went onto benefits and we also had what he was making coming in.

The pregnancy itself was easy enough. There were still no scans or anything, but I had no complications and Sixer was kind and considerate and carried everything for me and ran round to get me anything I needed. Around this time I was offered a place over in Dagenham because the maisonette was too small, but I turned it down, as it would've been too far for Sixer to get to work every day. I don't know whether that was good or bad fucking luck, but I found out later that Big H was living in the very same street where I was offered the place – who knows what would've happened if I'd gone there.

I was glad to have Sixer, we just looked like any other married couple with two kids and one on the way. It would've been much harder for me if I'd stayed on my own because, like I said, single mothers were considered the lowest of the low back then. And if people knew I was still married to Big H, and looked down their noses at me, they never said fuck all to my face because they knew me too well for that. I must've been happy, because I started to put on weight again and Sixer was all excited from the minute he knew I was expecting.

I went into labour in the middle of the night and Sixer was there with me. He took me to Lewisham Hospital, and he was so good it didn't feel like I was doing everything on my own this time. He stayed all night and he was a nervous fucking wreck. The hospital was different than in the mid-fifties, when I had Harry-Boy and Loveinia; Lewisham was busier and the nurses didn't seem to have as much time to give and weren't as caring. I was in labour for twelve hours and, when John was born, he weighed eight pounds. John was born with yellow jaundice and the doctors found out that I had a rhesus negative blood type. He had to have a transfusion to change his blood and we both had to stay in the hospital for two weeks to recover. Sixer came every day to see how we were and, once the doctors were convinced John was healthy enough to leave, we were discharged back to Hayden House.

There was this Scottish cow who lived upstairs and me and her never got on. I don't know why, it was just one of them things; she scowled at me and I scowled back. Once, when I was going up the stairs with the kids, she bumped into little John and almost knocked him flying. I was trying to behave, so I let it go, but she knew I wasn't happy about it. The next week, loads of water started coming through my ceiling, so I banged on it with a broom handle to let her know what was going on and I went out onto the walkway and shouted at her, but the fucker ignored me. That was it. I snapped and went marching up there to get her. She knew I was on my way and she was already coming along the walkway when I got to her landing. It was off! We fought like a couple of fucking alley cats and we were soon rolling round the landing. Then we tumbled all the way down the stairs and we landed with her underneath me. I hurt my back falling down the stairs, but you don't feel pain when you're angry. I carried on hitting her and managed to tear her dress off, so she had to run back upstairs to her flat in her fucking bloomers. She called the police on me, but I told them she started it and she pushed me down the stairs, and that's what it looked like, because I was holding my back with the pain that had kicked in. They believed me, but said if they were called out again they'd arrest us both. I never had no more trouble from the cow after that.

In the fifties we had the 'new look', fitted suits and long flowing skirts and women looked glamorous in them – they looked like women. The Twiggy girls of the sixties were too skinny and they looked like boys, with no fucking shape to them. But the hairstyles were good. I always liked to dye my barnet and in the sixties I changed my hair loads of times to keep up with the fashion – I ended up with a stern-looking 'Italian cut' and I dyed it black, then silver-grey. Sixer said it would all fall out if I didn't leave the fucking stuff alone. Contraceptives became more widespread as well and I had better control over whether I fell pregnant or not. It was a revelation for women of my generation; it gave us more independence and opened up other options besides just being a wife and a mother. I'd always been more than a wife and a mother, so life went on.

I got pregnant for Sixer again five years after John was born. Daniel was also born with jaundice, just like his brother and he had to go through the same blood-changing transfusion as John. They said there was some incompatibility between Sixer's blood and mine. Both kids took the Mackenney name, because Sixer and me weren't married. He was at work when I went into labour the second time and was taken to hospital, but the doctor rang up the job and told him he had another son. He was chuffed to fucking pieces and rushed over to see him – which is just as well, because they weren't to have much quality time, as they call it now, together.

Sixer had his accident early in 1966 – ain't that fucking ironic? Six wasn't his fucking lucky number, after all, that's for fucking sure. It happened in Peckham. He was coming out of a side road onto Peckham Park Road on a bicycle, of all fucking things, when he was hit from behind by a speeding car. Was it an accident or was it some cunt with a grief? We never found out. The car that hit him drove off without stopping and Sixer was thrown off the bike into the air and he landed on his head. People on bicycles didn't wear helmets in those days, so he took the full force of the impact on his brain. The doctors said it was a miracle he survived.

He had no ID on him, so I didn't find out what had happened until he didn't come home and I started ringing round looking for him. I'll never forget when I first saw him after the accident, in King's College Hospital, over in Camberwell. It was frightening. His head was completely bandaged and his face was swollen and covered in scrapes and bruises, like it'd been dragged along the ground. There were tubes coming from every fucking part of his body and all I could hear was the beep, beep, beep of the machines. It was fucking awful, just to think back on it now makes tears come to my eyes again. He was in a coma and I was told he probably wouldn't come out of it. Back in 1966, they didn't have the medical technology they have today and I was sure I was going to lose him.

I thought he was going to die and I felt so fucking helpless, so completely fucking useless. The last time I spoke to him we were arguing and now I was standing watching him die and I couldn't make him better to tell him I was sorry for fighting with him over nothing.

King's College was one of the best hospitals in London and Sixer got lucky when they took him there. The doctors were fantastic and didn't care whether he was poor or rich; they looked after him well and, when he didn't die like they thought he would, they tried to prepare me for what was to come. They told me he had severe brain damage and would live like a vegetable – I hate using that phrase, but that's how they explained it to me. They said he wouldn't be able to care for himself, not even his most basic needs and he might stay in the coma for years.

But he didn't. He came out of it and the doctors were taken by surprise. I was so happy when I heard the news and I remember me and the kids running over to the hospital to see him. He recognised us and I remember thinking that maybe it wouldn't be so bad as the doctors said, after all. But it was. I never expected Sixer to come home after the accident in the state he did. He had problems talking, his speech was very slow and he'd forget the words. He couldn't read nor write and this was a terrible thing to happen to him, because he was always a clever man and could read from the age of five and he was always in the library. His personality changed too; he became very aggressive and swore a lot and had mad outbursts of rage.

The doctors said it was caused by frustration, because he couldn't do all the things he used to do. After a while, when he could get out of bed, he used to walk around the house naked, because he'd forget to put his clothes on, and he was on so many fucking tablets that he fucking rattled when he walked.

Then he started refusing to take his medication and I used to have to crush up the pills and put them in his tea every morning and night. He'd call me names and he wouldn't wash himself and he'd lie in bed shouting at me to bring him his breakfast, dinner and tea. This was a very hard time for me. I wasn't used to it. I was having to be a wife, mother, fighter and thief, all at the same time – and now I was having to be a fucking mental nurse as well. It's a wonder I didn't need psychiatric help myself after all that bollocks. But I kept going because I had no choice. Sixer became like another of my children and not my partner any more, and it was the last relationship with a man that I was ever going to have. I was thirty-five years old.

I think John took his father's accident very badly. Daniel was only a baby when it happened and he couldn't remember how Sixer was before then. But John could and he didn't understand why his dad was acting so strange and why he wasn't the same as before. He became very rebellious and unruly. John was attending Kender Street Primary School in 1966 and, when I went to collect him one day, I was led into the head teacher's office. John had been 'naughty' and they wanted to see me about it. When I came into the room, I saw they had John tied to a bed – I mean, tied down so he couldn't fucking move! I didn't wait for no explanations, I erupted like a fucking volcano. No fucker on this earth was going to do that to my son! The head teacher's name was Miss Baker, and I jumped on the bitch. I was so angry, I can't put into words the absolute venom and rage I felt. Miss Baker was screaming for help and I could easily have killed the cunt, but I suddenly realised that John was watching. I untied him and left the slag on the floor with her clothes torn to shreds and her jewellery ripped off. On the way out, I heard her mumble: 'I'll make sure no school accepts him after this.'

So I went back and hit her again.

But Miss Baker was as good as her word. She got the school board onto me, and the local authorities, and Social Services, and they nearly took John away from me. But I fought the fuckers. When the school-board man turned up at the door, I laid into him, both verbally and physically, and, by the time I was finished with him, he actually apologised for what happened. He said he'd get John into a new school, but he wasn't able to – Miss Baker had spread her poison far and wide. Social Services came up with a boarding school in Chipping Ongar, in the Epping Forest area of Essex, and I remember going up there with him and the welfare people. I was wearing a duffel coat with a hood and he was all upset when I left him. As I was going down the drive, he came running after me and grabbed on to my hood and wouldn't let go. He was crying and saying: 'Don't leave me.'

And I couldn't do it. I took him home with me and to hell with the fucking consequences. He was my boy and he was staying with me. John never went to school again after that.

After Sixer's accident, I went out shoplifting full-time. I had lots of friends back then who were into the same thing as me and we'd take turns looking after each other's kids. The sixties were affluent for people after the war and the stingy fifties and people wanted to be able to spend the money they were earning and not save it like their parents. Like I said, all kinds of new department stores sprung up, which was manna from fucking heaven for someone like me. I was a professional by now and there's no mistake about that. I'd jump a train and go to different towns all over the south-east of England – Margate, Hastings, Ramsgate, Croydon, Lewisham, Catford, Peckham, Dartford, Bromley, Gravesend. I went everywhere on my travels to earn some money for the family. When I got off the train, I'd go to the high street to scope out the shops and see what was available and I did them all – Debenhams, John Lewis, Woolworths, C&A, Marks & Spencer, BHS, the list goes on.

I had a routine. I'd go in dressed up to the nines in a long, velvet, purple dress-coat with fur trim. I had leather high-boots, laced up the front, that were popular in the sixties and my hair and make-up would be done to perfection. On top of it all, I used to wear a big fancy hat, like the one Audrey Hepburn wore in *Breakfast at Tiffany's*. I looked like I just walked out of a fashion magazine and it was important that the store staff believed I was a reputable customer, or my scam wouldn't work. I'd browse for a bit, then tear a hole in a garment while no one was looking. I'd take it over to the counter and tell them I'd bought it there last week – you didn't need receipts back then and they had no CCTV, so I was laughing. I actually acted the part so well that I convinced myself I'd really bought a defective item and, because I believed it myself, the staff believed it too. They used to ask if I wanted an exchange or a refund. I always took a refund, saving me having to flog the gear later. I became a professional con artist and it was a licence to print money.

I was doing this every day of the week, and even weekends. I'd make breakfast for Sixer, take the kids to school, then go stealing. Sometimes I had to take Daniel with me, if I couldn't find someone to look after him who I trusted – and I trusted hardly anyone. I think I must have become addicted to it and I needed to get out of the house, away from Sixer – I mean, I loved him, but I was going fucking mad too and it was such a buzz to have a bit of money in my hand. I started to put some of it aside to buy things for the house, because I'd lost everything to the fucking bailiffs after Big H left. What was left had been broken when Sixer took a bad turn because of the accident. I started to furnish the house from the money I was making – curtains, carpets, furniture, a cooker and a freezer. It was like a long fucking birthday.

If I went on weekends, I'd take all the kids with me, down to the seaside towns on the south coast. They thought they were going on a little daytrip holiday and, after I got the money, we'd go for a meal in a local cafe and then on the beach so they could go on the rides and enjoy themselves. I took a lot of risks, but it seemed worth it to me when I saw my children laughing and having a good time. I know it wasn't right, but it was all I knew. The thought of what would happen if I got caught never entered my head – maybe I blocked it out deliberately, or maybe I just believed I'd never get caught.

I was wrong, of course.

It was late 1966 and my son Daniel was still just a baby. I was nicking children's clothes for the kids – handsome suits for the boys and pretty dresses and coats for Loveinia. Like I said, on the weekends I had to take the kids with me, because Sixer was ill in bed and couldn't take care of them and I didn't like no one looking after them. Someone had to go out and earn the greengages, and Sixer couldn't do it no more, so it had to be me. Daniel was so small I had to bring him into the stores with me, but I'd take Harry-Boy, Loveinia and John, who were about twelve, eleven and six at the time, to a local cafe and tell them to wait for me until I came back. I hated doing this, but I was desperate; I had to earn the money to feed them, the only way I knew how. I left them in the cafe, so they wouldn't see what I was doing – I thought they'd be ashamed of me and I didn't want them learning to do the same things as I did. So much for my dreams of a nice life and posh schools.

Anyway, I went into this department store in Croydon and I was lifting a load of leather coats that I knew would fetch a good price. But I was worrying about the kids all the time and not concentrating on what I was doing. Although I was an old hand at this lark, I made the beginner's mistake of looking nervous and that was enough for them to keep an eye on me. When I went to leave, the store detectives nabbed me and the police were called. The fucking coppers turned up in force and you'd think there'd been a major bank robbery, there was so many of the cunts. They were dragging me to the Maria and I was screaming that my kids were in the cafe next door. The bastards wouldn't believe me and were trying to get me into the back of the wagon when the kids came running out. They then threw us all into the Maria and drove us to Croydon police station.

They kept me in a holding cell along with the kids, while they went and searched my house to see if I was doing this shoplifting on a professional level. I wouldn't give them the address, but they soon ID'd me from previous and they went round and broke down the door, because Sixer was upstairs and wouldn't get out of bed to open it for them. They ransacked the place from top to bottom and all Sixer kept saying was: 'Where's Eileen? She hasn't brought me dinner.'

They found stacks of stuff under the beds that I'd lifted previously and they took it all away for evidence – clothes all brand new and tagged up; I kept them like that ready for me to sell when I got the time. When they got back, they brought me out of the cell for questioning and the kids all trooped out with me. As they did, one of the coppers took an interest in Loveinia's coat, which was sheepskin with a hood and fur trimming. It was obviously very expensive and I'd nicked it a few weeks before. The cunt tried to drag it off her while she was still wearing it, to look at the tag and see where it had come from. There was a iron staircase behind her and she lost her footing and went tumbling down the stairs.

Well, I was like a fucking woman possessed. I went for this copper, even though I was still holding Daniel in my arms. I tried to kick the cunt in the balls and head-butt him and bite him, but I couldn't get near him because the other fuckers pushed him away. We picked Loveinia up and she wasn't hurt bad, but she was scared and crying. I'd got the bastard's number and I demanded to see the commanding officer to log a formal complaint for assault on my eleven-year-old daughter. They didn't bother to interview me after that and the copper in charge took me to one side and said he'd let us go if I was prepared to see reason. I'd still have to go to court, but they'd take care of it for me. I agreed and got bail and we walked out of there.

I was bailed to attend Croydon court the following week and I remember going up to see where my name was on the case list outside. For fuck's sake, I couldn't believe it – my name filled the whole fucking list – 'Eileen Mackenney / Eileen Mackenney / Eileen Mackenney / Eileen Mac . . .', and next to it was a list of everything that was stolen. It amounted to seventeen counts of theft and deception being taken into account and I said: 'That's it, I'm fucked now! I ain't gonna be walking out of this one.'

I pleaded guilty on all counts, hoping for a lighter sentence. But then the judge called a welfare officer to give a reference for me before sentencing. I had no fucking idea who this woman was and I'd certainly never met her before and she stood up in court and started talking about the hardship I was going through and the way I was looking after my mentally ill partner and I was trying to provide for my children too. How the fuck did she know all this? Then she said I was being offered medical help for my nerves and they were arranging for me to see a doctor in Maudsley Hospital to try to calm down my temperament. That was a barefaced fucking lie, as I was never offered any help at all. I'm not saying the welfare officer knew it was a lie, but I could only assume the police had arranged all this to get their officer off the hook for knocking Loveinia down the stairs. Whatever it was, I had to give the woman her due, she made the judge feel sorry for me and the way I was living and I got a two-year suspended sentence.

I was so fucking relieved when I came out of court. I don't think I've ever had a nervous breakdown, but I was close to it at that time. But it made me realise that I needed to do things better at home with Sixer, as it wasn't just me who was suffering, it was the kids too – and I needed to change things.

It was too close a shave and I didn't dare risk bringing the kids out with me again. So, it was round about this time that I got a job serving tea on a building site. They were building a police station, of all fucking things, at Holborn and I had to make tea and rolls for the workmen and carry them down a ladder into a massive fucking hole in the ground. I was still living at Hayden House at the time and I travelled there by bus every day. I really liked the job too, which was unusual for me, but I had to give it up to look after Sixer when his mental state started to deteriorate further.

My children have always been very close; they stick together when one of them's in trouble. Maybe that's because we've always only had each other to rely on. Harry-Boy was a very responsible child and, when he got older, he'd do paper rounds and other little jobs to help me out. He knew how hard things were and he knew what I had to do sometimes to get money. He never actually said anything, but I knew he was clued up about it all. Sometimes he'd hop the wag from school to help me out round the house and look after his brothers and sister. He wasn't one to go out with mates and that; it was like he grew up before his time.

Loveinia was a bit of a tomboy, and growing up with three brothers was a bit like me when I was young. And she reminded me of myself, because she'd take risks and throw caution to the wind. She was extremely clever and talented but, when she was about ten years old, she was climbing a tree and she fell. I took her to the doctor and he told me she was OK, her hip was bruised, but nothing more than that. But she was in pain all the time and started to lose weight, so I went to the Greater London Council, which was the organisation that governed the running of all the schools. They were concerned because she was so thin and they told me it would be good for Loveinia to go away to a convalescent home for some respite time. The rest home was close to the beach in Margate and, when she got there, they examined her and found that her hip was broken and she had to go into surgery to have it repaired. I went to visit her and thought the place was nice. I thought she might enjoy her time there; it wasn't like the homes I'd experienced when I was young, she had her own room and her own things and I thought I was doing the best for her.

They sent her to school down in Margate and I used to go every week to see her. But she wasn't happy and didn't put the weight back on. The headmaster said she must be homesick and suggested that Harry-Boy should come down to keep her company. But he hated the place too. I didn't want them there, but I had Social Services on my back and, if I didn't agree, they'd have taken the kids away from me. I eventually found out that they were having a bad time there. The teachers were violent and they were being bullied. Harry-Boy stood up for Loveinia, just like I used to stand up for Ronnie all them years ago, and he was constantly in fights. History was repeating itself. I couldn't stand the thought of this, because I knew what it was like, so one day I went down there and took them home with me. We travelled back to London together on a coach – and we were so happy.

My father in Wiltshire wasn't used to the country in winter-time – the winters were cold back then – and he ended up with pneumonia and had to be rushed to hospital. Gracie contacted me, so I went up there to see him. I put on the best clobber I had and walked into that hospital like the Queen of fucking Sheba, all dressed up and strutting down the ward. Dad could see me coming and I heard him laughing and saying: 'Here comes Eileen!'

I brought him a bottle of the finest single malt and we were so happy to see each other, even though he was very ill. I went up there regularly to see him and he began to get better, but one day the cleaners left some water on the floor and Dad slipped on it. He broke his leg and never recovered after that. The pneumonia took hold of him again and he died in that hospital in Wiltshire. Gracie arranged the funeral and he was buried out there in the country. He was eighty-four. Although it wasn't as much of a shock to me as when my mother died, what with Sixer and everything, I felt like the sky was coming down on me. When my mother died, it was like someone had ripped my heart out, I'd never felt anything like it. With my father, it was like all the men I knew were gone and left me alone, to fend for myself. Big H was gone physically, Sixer was gone mentally and now my father was gone spiritually. It frightened me, more than it made me sad.

*   *   *

Like I said, things were very hard for me after Sixer's accident – years of poverty and hardship, looking after a seriously disabled man with four young children. Then, in 1969, I was out doing some Christmas shopping, the kind you don't need no money for, in Jones & Higgins department store in Peckham Rye. It was the in-place to shoplift, everyone used to go there. I'd already half-inched boxes of Lego and toy soldiers and I was looking for dolls and clothes for Loveinia. I'd left the kids at home because, after the episode in Croydon, I didn't like taking them out on the steal with me, just in case. Harry-Boy was about fourteen or fifteen and I usually left him looking after the others. He was a very responsible boy and I trusted him.

Anyway, I was in Jones & Higgins, doing my 'work'. I'd left the boys' stuff with a paper-seller and come back in with a cushion under my coat to make out I was pregnant. I was just about to ditch the cushion and replace it with clothes for the kids, when I was surrounded by a number of men in suits. 'Fuck it,' I thought, 'I've been fucking rumbled.' But they didn't look like police; they looked dodgy for some reason. So then I thought it must be some name who has a grief with me. I was into a bit of everything back then and I knew loads of villains. Then Big H come out from behind them and I almost lost my breath. He looked so smart in a suit and he walked up to me. The first thing I said was, 'My brothers ain't after you no more.'

They had been for a while, when he first fucked off and left me destitute. They were out for blood and looked everywhere for him.

'I don't care, Eileen.'

He said this without any emotion in his voice and I knew there was nothing there for me no more.

One of the others, who turned out to be a solicitor, handed me a piece of paper to sign – it was a divorce form. I didn't fight or argue or shout, I just signed it. I'd been ground down too much to protest, then he just walked away with his 'friends'. I followed them outside to see where he was going and he got into a car loaded up with Christmas presents, all wrapped in nice sparkly paper – but none of them were for my kids. I went back into the store to steal something for them.

He'd been round to Hayden House and knocked on the door, but the kids were told never to answer the door to anyone they didn't know. So, next thing Big H is talking to them through the letterbox and asking them where I was. They didn't recognise him and said I was down in Peckham Rye. Well, they didn't have to give him a fucking post code, he knew what that meant. But it was the coldness of the visit that amazed me – his two kids were in that house and he never asked them how they were or said Happy Christmas or anything. I couldn't believe it when I found out. I know me and him had our differences when we were together, but there was no need to take it out on the fucking kids, was there?

That's how I was divorced from Harry and I never seen him again until he got himself into serious trouble.

I tried to get some compensation from the state for Sixer – I even went to see a top Park Lane solicitor. He was one of the best and he took the case on. He referred me to Sir Roger Bannister, the four-minute-mile man, who went on to become a brain doctor. We went to see him and he assessed the brain damage done to Sixer. When he first came out of hospital, Sixer was very incapacitated. I had to dress him, feed him, wash him and sort out all his medication. It was awful, it was so hard to deal with the extent of the brain damage – I had to attend to his every need without any help from carers or anything and it was wearing me down. I couldn't go to work, I was stuck in every day and I nearly went fucking mad. The doctors said he would be brain damaged for life and he'd never be normal again.

I started to put together the case for Sixer's claim and Benny became my star witness. Benny looked the part as well, small and reserved, with glasses – you'd think butter wouldn't melt in his mouth. Most of all, he looked honest! Everything was going well, until some vindictive fuckers, who couldn't mind their own fucking business, told the court that Benny wasn't an independent witness. The judge was told that me and Benny were related, which we kind of were because Benny was married to a woman called Doll, who was my sister-in-law's sister. I had my suspicions who grassed us, and it had to come from inside the extended family somewhere, but I couldn't be sure, so I did nothing about it.

Anyway, the case went to the Supreme Court of Judicature in The Strand and I remember seeing Benny testifying. He was nervous as fuck and his glasses started to steam up and he had to take them off and give them a wipe. But he was so good I had to smile to myself; he saw it through with style and we won the case.

It had taken me many years to win this case and Sixer was awarded £9,000, which was a lot of money in those days.

But now I was standing outside the court in The Strand without a fucking ha'penny and wondering how I was going to get home. So Benny and me did a bit of shoplifting up there in the West End and we went to celebrate. But I would have given it all to have my old Sixer back, and the money didn't change the amount of work I had to do to look after him. I wasn't married to Sixer, and the children I had for him didn't even carry his name, so there were restrictions on how the money could be spent. It was held by the official solicitor, Mr White, in a trust fund and I had to apply to him for everything that we needed. I had to provide statements and receipts and they were very fucking thorough at checking everything. Then all my benefits were stopped and I was really no better off than before.

We did go on holiday once and that was new for us. The children had never been on holiday and we all went to Butlin's in Somerset for a week. But it was a constant struggle, because Sixer wasn't mobile and the kids were growing up and the maisonette at Hayden House wasn't big enough any more. So I asked the official solicitor if we could move to a bigger place. I wanted to go to Downham in Catford, to be closer to the centre where Loveinia was going to school after she came back from Margate. She was walking with a limp and she developed a stammer, which the doctors thought was a nervous thing, so they sent her to The Woodlands where she could have special attention from the teachers. A coach would pick her up and bring her home and I liked it out there; it was quieter than the inner city. They offered me 49 Crutchley Road in Downham, near Catford, south-east London and we moved there in 1971.

12

CRUTCHLEY ROAD AND THE SEVENTIES

Number 49 Crutchley Road was a three-bedroom semi-detached house, with a double lounge and a huge garden, something I'd never had before in my life. It was situated in a quiet cul-de-sac and I thought: 'Oh my God. I've hit the fucking jackpot!'

The local tenants' association was run by Roy Hicks, who was Tommy Steele's brother and he was a nice man who generally kept himself to himself. I really thought I would be able to relax now, after all the hardship. How wrong I was!

Daniel was seven now and he attended Forster Park Primary School; Loveinia was sixteen and going to The Woodlands; Harry-Boy was about seventeen and he'd left school and was working; John was eleven and just did his own thing, like riding round on his chopper bike. By then, the stress of Sixer on me and the kids was getting too much; the children were finding it more and more difficult to deal with him. I had to make a choice, so I was forced to take Sixer to Bexley Mental Hospital, also known as the London County Asylum, to become a resident there. It was 1972 and we'd been together for twelve years. I was forty-one.

Bexley was a big, stately home-type building, with nurses on hand twenty-four hours a day. I didn't really want to send Sixer away, but it was what he needed. In fact, it was what I should have done immediately after the accident, but I didn't know how to go about it then and I didn't have the resources to find out and, anyway, I kept believing he'd return to normal – like I'd get up some morning and the old Sixer would be back. But he never did. I went to see him at Bexley all the time and I took the children with me and I also arranged for him to come home on some weekends, because I missed him. But I couldn't keep him home full-time, because the years of caring for him had worn me out and I couldn't do it again.

Downham was different to the other places where I'd lived. It was still London, but it was the suburbs and not so built up as the inner city. There was lots of greenery around and it was pleasant and I was happier than I'd been for a long time. Harry-Boy became the man of the house and he took over that role from Big H and Sixer. He defended me and his younger siblings against anyone who crossed us. They all made their own network of friends and seemed to settle into the area quite well. My brothers used to come down from time to time to visit us and everything was cushti – for a while.

Within eighteen months of moving into Crutchley Road, my peace and quiet came to an end. Harry-Boy kept getting pulled by the police; they'd take him in over and over again and I'd be constantly up Catford police station. My children meant everything to me, no matter what people thought of them and the Mackenney reputation had followed us to Downham. Every two-bit copper saw a chance to earn his or her stripes by pinning something on my kids, whether or not they were guilty. I'm not saying they were angels, but if Harry-Boy was guilty of everything they pulled him in for, he'd be more notorious than Genghis fucking Khan. I started fighting the police with everything I had. At first I made complaint after complaint, but that got me nowhere, so I decided to fight fire with fire. I mean, they weren't just bumping into Harry and taking him in, they were brutal with it. He was a teenager and they were beating him with truncheons, loads of them, trying to get him onto the floor. Well, I wasn't gonna stand by and let that happen, so I laid into them and got them off him and stood toe-to-toe with them. If they wanted a fight, they came to the right fucking place.

Back in the seventies, the coppers could get away with that kind of stuff. *The Sweeney* was on the television, with John Thaw and Dennis Waterman driving round at high speed and being tough guys. So all the coppers thought they were the same, and the public did too. They could beat the shit out of people in the cells and say they fell over and laugh in court about it. It was the culture back then and it was widespread, along with police corruption. It was round the time that Sir Robert Mark said: 'A good police force is one that catches more criminals than it employs.'

And that was about it – hit the nail on the fucking head. Most coppers were on the take, right up to the very top and, if you didn't pay them off, they came after you. We never paid them off, we didn't see why we should. If we took the risks, then we kept the loot. There's an old saying, 'If you can't do the time, then don't do the crime.' The coppers wanted us to do the crime for them, without any risk of them doing the time. Fuck that!

After a couple of years went by, I realised the normality I wanted at 49 Crutchley Road just wasn't going to be. I reckon I just wasn't born for the quiet life. I went round the corner to the shops to get some fags one day and when I came back the first thing I seen was Loveinia banging some slag's head off the path leading to our house. The bird's husband came out and started to hit Loveinia, who was about eighteen at the time. What happened was, John, who was about thirteen, got a bit cheeky with the bird's kid and she come round our house about it. She must have thought Loveinia was John's mother and went for her. But Loveinia was a bit like me and she wasn't scared of anything or anyone, so she fought the bitch onto the floor. Loveinia made mincemeat of her and, by the time I got there, the woman was bleeding all over the place. I took on the husband and neither of them ever came near our house again.

But things just kept happening. Boy-Boy, my dog from Hayden House, came with us to Downham but because we were new in the area people did try to push their luck with us. Boy-Boy used to go roaming and he got on the nerves of some Gypsies who lived opposite us in the cul-de-sac. They came to the door one day and threatened to kill the dog. My brother Jimmy came down to help me sort them out and he went straight over there and banged on the door. A woman answered and Jimmy said: 'If there's a man in there, bring him out!'

A geezer came out and Jimmy scared the living daylights out of him, and he ended up coming over to our house to apologise. But we'd made enemies.

After that, my brothers used to come down so often that some idiot neighbour reported me for running a brothel. Now, my children had seen the hardships we'd suffered and they'd seen me fight and they'd become tough themselves and weren't the sort of people to be pushed around. They took no shit from no one – just like me! But the police had us in their sights and were determined to hound us and intimidate us, no matter what we did and no matter where we went. Like, one time I was shopping in Tesco's with young Harry and we were walking round the aisles minding our own business. Suddenly, all the alarms went off and all the doors were locked and the place was surrounded by police. Gradually, the other customers were ushered out of the store and me and Harry were surrounded by armed coppers. We were taken to the police station and strip-searched. They said they'd received a phone call saying Harry was carrying a gun and was going to rob the place. We were released without charge after being held for several hours.

My old mate Peg the Leg was into forgery back in the old days, but it was something I'd always kept away from, because it carried too much time if you got caught. Harry-Boy was nineteen in 1973 and he got in with certain people when we moved to Crutchley Road, who were forging post-office savings books and bank cheque books. Security wasn't as tight as it is today and there was no chip-and-pin shit, so it was a way to make a lot of money – fast. I suppose he reckoned if the coppers were onto him all the time, he might as well be guilty of something, so Harry-Boy got up a team to work for him. The crew included Benny the Bull and a mate of Loveinia's and the scam was going on for a couple of years. I knew about it, but I wasn't directly involved.

Someone on the inside must have grassed, because we started to see suspicious-looking cars parked close to the house and we were told that the police had set up surveillance inside some of our neighbours' houses as well. Every move we made was being watched and the money started to dry up. The crew really needed to get out and do some business, but there was no way to get in or out without the CID knowing about it. Anyway, I telephoned the local coppers and told them there was a suspicious-looking geezer hanging about the area and he was approaching little kids in the street. It worked. The Downham coppers came down in a squad car and took the undercover geezer away.

The crunch came when Harry-Boy asked me to go along with him down to Deaf Hill in Kent, just to help him suss out some post offices – 'Deaf Hill' was a nickname we had for the area around Swanley, near Brands Hatch – I can't remember why we called it that, probably something to do with the noise of the racing cars. Anyway, we were driving on the motorway when, suddenly, we were surrounded by police motorbikes. We were taken to Dartford police station and interrogated. I told them I was going to visit my brother Jimmy, who lived in Dartford at the time. They searched the car, but they couldn't find anything, so they had to let us go. But things were getting hot and it wasn't long after that Harry-Boy and me were taken in for a line-up. Somebody was grassing, and we got identified by people we couldn't see. We were charged with fraud, even though I wasn't involved, and sent to trial at the Old Bailey.

I was defended by a solicitor called Michael Relton, who was later given twelve years for laundering money in the Brinks Mat gold-bullion robbery of 1983. They had a list of charges against me and Harry and a list of bank books they said I'd forged. Harry told my solicitor that I couldn't have forged the bank books, because they were in men's names, not women's, so how could I have gone in and drawn money in a man's name? He admitted organising the fraud himself and said I had nothing to do with it. After that the prosecution changed the fraud charge against me to conspiracy to commit fraud, as they said I knew what was going on and helped the fraudsters. I pleaded guilty on the advice of Michael Relton and I ended up with a two-year suspended sentence. Harry was found guilty on sixteen counts of fraud and went to Hollesley Bay Borstal in Suffolk for a year. Harry took most of the blame on himself to protect me and he refused to name any of his accomplices.

I visited Harry-Boy all the time he was inside. It hurt me to see my son in there. I was in borstal myself and I wanted better for my kids; it wasn't something I wanted to see. But I knew Harry could protect himself and wouldn't take no shit. He got out in 1974.

I never wanted to get mixed up in the fraud thing; it carried too much of a risk for me and now I had a two-year suspended and my family to look after. I just couldn't chance it. However, there was a way I could get money in advance from the social if I needed it, the way the benefit books were printed back then. If I was having a bad week, all I needed to do was crumple up the section with the date on it – all it needed was a little crease in the right place. The date then became so hard to see that the post-office people would just put it through without questioning it. It made it harder the week after, of course, because I'd have already got my money for then. But next week was next week and could take care of itself. Now was now and, when necessity calls, the devil fucking answers!

But it wasn't all bad news – round about the mid-seventies, my brother Ronnie used to take us all pea-picking. Loads of us used to go, neighbours and friends from the Downham Estate. Even one of Loveinia's mad boyfriends, who we nicknamed 'Little-Legs', came once and had a fight with the farmer. It was more a laugh than anything else, a break from the realities of life. It wasn't like back in the thirties when we went hopping, it was like a day-tripping kinda thing: we'd drive down there in the morning in Ronnie's van and come back home every night. There wasn't the same pressure as when I was a child; then we did it to survive, but now we did it out of choice. And it wasn't just peas; we'd go picking all kinds of fruit as well, like strawberries and apples. I used to do the recruiting, going out and getting people to come with us and they all loved to get away from London for a day or two and get paid for it as well. We went to Ashford in Kent and to Hayes Farm and we looked a right old gang. It wasn't strict like in the thirties; we'd pick as many as we wanted to and the farmers would pay us for doing it. Simple.

But I always had to come back to life in London. I remember coming back to Catford with Ronnie in the van once, about 1975 or 1976, and there was a massive commotion going on and all the traffic was being held up and there were police everywhere. Someone said a jewellers had been hit by a man and a woman pretending to be an engaged couple wanting to buy a ring. When the assistants brought out the trays of sparklers, the pair held them up and took all the diamonds and scarpered. I was telling the rest of the family about it when I got home, but they laughed and said they already knew. They said it was Harry-Boy's girlfriend and Loveinia's boyfriend who done it, but I took that with a pinch of salt. Anyway, whoever it was, all the gear got sold and nobody ever got caught for it.

In 1977, a supergrass whose name I can't mention was moved onto the Downham Estate and his flat was being watched by police all the time – then his wife started having it off with a local geezer called Frank. Now, I'd had a few run-ins with this Frank character and he didn't like me one little bit. When he started knocking off the supergrass's wife, it must've made him think he was bigger or something because, one day, he set his dog on me. I gave the fucking dog a good kicking, but Harry-Boy was furious when he found out about it. He went round to see Frank and I went with him to keep him calm – believe it or not, I hated to see my kids fighting. When we got there Frank came to the door armed with a crowbar. Harry asked him why he set the dog on me but, before he got two words out of his fucking mouth, Harry-Boy laid him out on the floor and we walked away. Then, Ronnie got to find out about it and he went round to see Frank with a pickaxe handle. I tried to stop him and told him Frank had learned his lesson, but he wouldn't listen, so I followed him round to Frank's flat, which was on the top floor of a three-storey block. Frank must've have seen us coming, because he jumped out the window, trying to get away, and broke both his legs.

Some time after that, Frank was in the local pub, called the Downham Tavern, and was telling everyone what the fucking Mackenneys had done to him. He ended up rallying a lynch mob round him and he had to have a load of them, because he'd never do anything if he wasn't mob-handed. Some of them were known in the area at the time; there was a geezer called Dave White who went on to kill a bloke called Johnny Walker in another dangerous pub called The Squires. The lynch mob was outside the house and I could hear them all shouting for us to come out – so we did. Harry-Boy, John, Ronnie and me went out there to sort them out. When they saw us coming, the fuckers turned and ran out of my garden and fucked off down the street. I never heard no more about it and I never had no more trouble from Frank.

The kids were getting older and Harry-Boy moved to Evans Road, a couple of streets away, to live with his girlfriend. It was a large block of flats on the Downham Estate; there were rows and rows of them and they were all the same. They were still building blocks like that in the seventies, to house working-class people, and I say 'working class' with a tongue stuck in my cheek, because most of the work we done was hooky. Loveinia had a son called

Thomas for her boyfriend, Little-Legs, and they moved into a flat opposite me in the cul-de-sac.

I was asleep one night, when I was woke by what I thought was the faint sound of church bells. It unnerved me and I had to get up to see what it was. There was a window on the landing that looked out over the road to the flats opposite, and when I walked out of the bedroom I could see directly towards Loveinia's flat. There was meat wagons full of police outside, they were all armed and were beginning to enter the block. I knew Loveinia was out working nights and my grandson Thomas was in there, so I grabbed a dressing gown and ran to get over there to find out what was happening. As I was crossing the road they were dragging Little-Legs out in handcuffs – the bastards weren't going to let me in, but I kicked up such a commotion that they had to let me take Thomas back across the road to my house. I later found out the flat was raided in connection with stolen diamonds, but Little-Legs was never charged with anything. And that's the way it was – if you were connected in any way to the Mackenneys, you were in for trouble from the police, no questions asked.

One day, I went round to Evans Road to see Harry-Boy and there were armed police everywhere. The first thing I saw was a copper lying on his stomach with a machine gun on a tripod, aiming it straight at me. They came raiding for Harry and Loveinia's man, Little-Legs, because there had been a shooting at a jewellers and half-a-million quid's worth of diamonds had gone missing. The jeweller had been killed. Some narks had given Harry-Boy's and Little-Legs's descriptions and put their names in the frame – there was a lot of bad feelings in the area, due to the reputation my family had. Harry-Boy and Little-Legs were good mates then and they went everywhere together and they got known as 'Simon and Garfunkel', because Harry was tall and lanky with curly hair and Little-Legs was short and dark with a baby face. Harry was a good-looking boy, like his father, and the birds were always flocking after him and some geezers were either afraid or jealous – or both. So when things went wrong he always had the finger pointed at him.

Neither Harry-Boy nor Little-Legs were there and I wasn't allowed in. I tried to get through, because I knew Harry's girlfriend was in there and the bastards were tearing up the whole place, floorboards and everything. But the cunts forced me back and warned me I could get shot if I carried on. I went back to Crutchley Road to see if Harry had come round there, but the police had beaten me to it. There were loads of them, completely surrounding the house. Sixer used to visit now and then, so he could stay in touch with the family, and he and Daniel were inside the house. The coppers were turning the whole place over and digging up the fucking garden and everything – they were tearing the place apart. I went in there and started shouting at them, but they just grabbed me and pushed me to one side. I didn't want to start a full-scale ruck with them, because Sixer still wasn't very well and Daniel was only thirteen and I was worried the fuckers would beat them up as well as me – they were well capable of it when they were mob-handed.

It was like being fucking molested. They went through every drawer and cupboard and I was going fucking mad. I demanded to speak to the copper in charge and this sneering geezer came over and told me they had their eye on my family and they were going to keep it there! He also said they knew my ex-husband, Big H, and they were going to sort him out good and proper. That's how cocky the cunts were back then; they could say what they liked and they knew you couldn't do nothing about it. I hadn't seen Big H for some time and I didn't know what he was talking about. But I soon found out.

They turned up nothing at my house, so they fucked off. They found three replica guns and a rifle at Evans Road and a warrant was issued for Harry-Boy. They got him six months later, and this started an endless circle for me, of going to police stations and solicitors' offices and courthouses and prisons, that was to last for the next twenty years. When they did take Harry-Boy to court for the jewellery blag he was found not guilty – but that didn't cut no ice with the police. We were earning a reputation in the Downham area; Harry was very much like me and it wasn't long before John and Loveinia followed in the same footsteps.

Sixer had good days and bad days and he was eventually moved from Bexley Mental Hospital into sheltered housing with a carer to look after him. I went to see him all the time and I could see gradual improvements – very gradual, over the years. He started to get better, he learned to read and write again. Little signs of the man he was before came back and, after staying with me on and off temporarily, I helped him get re-housed and he lived down the street from me in Crutchley Road. He did get better and he lived as an independent person and was one of the wisest people I ever knew. Although we weren't together no more, he was still a part of me and I was devastated when he passed away in 2003.

13

BIG H GOES ON THE RUN
– I GET HOUNDED

The coppers were as good as their word, and Harry Mackenney was accused of robbery and murder in July 1979 and he went on the run. I was sitting in Loveinia's house at the time and a report came on the radio about a manhunt for a vicious East End villain, who answered to the nickname 'Big H'. I couldn't fucking believe it. The report said he was armed and dangerous and shouldn't be approached by members of the public. I said to Loveinia: 'They can't mean your dad, for fuck's sake!'

But they did. We tried to get in contact with him, but he was nowhere to be found. I didn't know what was going on or what to do. I just listened to the news on the radio for the rest of the day, in total disbelief.

The next day, all hell broke loose. The case was in all the papers. Suddenly we were the most notorious family in London. Reporters came out of the woodwork, because Scotland Yard told them where to find us and they were digging as much dirt as they could find and what they couldn't find they made up. It was like some fucking detective drama on the television; I couldn't believe what I was hearing and seeing. I was surrounded by reporters saying all these horrible things about Harry and I knew he wouldn't do anything like that. I knew he wasn't capable of the things he was being accused of. The fuckers were all in my front garden and I had to pull the curtains to keep them from staring in at me. No fucker could get in or out with them there.

They camped out there twenty-four hours a fucking day. The bastards were even brazen enough to come and knock on the front door over and over again. No matter what I did, they wouldn't go away and they loved it when I got angry with them and they took pictures to prove what a violent woman I was. This kind of in-your-face tabloid journalism was new, to some extent, back then, like when sensation takes over from the truth. It's all over the place nowadays, of course, with all these half-arsed celebrities constantly getting their fucking physogs on the front pages – all these reality TV shows and stuff. Back then was the beginning of it and we weren't exactly celebrities; we were made to be notorious, like when these geezers go on the rampage now and shoot up villages and stuff and the media come down there and pick their lives apart. That's what it was like for us.

All the fucking neighbours were out whispering and pointing fingers. At one point some leary bitch knocked on the door to tell me the people in the area didn't want 'scum' like us living near them. Well, Loveinia answered the door to her and knocked two types of fuck out of her and banged her head on the doorstep. Of course, this only played into the hands of the reporters; it gave them a licence to print anything they liked about us, truth or lies, and there was nothing we could do about it.

Big H was labelled as 'Hit Man Harry' and 'Danger Man' in the papers and anyone with the name Mackenney was automatically a 'monster' and a 'savage' and a danger to all law-abiding citizens. Reporters followed us around everywhere, hounding us and harassing us. People were interviewed who didn't even know us and then sold their fucking stories for money, which were then twisted to suit the witch-hunt that had been stirred up.

Vigilante gangs were organised in the area and, because they knew we couldn't go to the police for help, they thought we were fair game for their harassment and violence. When the Big H scandal hit the papers, Daniel was still at school and he was bullied non-stop over it. Even though Big H wasn't his father, I'd given him the Mackenney name and that was as good as calling him Jack the fucking Ripper! The hunt was on for Big H and he was labelled Britain's 'Most Wanted Man', a deadly assassin that must not be approached at any cost. The name Mackenney was everywhere, on all the news channels and in all the newspapers. Everyone knew we were related to him and that Harry-Boy and Loveinia were his kids and, anyway, they were both the spitting image of him.

The reporters even went up to Wiltshire to harass Gracie. Her and Ale had adopted two children, because she couldn't have any of her own after the accident in the factory, like I told you. One was a girl and the other a boy, but the boy committed suicide and, even though it was completely unrelated to anything going on in London, the reporters tried to make out that Big H had killed him. It wasn't only ridiculous, it was criminal. Nobody was spared.

The thing is, I always loved Big H and, even though I settled down with Sixer and was angry and hurt and heartbroken after he left me, I still loved the man and I think I probably still love him to this day. I'd kept his name and I'd given it to Sixer's children and, in doing that, I'd made us all targets of the hatred directed at him while he was on the run. Terrible, gruesome things were being written about him and the kids were getting abuse from people who just wanted to see if the family was as big as was being reported. Everyone was talking about how Big H killed a little boy, amongst others, and it made it worse when I stood up for him, because I knew him better than anybody and I knew he was no cold-blooded killer.

All I could hear everywhere I went was 'murderer', 'murderer', 'murderer'. In the end, me and Harry-Boy and Loveinia decided to talk to the reporters, to try and put across our side of the story and tell them what Big H was really like. It meant saying that the police were trying to fit him up and that made us targets for the police, even worse than it was before. They never left us alone after that, right to this day. It gave the police a new licence to step up their campaign against us. They taunted us continuously and believed they could get away with whatever they liked – and they were right! I used to make complaint after complaint against the coppers, but they just laughed in my face.

I believe it was the police who were 'leaking' all this information to the press and building Harry up to be this outrageous, cold-blooded villain. They knew it would make their job of getting him banged up all the easier when they caught him and brought him to court – half their work would be already done and their evidence wouldn't be scrutinised all that much, because the public would be demanding justice and the courts would be only too willing to give it to them and it wouldn't matter that a man who might not have been totally innocent in his life, but was definitely innocent of what he was being accused, could go down for life.

Once, during this time, as Harry-Boy was leaving the house, there was this copper we knew well waiting for him. He grabbed Harry-Boy and handcuffed him as he came out of the garden. I saw this and ran out to see what was going on. I shouted at the copper: 'Why are you hand-cuffing him?'

He just laughed at me and said, 'I don't like the name Mackenney!'

At the same time, Loveinia came out of her flat opposite; she was with 'Little-Legs', who had a broken little leg at the time and was on crutches. I was shouting at the copper and telling him he had five minutes to take the cuffs off Harry-Boy or I'd report him, so Loveinia and Little-Legs came across to see what was happening. The copper was laughing at us, so Little-Legs shouted to Loveinia, 'Knock the cunt out!'

She punched the bastard so hard she knocked him over the hedge and he ended up in the neighbour's front garden. He was trying to call for help on his radio, so I grabbed it from him and stamped on it and smashed it to pieces. Harry-Boy was handcuffed, so he couldn't do anything, and Little-Legs was on crutches, so it was down to me and Loveinia – two women. We laid into this cunt and the whole street could hear him screaming, 'Help me! Help me!'

Eventually, his mates turned up in force and we were all taken to the police station. Me and Loveinia were charged with assault and taken to court. We were found not guilty.

Another time, I heard this commotion outside the house; it was dark and raining really hard. I went out front to see what was going on and I could see a Mini parked in one of the bays in the cul-de-sac. A gang of riot police had the car surrounded and they were bashing fuck out of it with truncheons. They'd broken all the windows and they were smashing in the roof. I could see all the dents in it. The noise was so loud, everyone was looking out their windows by now. Then, suddenly, I saw an arm stick out through one of the broken windows and I realised someone was in there. I went closer and saw it was Harry-Boy; the horrible fucking bastards were smashing the car in on him. I could see blood smeared on the broken glass and I thought they were trying to kill him. Well, I didn't wait to find out what he was supposed to have done, I went screaming like a banshee at them and started pulling them away from the car. But they threw me to one side and went back at it again. The only way I could stop them was to put myself between them and the front seat and I'm sure they would have beaten me to the ground if a crowd hadn't gathered by now and they knew there was plenty of witnesses. So they stopped beating the car and dragged

Harry-Boy out and took him away. He was released later, without charge.

It wasn't just us; the few friends we were left with got hounded too. John had a friend called Mickey who had serious asthma. Mickey looked just like Jesus, with long shoulder-length hair and a little beard. Anyway, Mickey was coming round to us one day, walking along the footpath, when a panda car came chasing after him. It mounted the pavement and almost ran him over. Mickey took out to run and the car chased him all the way into the cul-de-sac and, when he came through my door, he collapsed in the hallway. I ran to help him, but he was vomiting violently and hyperventilating and couldn't seem to catch his breath. I thought he was having a heart attack. The cunts in the panda car fucked off after doing this and eventually I got Mickey into a sitting position on the sofa and he recovered. But his hair was all covered in vomit and he looked like he was at death's fucking door.

I tried to find out where Big H was when he went on the run, so I could try to help him, but I wasn't able to. None of my connections knew, or they said they didn't know. People told me he was gone abroad to negotiate deals for selling diving equipment from a factory he was running. Others said he was dead, that he'd been murdered in a contract killing. You might think that I'd have been glad that Big H got himself into all this bother, after the way he left me, but I wasn't. I couldn't believe the things they were saying about him and the names they were fucking calling him and I wanted to scream at them, 'You're wrong, you fucking bastards! You're fucking wrong!'

I wanted him to come to me – to come back to me, and we'd be able to show everyone that it was all a mistake. I'd be his alibi, I'd be his witness, I'd be his getaway driver, just like before. Then the police started watching my house, hoping that he'd show up here and they could nab him, and I didn't want him to come. I wanted to be able to get in touch with him and tell him to stay away, to meet him in some hideaway place and make a plan for us to get out of the country together, with the kids. All this stuff was going through my mind and it was driving me insane.

I started getting strange phone calls – when I'd pick up the phone it would be all silent on the other end. I didn't know whether it was Harry or the police or the newspapers or some sick bastard being a fucking nuisance. I'd speak softly: 'Harry? Is it you?'

But whoever it was they always hung up and that wound me up worse than anything.

Harry being on the run was stirring up a lot of heat for London villains. Addresses were being raided all over the city and even outside it and plenty of people were going to ground, not wanting to be involved. Even Interpol flashed Big H's description to over a hundred countries and an extensive search was carried out in the south of France, because they said he had connections with the notorious criminal underworld there. *The French Connection* films had come out not so long before and Harry's reported connection made him seem more of an international crook. They said he was slipping in and out of Britain in a private plane, which he flew himself, and that he was an expert sub-aqua diver and pistol shot and all this gave him 'a James Bond reputation'.

All sorts of stories were surfacing, about what Big H had been up to since me and him parted. He was supposed to be living with a woman called Gwen Andrews, who was the wife of Ron Andrews, a man who'd disappeared about a year earlier and who was a good friend of Harry's. Reports said Big H had taken her and her kids on holiday to Marseilles and she'd acted as his alibi while he somehow came back to England and carried out a half-million-pound security-van robbery. Gwen Andrews was arrested and held in police custody for a week, before being given bail on £10,000 surety and the surrender of her passport. They said she provided aid, comfort and a Volkswagen car to Harry. This stung me and resurrected the old green-eyed monster inside me, but I still wanted to help him in any way I could.

Big H was on the run for three months. He ended up at a house in Plaistow in East London. The house belonged to Bill Woodcraft, a friend, and Big H lived there for about a week. Then Chief Superintendent Frank Cater, in charge of Scotland Yard's Serious Crime Squad, got tipped off and the house was surrounded by a team of armed police from the 'Special Squad'. When he realised there was no escape Harry gave himself up quietly and without a fuss. He was unarmed. Harry told me later he believed the police would rather have shot him dead than arrest him and save themselves the trouble of a court trial – and they probably would have, if the Woodcraft family hadn't been there.

I'd been through a lot in my life, but nothing compared to this. I knew Harry didn't murder anyone and I told everyone who pretended to listen, but no one believed me. I made myself a nuisance to the police, wanting to know why Big H was held for such a long time without being charged. I even stood outside Bow Street court and demanded a full inquiry into police methods of interrogation. I was laughed at, of course, and my family was accused and abused by police, newspapers, neighbours and everyone and anyone who wanted to take a cheap shot at us – it was as if we'd killed those people ourselves, me and the kids. I didn't know how I'd have the strength to keep on fighting – it seemed like the whole fucking world was against us. Every day there was another fucking incident against us and it seemed like it was never going to stop. It felt like I was talking, but everyone had suddenly gone deaf – or I could hear the words I was saying, but nobody else could.

We told the newspapers what we thought, what we knew, that Big H was no monster, like they were calling him. But it was no use. He was tried and found guilty, before he ever set fucking foot in the Old Bailey.

14

THE FRAME-UP AND OTHER
ATTEMPTED FRAME-UPS

When the case opened at the Old Bailey in 1980, the whole family was getting non-stop attention from the press. Loveinia's boyfriend Little-Legs was the jealous type and he wasn't happy about reporters following his girlfriend around all over the place. Loveinia was twenty-five and beautiful and the tabloid hacks loved to flock round her and take her picture and try to get a story from her. Little-Legs was a controlling cunt and watching this made him seethe inside. But, being the only girl amongst three brothers, Loveinia was a strong woman and wouldn't be controlled.

She originally met Little-Legs at a hostel, where she stayed for a while. She wasn't happy at 49 Crutchley Road, so she managed to make contact with Big H and went to Dagenham to live with him. But that didn't work out either, so she got herself a place in the hostel for a while and eventually settled down with Little-Legs in a flat just across the road from my house in Crutchley Road. The relationship was a turbulent one, to say the least. I thought they just liked to argue, like me and Big H used to, but it was more than that. Little-Legs was an out-and-out fucking nutter. I mean, I was well used to hard cases and I got on well with him, but when it came to being jealous of Loveinia, he just couldn't control himself. It was only a matter of time before it kicked off big time, as it did one night in 1980.

I was at home with Sixer, who was getting better and spending more time with me. The first thing I heard was the noise – a massive bang, and the sound of smashing glass. Daniel was fifteen then, upstairs in his room, and Sixer was asleep in a chair. I had two dogs at the time and they were going fucking mad, howling and growling at the front door. I ran upstairs and looked out the window, to see what was going on. There was Little-Legs, with his face so contorted in rage, he looked like a fucking gargoyle or something. He was normally a nice-looking man, with a baby face, but now he was the fucking devil incarnate. Not many things scare me, but Little-Legs did that night. He was no longer the bloke who used to come in with Loveinia for a cup of tea, he was fucking possessed.

Little-Legs was smashing our windows with an iron bar. Every one of them went in and, because the house was semi-detached, I was worried he'd get round and come in the back door. Neither Harry-Boy nor John were in the house and Little-Legs knew that, otherwise he wouldn't have started to do what he did. But it was only me, a semi-retarded man and a fifteen-year-old boy. I immediately got Daniel out of the house. He jumped the fence into a neighbour's garden and kept well out of sight. But Sixer wouldn't leave. I'm not sure if he knew exactly what was happening, but he showed no signs of fear. I went back upstairs and looked out the window and saw that Little-Legs was preoccupied with something. It was pitch-black and I could barely make him out. Then I heard him scream-ing and shouting: 'You only fucking die once!'

And he started crawling on all fours up to the front door.

He smashed the door with a sword and threw some-thing in – it was a petrol bomb. Flames began to engulf the hallway and Little-Legs was slashing at the door with the sword, trying to make a hole big enough for him to get through. His hands were coming through the hole into the house and he was pulling bits of wood away from the door. I was really scared now. Sixer realised something was wrong and began to throw buckets of water on the fire to put it out. I didn't want Little-Legs to get in and, if the fire was out, it would make it easier for him. But Sixer was determined and he fought the flames back so far, until he could see Little-Legs' hands coming through the hole in the door. Then he ran and got a club hammer from Harry-Boy's toolbox and started walloping Little-Legs' hands with it. I could hear the crunching bone sounds and Sixer used the hammer non-stop, until Little-Legs drew back. I could hear him screaming and cursing and there was blood everywhere, all over what was left of the fucking door.

Little-Legs ran away up the road but, by now, the police and fire brigade had arrived – the neighbours must've called them – and I was outside the front of the house now, because I was worried about Loveinia. What happened was, she and Little-Legs had a bull-and-cow and she walked out. He thought she'd come over to my house and wouldn't come out to talk to him and he went berserk, but she didn't, she just went for a walk to cool down. Like I said, he was a complete fucking nutter. Anyway, more police were coming up the street, and they had Little-Legs in handcuffs. Just then, a Mini Cooper car came driving into the cul-de-sac at high speed – and it wasn't slowing down. It mounted the kerb and headed straight for Little-Legs. The police pulled him out of the way just in time and the car missed them by inches. The Mini then reversed and went at them again. I didn't know what the fuck was going on. The police scattered like flies and Little-Legs was trying to dodge the car, with his hands handcuffed behind his back. It was his turn to be fucking scared – and he fucking was! The police were calling for help on their radios and, at this point, the Mini raced off into the night.

Well, as it happened, the Mini used to belong to me, but I'd sold it that very morning to a geezer named Harry MacDonald. But, when they found out, the police didn't believe me and started looking for Harry-Boy. They found him and arrested him and he was charged with attempted murder. We fought the case in court and Harry was found not guilty. Little-Legs was never charged with the fire-bombing.

And that's how it was during the trial of Big H. To my mind, the coppers were only interested in crucifying my family, nothing else mattered to them.

In the middle of all this, my granddaughter Shelley was born to Harry-Boy and his girlfriend.

When the trial began, me and Harry-Boy and Loveinia went to the court every day to protest his innocence and show support for him. Once, while I was there, I got to see one of the police 'manhunters' who went after Big H when he was on the run and I asked him why we were getting so much harassment and how the reporters knew where I lived and kept camping outside my house. He laughed and said, 'I didn't think that kind of thing would bother someone like you.'

In other words, we were less than human in his eyes, we were the scum of the earth and deserved anything we got.

All this fucking supergrass stuff began in the early seventies with Bertie Smalls and anyone who turned super-grass could expect a 'tariff' sentence of five years, most of which would be spent in isolation so they couldn't be got at. Narks and grasses told lies to get off heavy sentences and sent hundreds of people to prison during this time. It was a convenient way for the coppers to verbal anyone they wanted, without having to come up with any real evidence.

John Childs turned supergrass against Harry and Terry Pinfold, in order to save his own worthless skin. It was part of the trend back then and the tabloids perpetuated the illusion that these narks were doing a public service. In the end, it was grasses informing on grasses and no fucker knew where they stood. The coppers who ran the show were as bad as the villains, but they never got put away, because they had the 'law' on their side. Harry was one of the victims of this diabolical system.

I remember pushing my way through the lynch mob of reporters and screaming idiots outside the courthouse and making my way to the famous court number 2. I sat with Harry-Boy, who was twenty-six at the time, and Loveinia, who was twenty-five, waiting for Big H and the others to be brought up into the dock. Harry and three other men – Terry Pinfold, Paul Morton and Lenny Thompson – were finally going on trial for the murders of Terence Eve, Freddy Sherwood, Ron Andrews, Robert Brown, George Brett and Terry Brett. Terry Brett was only ten years old when he disappeared.

The chief prosecutor was John Mathew QC and Harry's barrister was Michael Mansfield QC. The cunts all looked happy and cheerful in their wigs and gowns, as they chatted to each other and cracked jokes and waited for their lordships to take the bench. Reputations would be made and careers enhanced and the proceedings talked about in posh wine bars for years to come. I, on the other hand, was filled with fucking dread – courthouses weren't friendly places for the Mackenney family. They were hostile and dangerous and this occasion was to be no fucking exception.

I came to the Old Bailey every single day of that fucking trial – that fucking frame-up. I felt sorry for Harry, in the dock, chained like an animal, handcuffed to a couple of CID slags, like he'd try to make a break for it if they didn't chain him up, or he might try to cut the judge's throat or turn into Jack the fucking Ripper. He was made to sit on a chair that was fixed to the floor and surrounded by prison screws. That's how they made it look, like he was what they'd been calling him – 'Britain's Most Wanted Man'.

We were his family, the only people who knew he was innocent. We wouldn't desert him, like he'd deserted us. But I could see the despair in his face; I knew that he knew the odds were stacked against him. It all seemed stage-managed to me, like some horrible fucking farce – only there was nothing funny about it. Maybe it was funny to the toerag reporters who blew the story out of all proportion, but I wasn't fucking laughing.

For over a year, the newspapers ran headlines like 'Hit Man Harry' and 'Dial H for Murder' and 'Gangland Killer' and 'Danger Man' and 'Monster' and 'Child Killer' and 'Evil Hitman'. The jury read all them headlines, so what fucking chance did he have? It didn't matter that there was no real evidence – no bodies and no weapons and no forensics, just the word of a pathological liar who'd cut a deal to send innocent men away for life, so he could get off with a light sentence. But all that didn't matter, the papers had already tried and convicted Big H, it just needed the jury to make it official.

John Childs was the prosecution's star witness – Harry called him 'Bruce' when I knew him all them years ago. They met up in prison, back in the old days. His real name wasn't even Childs; he was a Welsh cunt called Martin Jones and he stole the name Childs from the previous tenant of his flat in a tower block in Poplar, East London. I never liked Childs, right from the first time Harry introduced him to me. He was shifty sort and I didn't trust him. He was a petty crook who got involved in the big-time and then couldn't take the consequences when he got collared.

Harry was always good with his hands and always making things and, after he left me, he started up a factory with Terry Pinfold in a disused church hall in Dagenham, making underwater diving equipment. It was back in 1973, four years after our divorce. They called the business HJM Marine and when Bruce Childs came out of prison Harry gave the fucker a job – and see where it got him! Anyway,

Terence Eve was another ex con, who shared the factory. They called him 'Teddy Bear Eve', because he made children's stuffed teddy bears. In 1974, Eve became a suspect in the hijacking of £75,000 worth of stereo equipment. He found out he was facing a five stretch before he could be arrested and did a runner. He was never seen again, and that was the end of that – until 1979.

Childs was arrested in 1979 for being involved in a series of Hertfordshire bank robberies, including a security-van robbery, that netted over £500,000. He was looking at a fifteen stretch, at least – so he decided to become a fucking supergrass. He testified that Terence Eve was dead and that he killed him, along with Harry and Terry Pinfold, on the day he disappeared, because they wanted to take over his factory. I knew this was complete fucking bullshit. Even though I wasn't with Harry during that time, I knew he'd invented and patented a unique diving valve that he called the 'aqua valve'. He stood to make a fucking packet from this invention and he didn't need no half-arsed teddy-bear business.

Childs testified that Teddy Bear Eve was strangled and battered to death in the factory, then his body was brought to the ground-floor flat in Poplar and butchered, after the cunt had supposedly sent his wife Tina and their two young children away for the day. First, he said, the body wouldn't go through the industrial mincer that Pinfold was supposed to have procured somewhere, although nobody said where – so they started flushing it down the lavatory. But this was taking too long, he said, so they burned what was left in the small grate. I couldn't believe what I was hearing. I looked at the jury, they were hearing it too – only difference was, they were fucking believing it. The hacks were scribbling like mad, wearing out their fucking pencils and grinning at each other like fucking ghouls.

Childs also admitted to killing five other people with Harry and Pinfold – these people had disappeared during the seventies and he said they were 'contract killings'. Pinfold was supposed to have been the 'procurer' who got the contracts and Harry and Childs were supposed to have been the killers. Anyone who knew Harry knew he wasn't a killer – he might have been a lot of things, but he was no fucking murderer.

The court was told that Harry was lusting after Ron Andrews's wife, Gwen, and that's why Ron was killed, so Harry could have her. The fact that Harry knew Ron and was with Gwen before he was arrested didn't help his case, and they really didn't need any more evidence than that. But I knew it was a complete load of fucking rubbish – Harry could get any woman he wanted, he never had to kill nobody to pull a woman, for fuck's sake! According to Childs, Andrews was supposed to have been suspicious of his wife seeing other men, so Harry told him there was this private detective waiting to see him at the flat, a man who'd keep an eye on his wife when he was out of town. He was shot through the head when he got there. Childs said he and Harry then drove Andrews's car to the River Nene at Wisbech, Cambridgeshire, a hundred and twenty fucking miles away. Harry was alleged to have dressed in diving gear and drove the car into the river, then swam ashore, where he was picked up by Childs, who said they hoped the police would believe Andrews drowned and his body was carried away by the current and out into the Wash.

They then went back and burned the body but, Childs said, he had to drink two and a half bottles of whisky to do this – I don't know of any cunt who could even stand up after drinking two and a half bottles of fucking whisky, never mind burn a twelve-stone body.

Freddy Sherwood ran an old people's home and Childs said the contract came from a rival who wanted him out of business – the rival's name was never mentioned. Sherwood was lured to the factory, according to Childs, on the pretext of selling his car. Then he was shot and bludgeoned with a hammer. He was cut up on the factory floor and the body parts were transported across London to the flat for burning. How could anyone believe that? Would you? Childs said all the burning was affecting him so much he had to get drunk every night to be able to sleep. What about the smell, the fucking residue, the grease, the bones – never mind the rest of the fucking fairy tale? Nobody bothered to ask about that.

Robert Brown had escaped from the nick and he was hiding out in a room at the factory. Childs said Brown witnessed some of the killings and they couldn't trust him not to blab if he got caught, so he had to be dealt with. He said Harry told Brown his cover was blown and the police would be there soon to pick him up. That convinced him it would be safer for him at Childs's flat. Once they got him there, they shot him twice in the back. But, according to the lies, Brown didn't die from the shooting, so Childs and Harry finished the job with a knife, a sword and an axe. Then they burned him.

George Brett had testified for the prosecution at the trial of the infamous Tibbs gang back in 1972 and he was killed, according to Childs, because he was sticking his nose into the Mountnessing silver-bullion robbery that happened in the same year, and for which his brother Johnny got a fifteen-year stretch. Again, the person who took out the so-called 'contract' wasn't named. George brought his ten-year-old son along when he went to meet the 'killers' and the boy got topped just because he was there.

Childs swore he convinced George Brett to go to the factory with him from Brett's farm in Essex, on the pretext of having some haulage business for him. Harry was supposed to have 'blasted' him with a sten gun and then shot the boy, who was crying and holding one of the teddy bears. George Brett was a tough man. He was known as 'Big Georgie' and people didn't take liberties with him. The tips of both of his little fingers had been lopped off in some previous grief and he carried a bullet scar on one knee, where he was shot during a fight with a sword. He had many convictions for violence and carrying firearms. George was street-wise and tough and he would never have fallen for a story from a fucking muppet like Bruce Childs. Even if he had, he would never have taken his ten-year-old boy along with him to a meet that was a big dodgy – anyone who knew George Brett would have known that. Also, with bullets from a sten gun blasting round the factory, there was bound to have been some fucking ballistics – but the police never found nothing.

This was manna from fucking heaven for the tabloids. They printed stories of bludgeonings and slicings with swords and knives and hatchets and the flat was compared to an abattoir, with blood and guts everywhere. When the defence questioned the logistics of burning the bodies of five men and one boy in a small fire grate only eighteen inches wide, using ordinary household fuel, police scientists testified that they'd killed a 160lb pig and burned the carcass in Childs's grate, which took them thirteen hours. Childs said the mental torture of burning the bodies like this was driving him crazy and that's why he confessed.

The only crazy cunts were the ones who believed him!

Childs couldn't explain how he and Harry had got away with it for all those years, or how his wife or his neighbours didn't smell the human flesh burning in his flat for days on end. I knew about Bruce Childs; he was a liar and a coward. He'd even tried to rape my daughter Loveinia when she was younger and he was the worst kind of scum you'd find in a fucking day's march. He wouldn't have had the imagination to concoct a story as elaborate as that. It was clear to me that he was briefed – he was tutored – he was coached for a long time. Who wrote the story for him? Well, that would be supposition, as they say in court – but I'm sure you can fucking work it out for yourselves. There was nothing fucking surer to me, than Childs had been rehearsing his part for months, before he went into the Old Bailey in November 1980 and gave a fucking Oscar-winning performance for his audience!

Tina Childs wasn't proved to be in on any conspiracy, but surely she would have known about all those bodies being burned in her flat? She told the newspapers that she'd be living in fear for the rest of her life and that she'd never be safe, because of what we, the Mackenneys, might do to her. The police even put her and her kids under protection, supposedly to make sure we didn't get near her – in my opinion they did it to blacken the Mackenney name even more than it was already and make us all out to be some sort of fucking 'serial-killer' family. I didn't give tuppence for that little cunt; I knew she knew her husband was a lying nonce, yet she never opened her fucking mouth to contradict him. But that didn't matter to me. I believed she was probably more scared of what the fucking police would do to her than she was of the Mackenneys.

Childs was the prosecution's entire case, they had nothing else, no bodies and no weapons. Harry's defence lawyer focused on the inconsistencies in Childs's story and told the court that he had a solid alibi for the weekend Terence Eve was supposed to have been murdered – he was on a course, training to be a flying instructor, which was one of Harry's many ambitions. Terry Pinfold could prove he was in Clacton the whole weekend the murder was supposed to have been committed and this was corroborated by witnesses. Eve's wife, his mother and one of the factory workers said they were in the factory on the Saturday morning Terence went missing and they saw nothing out of the ordinary. They also said they never saw Pinfold nor Harry that day. But the jury ignored all that; they'd read in the papers that Harry was a heartless child-killer, they'd read he was a marksman and a classic schizophrenic, they'd read he was Jekyll and Hyde – and that was enough for them!

There was one man, however, who knew that none of it was true. He knew, as the trial dragged on for thirty-seven days, yet he never opened his fucking mouth to end it. That man was Commander Bert Wickstead of J Division, CID – the man the *Daily Telegraph* called 'the incorruptible Old Grey Fox'. In 1976, Chief Inspector

James Harrison-Griffiths had tried to investigate Terence Eve's disappearance, but was warned off by Wickstead. Wickstead told him that Eve was alive and living under an assumed name in West London. Harrison-Griffiths was told his career in CID would be short-lived if he didn't drop his inquiry. This meant that Wickstead knew full well that Terence Eve was alive more than two years after Harry was supposed to have killed him, according to Childs's testimony. And, if Eve was still alive when he was supposed to have been dead, what about the other five 'victims'?

I listened to the horrible fucking details of the 'killings' being picked over, one by one, day by day. Going into that courtroom to see how Harry was being crucified was torture for me, but I never missed a fucking minute of the lies and perjury and viciousness. I watched the families of the missing 'victims' and I could see their hatred for the men on trial, I could see they believed all the lies, they believed Harry murdered their sons and husbands. But I knew he didn't. But I was a monster too, by association, and so were my kids. The ropes and the burning crosses were out, the baying fucking mob was on the rampage and there was no stopping it.

Life would never be the same for any of us again.

Like I said, Harry's so-called trial was a complete fucking farce from start to finish. He never had a fucking chance. I could tell, right from the start, that there was never going to be fair play and the court proceedings were just a fucking charade, so the CID could close the books on six so-called 'killings' and go get drunk celebrating putting Big H Mackenney away for life. The stinking lies that were told by Childs in court were ludicrous, to put it mildly. But it was the way things were being done during the seventies and eighties – more than one innocent man had been fitted up for crimes they didn't commit and left to rot in prison for years. The public didn't care, because they saw the police force the way it was portrayed on TV in *The Sweeney* – with hard-working officers risking their lives to combat crime and, if they bent the rules every now and then, like John Thaw and Dennis Waterman, what matter – the criminals deserved every fucking thing they got!

Another fucking thing. If Childs was telling the truth, then all four defendants should have been found guilty on all charges. But the verdicts were different and confused every fucker. Harry was found guilty of murdering Freddy Sherwood, Ron Andrews, George Brett and ten-year-old Terry Brett. He was found not guilty of murdering Robert Brown and Terence Eve because, they said, there was 'a lack of corroboration' – whatever that meant. Terry Pinfold was found guilty of murdering Robert Brown and hiring Harry to murder Terence Eve, even though Harry was found not guilty of Eve's murder. How the fuck could that be right? The other two defendants were acquitted.

Childs's sentence of life for the six murders conveniently didn't carry a minimum recommendation, which was usually a mandatory stipulation by the bench in murder cases. Childs's wife, Tina, said in court that she expected him to be out in six. Harry was given a 'whole life' tariff, which meant he could never expect to be released.

Harry wasn't allowed to give evidence. When they asked him if he had anything to say after they'd done their dirty work, he just replied: 'Get this fiasco over with. I've killed no one. I've saved plenty of lives.'

Which meant his 'aqua valve' had saved the lives of divers. I even tried to get up and speak for him; I mean, how could the bastards get away with what they were doing? Somebody had to tell the truth! But they stopped me. They warned me it would make things worse for him – how could it possibly have been any worse? They threatened that I'd be evicted from the court. I called them cunts and swore at them for what I believed they were doing – at the prosecution for what looked like their collusion, and at the defence lawyers for what they seemed to be allowing, in the name of the fucking law!

Harry was defiant in the dock, when they eventually brought him up for sentencing, even though I could see the hopelessness in his eyes.

'Do your worst, you mongrels!' That's what he shouted when they sentenced him, before the grinning screws dragged him from the dock. I was there on that day and he turned and looked at me and it was the first time he'd looked at me like that for many years. He looked lost and sad and his face was full of sorrow. I wished I could have done more to help him, I wished I could have proved he was innocent. I felt so helpless, I couldn't do anything to stop what had happened and that was the worst thing of all. I felt guilty too, for driving him away, for leading him a dog's life when he was with me. I felt guilty for every time I'd accused him of being with another woman and for every time I'd hit him and for every row we ever had. Maybe if I'd been more reasonable, he'd have stayed and he wouldn't have fell in with these people and all this would never have happened.

When I left the courthouse, I was in tears. The press surrounded me and hounded me down the street. Harry-Boy tried to keep them back, away from me and Loveinia, but that only made them worse – they were like a pack of fucking wolves. Our car was surrounded and Harry-Boy had to almost drive over some of the fuckers to get us out of that evil place.

The trial itself is a matter of record, but what ain't a matter of record is Big H's pain – and what me and my family were put through before, during and after it. We were abused and abandoned by everyone, even people we knew for years and even villains who'd done far worse things in their lives than we ever done. But none of that was reported in the papers. That side of the story's never been told – until now! Harry was labelled as one of the most infamous murderers of all time and, because we didn't disown him and didn't abandon him, we became a target for the haters. Harry was out of their reach now, so they turned on us!

15

MACKENNEYS AGAINST THE WORLD

The eighties was the era of Thatcherism and the poll tax and the miners' strike and the yuppies and the 'greed is good' culture. It was the end of the old-time villains in London. New mobsters from Eastern Europe were moving into the manors and drugs and vice were the ways of making big money. I wanted nothing to do with that. The smart crooks were moving across the river, into the City of London, into investment banking and the stock market and places like that, where they couldn't be called to account for their fucking crimes.

Harry was wrongly accused of six murders and wrongly convicted of four of them – and one of them was a child. The killing of a child arouses huge emotion in the public and, when it's sensationally reported by the tabloids, it can stir up vigilantes and lynch mobs. We knew Harry was innocent, but no one wanted to believe us. The London villains knew well how people were being fitted up by the supergrasses, but they didn't believe us either. Me and my family were found guilty too – of being related to Britain's most wanted man and a child-killer.

I went to see him in Parkhurst Prison on the Isle of Wight – I went about five times altogether. Like I told you already, the first thing I said to him was: 'I still got your dinner in the oven.'

It's hard to understand, but I never stopped loving him and it was like having my heart ripped out to see him in that place, to see the stress on his face and the weariness that was all over him. He looked so sad and so broken. If I didn't have my kids back then and if I didn't have to deal with all the shit that was happening to them, I'm not sure if I would have survived it. I asked him about Gwen Andrews and he told me they were never an item. She turned against him like all the rest after the trial, after they said he'd murdered her husband in that horrible way.

After the fifth time, I couldn't go on visiting him, I couldn't go back again. It was just too hard, watching the change that came over him, like he was wasting away. He was a broken man, just the shadow of what he was before. He lost so much weight and his face was all gaunt – it was just too hurtful to see. I wanted to take him away from it, to rescue him, to help him – we were happy when we were good together and I couldn't help thinking if I'd done things different, maybe it would have worked out different.

Harry's father telephoned me and thanked me for going to see him and for not jumping on the bandwagon like all the rest of the cunts and slagging him off. How could I do that? It was never a question of whether I'd stand by him or not. We may have been parted, but he was still the father of my children and I loved him regardless of anything in the fucking world. But I couldn't go back to see him no more. I still did everything I could to clear his name, but the hurt was too strong and too raw to see him chained up and I felt so fucking useless.

Big H did marry again while he was in prison. He married a woman who used to work for him in his aqua-valve factory, or so I believe. To be fair to her, she did stand by him, as much as it hurts me to admit it and, as far as I know, she's still with him to this day.

Life was never the same again after Big H got sentenced. My brothers used to visit me all the time and now they never came round no more. I was left out of all family functions and celebrations like weddings and stuff. They never telephoned nor sent Christmas cards nor nothing. I became the black sheep. I didn't have any friends neither – all the people who'd been my partners in crime over the years, none of them wanted to be seen with me. It would have brought too much aggravation down on their heads. Johnny Kellard, Mad Frances, Peg the Leg, Millie, Shirley Pitts, Fat Mike – even the hardened villains like the Richardsons and the other big gangs – they all avoided me like the fucking plague. I can't say I blame them – if I could have got away from it all, I would have too. My mate Sissy was the only friend who stood by me at that time – she was my real mate.

Big H was inside, but the real shit was hitting the fan on the outside. We were now prime targets for the police. We had a reputation, and anyone with the name 'Mackenney' was fair fucking game. The police were out for blood, with every tuppenny-ha'penny copper wanting to earn his stripes the easy way – by putting something on us. They all wanted to have a go.

During 1981, the police went for Harry-Boy a number of times. He was twenty-seven and he was outspoken in defence of his father, giving interviews to the newspapers and accusing the police of criminal conspiracy and he wouldn't let the thing drop. They really wanted him sent away for a while, where he'd have to be quiet. On one occasion, I was outside in the cul-de-sac, talking to the milkman, and Harry-Boy was walking round the corner, coming towards me. Just then, an unmarked car pulled up with CID men in it. They stopped Harry-Boy and said they'd come to return some property of his that was left behind the last time they arrested him. So they pulled out a big bag and handed it to him. Harry opened the bag and saw a shotgun inside. This was in broad daylight in front of witnesses and it went to show how fucking brazen they were and how the bastards thought they could get away with anything.

Anyway, Harry-Boy never touched the gun to leave his fingerprints on it. I called Loveinia and got her to take the gun straight down to Catford police station. They never done any more about it, because we had loads of witnesses – all they said was they must have made a mistake. That's all they ever said, every time they tried it on and failed – 'Oh sorry, we must have made a mistake.'

The Director of Public Prosecutions investigated this episode, but decided there was insufficient evidence to take the police involved to court. We didn't expect it to be any different. I was becoming paranoid, watching over my shoulder all the time. I was constantly waiting for the next bizarre event, and the next, and the next.

And they kept coming. Harry-Boy was called to the local social-security office in Catford for a meeting over something or other. I went in with him and John waited outside. I noticed straight away that something was wrong, because the place was empty and the staff were being very polite, which wasn't like them at all. While we were in there, the police surrounded the building – but John was outside and he saw what was going on. He got in before the police could seal the place off and he told Harry-Boy what was happening, then he gave Harry the keys to his place at the back of Catford, where he'd just moved to. John then pretended to be Harry-Boy, while the police moved on us and Harry got away in the confusion.

I couldn't even tell you what it was all about. The whole of the eighties were a blur of attempted fit-ups, allegations, warrants and arrests. My house was raided so many times, I might as well just have given the police a fucking key to the front door. They used to sit there in their cars and wait for us and try to wind us up so we would do something and they could arrest us and keep us banged up in the cells for fucking hours on end. The physical effects were bad enough, but the psychological effects were worse, just to know they were there, watching you all the fucking time. It was hard to be a friend of ours then; if you were, you got targeted too. That way, they could isolate us and we'd have nowhere to turn. So we ended up sticking together, when one of the family got beaten or arrested or attacked, we'd all be there to stand up for them. I've been inside more fucking police stations than I've had hot fucking dinners.

I was convinced our phones were all tapped, mine and Harry-Boy's and Loveinia's and John's, even though I couldn't prove fuck-all, and we were constantly being stopped in the street by the police. They had a licence to do it and they thought it was a right laugh. I'd be going along, minding my own business and a panda car would pull up and the slags would jump out and start asking me twenty fucking questions about what I was doing and where I was going. They'd keep me standing on the street while they got back in their car and smoked a fag and all the cunts passing by gave me an eyeful.

We were the murderer's family and we might as well have gone and killed those people ourselves, the way we got treated. We were complete outcasts, notorious. But what people didn't realise was that they made us what we were. Over and over we took the abuse and, when we fought back, we confirmed their prejudices that we were a bunch of violent nutcases, without any feelings and without any human intelligence. We didn't want to be seen that way, but what do you do when people keep trying their luck? You have to fight back – don't you?

Catford police station was bombed in the early eighties – it had nothing to do with us, I swear! But the police came round with sniffer dogs and searched the house for explosives. Would you fucking believe that?

Harry-Boy moved into 17 Crutchley Road in 1982, but there was no let-up from the media or the police and things were anything but plain sailing. His girlfriend couldn't take the harassment and intimidation any longer and, in 1983, she left. She left my granddaughter Shelley, aged three, behind her and I went round and took the little girl back with me to number 49 and she lived with me every day after that. I was fifty-two at the time.

I went to all of Big H's appeals, but it was always the same – they refused to see the new evidence and they wanted him to be guilty. He had to be guilty, otherwise the whole system was wrong, and how could they admit to being part of a completely corrupt system, where people got sent down for life just because they were getting on some fucking bent policeman's nerves. But it was the way it was, and I didn't think it would ever change.

Shortly after Big H got sent away and Harry-Boy was up visiting him in Leicester Prison, Daniel and one of his mates were round the back of the flats in Crutchley Road and they found an old ladder that was dumped where the bins were. They messed around with it for a bit, then they brought it home and left it in my back garden and Daniel went up to his room. About an hour later, there was a knock on the door and two fully grown men were standing there, saying they wanted Daniel. They said they were CID and wanted to question him, but they wouldn't say what about. I wasn't about to let no fucking geezer take my son away; they didn't look like CID and, after all the shit we'd been through, they could've been some dodgy fuckers from the area trying to do him in, for all I knew.

I wouldn't let them in, so they barged past me and started searching through the downstairs. My friend Sissy was visiting me and she was in the front room and Daniel heard the commotion and got out the window into the back garden. They saw him and rushed out through the back door and tried to grab him, but he picked up a piece of wood and let the first one have it across the side of his ugly fucking head. The other one tried to wrestle him to the floor – don't forget, this is a full-grown man against a sixteen-year-old boy, so I started laying into him, punching the geezer and trying to get him off Dan. Sissy rang for the police from inside the house, but the one Dan had hit with the piece of wood came at me from behind and got me in a stranglehold round the neck. He started dragging me back inside the house, while the other one was dragging Daniel. I had no shoes on and I was choking and struggling and my face was being scraped along the wall as he was dragging me.

He'd just got me to the front door and was trying to pull me outside, when the uniformed police arrived. They turned up within minutes and that was a surprise, because they were never that quick before whenever we were being attacked. It seemed to me as if the cunts were waiting down the street so they could have a good laugh. Sissy was shouting and cursing the whole time and telling them to let me get my fucking shoes on. For once, I was relieved to see the uniforms, because I honestly thought these two geezers were villains, out to do us. It turned out that they were really CID and they were spying on the house when they saw Daniel with the ladder and decided he'd been burgling or some fucking thing.

We were all carted off to the police station and held there for hours in the cells, while they made their 'enquiries'. In the end, they let us out and said: 'Sorry, we must have made a mistake.'

And, as I was leaving, one of the CID bastards laughed at me and said: 'You've had an exciting life, Eileen. You should write a book.'

I wonder if the cunt's laughing now!

In prison, Big H was housed with IRA terrorists and was accused of all sorts of things, from being a terrorist himself, to being responsible for the disappearance of Lord Lucan. It'd be a good joke – if it wasn't so fucking tragic! One Christmas Eve, I was leaving the house when I was stopped by some dodgy-looking geezers. They didn't look like anyone from around the area – they were real tall, with long black overcoats and proper formal, not like the usual coppers either. They asked me if I lived at number 49 and I said yes, because they'd seen me come out of there and they asked me to go back inside with them and answer some questions that were of the utmost importance. I didn't ask them for ID, because, from experience, I never got shown any and, whenever I refused to let them in, the CID usually barged their way in anyway. They wanted to know the ins and outs of a duck's arse – my maiden name, where I was born and family connections and all sorts of other stuff. I finally got to ask them what they were fucking getting at and they said were investigating possible connections to the IRA.

The fucking IRA, for fuck's sake! It turned out that Loveinia had gone to see her dad in prison and, while she was in there, she started talking to one of the people in the waiting room who was known to Special Branch as a gunrunner, with IRA connections. I thought, fuck it, the cunts are going to frame me for plotting to bomb Buckingham Palace or something. But, in the end, they seemed satisfied I wasn't going to kill half the fucking government, so they left. All the same, I was at my wits' end for a while after that, because I knew the bastards could do what they liked to me and nobody would help me – and I told Loveinia to be careful who she spoke to from then on!

A few years after Big H went inside, maybe around 1984, my son John was in a local pub called the Governor General, with one of his mates – it was actually the pub they used in the film *The Long Good Friday* and it was eventually knocked down, because there was far too much trouble there. Anyway, John was twenty-four now and he was just having a drink and minding his own business. Suddenly, a rough gang from the area surrounded him. They were known to be knife merchants and were out to make a name for themselves. Since Big H's trial, we were classed as a family of murderers and, if someone could get one of us, it would show how hard they were. Even though John wasn't Big H's son, he was a Mackenney and that made him a prime target. The gang boxed John in so he couldn't get out, but his mate managed to escape and ran round to my house to tell me he was in trouble. I immediately went round there to try and stop what was going on.

The geezers were all tooled up and I'm sure they intended to kill him, but John was no walkover and, as they were coming at him, he was knocking them out. Then, in the scuffle, one geezer ended up getting stabbed with his own knife. This made the others think twice and I was able to get John away. I took him back to the house, because Shelley was there asleep and it was late at night. But, when we got there, I was afraid they'd come after John, so I told him to go out the back and get round to Harry-Boy's, which he did.

John wasn't long gone when I heard it, a commotion outside in the cul-de-sac. I could see through the side window and the only way I can describe it is like you see in the old horror films, when the lynch mob of villagers are coming to the haunted castle with their pickaxes and pitchforks and shit. There was loads of them and the noise was like at a football match, all the shouting and hollering. I ran out of the house with Shelley in my arms before they could get to the door, and went straight to my next-door neighbour's. She was a decent woman, not like the rest of them, and she let us in. I knew they were coming to do over my house and I couldn't handle them alone.

The neighbour called the police, but the mob must have seen me in the dark, because next thing they were in the woman's garden and I remember standing in the hallway and looking at the front door. One of them was a geezer called Lenny Kempley and he had a gun. He had a grief with my sons for a previous fight where a mate of his got cut up – Lenny would be stabbed and killed in the Downham Tavern in 2010. Anyway, my neighbour's front door had a glass panel in it and I could see them coming to it and standing outside. Then they started trying to smash the glass, which was tough and didn't go in easy. But they kept on at the front of the house; all the windows went in and, eventually, so did the door. My neighbour was hysterical by then and had called the police three times – but nobody came.

Then, all of a sudden, the mob dispersed. They went away and it all went quiet. I was too scared for Shelley to go see what was happening, there was glass everywhere, over everything and my granddaughter was crying her eyes out. Then Harry-Boy appeared at the door, with John behind him and Loveinia – and the mob, like all cowards do when they're confronted, ran away.

The coppers eventually turned up, like when it was too late, and they arrested John and charged him with attempted murder. They didn't seem interested in the fact that the geezer was stabbed with his own knife, or that John was only protecting himself, or that the mob had trashed my neighbour's house, or that we were the victims here. It seemed to me they were only interested in another chance to send a Mackenney down for something he didn't do. It meant more trips to solicitors, more trips to courthouses – whenever they took my children to court, I was always there, right beside them. John was sent to Crown Court and was found not guilty.

I was endlessly going to court throughout the eighties – one court after another, local, Crown, the Old Bailey, over and over. I even had a family solicitor now and I recorded conversations I had with the police because I knew, if I gave them the slightest chance, they'd send us all down after Big H – that's what they wanted to do. I can't stress enough what it was like – they all knew me by name and they'd drive their pandas alongside me as I was walking to the shops or somewhere and they'd shout: 'All right, Eileen? How's Harry-Boy?'

Or they'd pass some comment about Loveinia or John and they did this all the time. For every court case we won, the police would try harder and dig deeper. I would wake in the morning and wonder what shit would come my way today. It made me so angry, but it also made me harder than I already was.

During this time, Big H was appealing against his life sentence. He went to court again and again and the farce continued again and again and he was always sent back to prison. I even went to see the Conservative MP for Lewisham at the time, Colin Moynihan, to see if he could help. I brought some tape recordings of a police conversation, where they seemed to be saying they were going to fit Harry-Boy up, just like they fitted up Big H. The MP said he couldn't hear what was being said on the tapes properly. He said it wouldn't do any good, because the evidence wasn't strong enough. So I got independent solicitors to investigate the case. I went to Scotland Yard, I even went to see Commander Carter, who was in charge of the investigation, to try to get my evidence listened to. But nothing worked and I slowly began to lose hope. It was like banging my head against a brick wall.

But I'd been a fighter all my life and I didn't know how to do anything else. I made complaint after complaint to Scotland Yard that are a matter of record. I met with all the coppers who tried to warn me off and told them where they could fucking go. I kept fighting in the courts and on the streets, not only to clear Big H's name, but my family's name as well. I even got a letter from John Childs to Michael Mansfield QC, confessing that he lied in court, but it was ignored. Harry had two appeals turned down, where new evidence was presented, and it seemed to me the courts ignored it because to acquit him would mean having to admit they were wrong in the first place.

Because of my persistent campaigning for Big H, our house was continually raided and Harry-Boy was pulled in more than twenty times. I knew all the coppers involved and this treatment was to scare me off, to stop me from complaining and going to see this one and that one and telling the truth.

But I didn't scare easily!

I was in the house one day in the late eighties, minding my own business, when I heard a helicopter overhead. I didn't take much notice of it at first but, when it didn't go away, I decided to have a look see what the fuck was going on. Well, the whole fucking cul-de-sac was filled with armed fucking riot police – it looked like a fucking SWAT thing that you see in America. They were everywhere and they had flashlights and shields and the whole fucking tommy-rollocks. I was enjoying watching the lark for a while, because I thought it's a bit of gossip and you can't help being nosey, can you? But when they started coming towards my house, it wasn't fucking funny. They said they were looking for Harry-Boy and I asked them what they wanted him for. The geezer in charge came up to me and I thought he said they were delivering a summons for a death threat.

'What death threat?'

'Breath test, we're delivering a summons for a breath test.'

I thought I must have heard him wrong the second time, so I made him say it again – 'We're delivering a summons for a breath test.'

Yes, he definitely said 'breath test'. They didn't have a warrant to search my house, so I wouldn't let them in. Then the whole lot of them fucked off round to Harry-Boy's house and raided it, along with his neighbour, for good measure. A helicopter and fifty riot police to deliver a summons for a breath test? Harry-Boy was never arrested and never charged. It was just a show of force, to let us know what we were up against.

In 1988, John decided to go out for a drink with a good friend of the family called Bill Kyneston, who was visiting. Bill had been Harry-Boy's friend for years, he came from Sheffield and he used to be in the Queen's Guards. We thought of him as one of the family and they decided they'd go over to Lewisham. I had a really bad feeling about this, I don't know why, call it intuition or sixth sense or whatever you like, I just felt it and I begged them not to go to Lewisham, but to go to Bexley Heath instead. In the end, I went round to Harry-Boy's house and asked him to go with them, because I just had a bad feeling about it. Harry had settled down again at 17 Crutchley Road and had two kids with his new partner. He agreed to go with John and Bill and they all left about 8.30 p.m. That was the last time I ever spoke to Bill Kyneston.

The next thing, I got a phone call about 11.30 p.m. There'd been a massive fight in the Joiner's Arms over in Lewisham – John had been stabbed, Harry had been arrested and Bill was fighting for his life in Lewisham Hospital. I felt sick to the bottom of my stomach. I knew something was going to happen and I should have done more to stop them going over there. I got to the police station as fast as I could and they told me there was a fight involving a large gang that had spilled out onto the high street. They had Harry-Boy in a cell and they'd put John in a cell too, even though he'd been stabbed, but he passed out, so they had to take him to hospital.

They wouldn't let me talk to Harry-Boy, so I went to the hospital and John was able to tell me that a large gang of geezers from the Downham Estate saw them in the pub and decided to take them on. Harry-Boy was on the phone trying to get a cab, when they attacked John and Bill. Harry saw what was happening and rushed back over and waded in, trying to get John and Bill to the door and it all spilled out onto the street. By this time, Harry could see blood pouring down John's legs from his stomach, so he stopped a passing car and pulled the driver out and put John in, so he could get him to hospital. He called to Bill to get to the car, but Bill was surrounded by the gang and, by the time Harry-Boy could get back over to him, they were on him like a pack of wolves. They used bar stools to smash him to the ground and then they repeatedly hit him on the head, over and over.

The police arrived and arrested everybody involved. Harry-Boy and John were charged with affray, along with the gang that started it all. Bill was in a coma. He remained like that for six months. I went to see him every day, I took music tapes and played them to him and I talked to him and done everything I could to try to make him come out of it. I saw every doctor under the sun, but they all said the same thing: he was severely brain damaged and he'd never lead a normal life again. I thought about Sixer and I cried. They took him off life support and he continued to live, even though he stayed in a coma. Sometimes I'd talk to him and his eyelids would move and once I thought he tried to lift up his head. But he never recovered and eventually he died. Bill was thirty-five. It was like losing one of my own sons.

Harry-Boy and John were held on remand at first, then John was given bail. Harry was denied bail for a long time, but eventually he got granted it too. Then the fight was on to get a fair trial – fair trial for a Mackenney? Who the fuck was I trying to kid! The whole thing was a fucking farce. It came to court after a year and John was found not guilty, so that was a good thing at least, but Harry-Boy got three and a half years for violent disorder – section 2, causing an affray. The bastards who started the fight got eighteen months.

Harry-Boy was sent all over the country, constantly being moved from one prison to another. I visited him everywhere and the cunts wouldn't even let him out to attend Bill's funeral – it broke his heart. Harry-Boy also had two little toddlers, who were without a father, and John was seriously affected by it all; he couldn't come to terms with it and started drinking heavily to try and forget. After Harry-Boy done two years, he was categorised down and was eventually allowed out on home leave. He looked terrible, like he'd aged prematurely; he'd never been able to grieve for Bill and the stress was getting him down. He decided not to go back and he went on the run.

The family would never be the same again.

Shortly after, my house was surrounded again by armed police, who told me they had a warrant to search the place because they had a tip-off we had guns on the property. They took me and Shelley out of the house and cordoned off the whole street – nobody was allowed in or out of the cul-de-sac. We were made to sit and wait in police cars for hours on end, while they searched the house and dug up the garden. No guns were found and the house and garden were left in a terrible fucking state. As well as that, the whole area had front-row seats to the spectacle of the Mackenneys being harassed again by the coppers.

Harry-Boy stayed on the run for four years, then they finally captured him taking Shelley to school one day. She was a teenager by then and going to secondary school. Harry-Boy had eighteen months of his sentence left to serve when he absconded. After they got him back, he didn't come out again till 1996 and when he did, he was a different man. His life was in tatters.

John was in prison constantly on remand, but he won every one of his cases. The cases against him were endless back then and he was repeatedly charged with everything they could think of. But he was always found not guilty and they could never pin anything on him.

Daniel has never been in prison, or held on remand. The police tried over and over to get him for something and he was pulled in repeatedly but, like John, they were never able to pin anything on him.

Fit-ups and arrests, court cases, GBH, ABH, attempted murder, sawn-off shotguns, threats, beatings, mental torture – the list goes on and on. It was like open season on the Mackenneys. The police and the papers loved to hunt us more than anything or anyone else. Our neighbours and friends turned on us and we became outcasts. We had to fight to survive – literally! The more we fought, the more notorious we became.

16

KEEPING A SENSE OF HUMOUR

I had a saying at one time: I called it 'the curse of Crutchley Road'. Everything that could go wrong, did go wrong – and more. I really mean it, you name it and it fucking happened to me. For fuck's sake, I even got hit by lightning! I've known a lot of strange people who did strange things and who had strange things happen to them, but I don't know anyone else who's been hit by fucking lightning – inside the fucking house!

It was in 1995 and it was the loudest noise I've ever heard, outside of the fucking war. You can check it on the Google map and you'll see a dull orange streak running from the top of the roof to the bottom of the roof. It struck the aerial and ran down the electrical cable, then went through all the wiring in the house and blew up every electrical appliance that was plugged in. A great flash came out of the fucking television and hit me on the side of the fucking head and my barnet stood up on end.

I know you're fucking laughing, but I wasn't worried about that, because I was sixty-four and I was going fucking grey anyway. I was worried about all the gear that got destroyed, television, video, stereo, fridge, every fucking thing. We didn't have a circuit breaker, so every transformer in all the appliances was fucked and everything had to be thrown out. They weren't even insured, because it was an act of God, so I had to go out and nick everything all over again.

Then I got infested with fucking wasps. I woke up late one night because I could hear this really loud buzzing sound. I thought some mad fucker in the street was mowing the fucking lawn in the middle of the fucking night. I came out of my bedroom to see the whole landing ceiling covered with wasps – and it was a big fucking landing. They were swarmed round the pendant light and they looked like a big buzzing teardrop. The bastard things were everywhere, crawling on the walls and I didn't know what the fuck to do. Me and Shelley ran out of the house with a blanket over our heads and we woke up the geezer from next door called Nigel. By now we had an audience, because every fucker in the cul-de-sac was out looking, wondering what was going on and saying to themselves: 'The Mackenneys are at it again.'

Nigel got hold of insect-repellent sprays and ran into the house spraying, just like Butch fucking Cassidy. But he soon ran back out again screaming, because the wasps attacked him left, right and centre and flew up his trouser legs and down his shirt. It was comic to see him dancing around in the front garden and trying to rip his clothes off.

The next day I rang up the council, who sent proper pest-control people round with fumigators and they soon got rid of the swarm. But Nigel's legs were swollen up like balloons for a few days.

I told you about John's mate Mickey, who looked a bit like Jesus, and also about Bill Kyneston, who died after the fight in the Joiner's Arms. Well, before that, Mickey and Bill got into a bit of a scuffle in the local fish-and-chip shop. Bill got stabbed and was taken to Lewisham Hospital and me and Harry-Boy went over there to see how he was. The wound wasn't critical, but Bill was in a lot of pain while he was recovering. I brought him home with me and he stayed in the spare room. He had to sleep sitting up for a while and I nicked a rocking chair for him. He swore to me one night that he'd just seen Jesus walk into the room. I thought it was probably the painkillers and other tablets he was on had made him fucking hallucinate, but he was adamant. Mickey got caught doing an armed robbery a few weeks later and went down for ten years. Well, one night Bill and me were watching *Songs of Praise* on the television and who do we see? Only fucking Mickey, singing with the fucking prison choir and he looked like a little fucking saint. Bill pointed at the TV and shouted: 'That's him! That's Jesus!'

I told him it wasn't, it was the geezer who stabbed him in the fish-and-chip shop, but he wouldn't have it. It must have been some kind of association thing and a psychiatrist would have a fucking field day with it, but Bill was a strict Catholic and really believed what he saw. The strange thing is, in the years after Bill's death, things started happening in my house that I can't explain. Clocks started acting funny, like changing time on their own, and things started moving about, like cakes on a plate, and a voice calling me when I'm alone in the room. I'm not the only one to have seen these things and sometimes I think it might be Bill, keeping an eye on me. Who knows?

During the nineties, the coppers were all the time trying to pin something on Daniel, but they never succeeded. Daniel is the quietest of my sons and he never gave them any reason to arrest him, except that his name was Mackenney – but they kept on trying. He was continuously stopped and searched and taken into police stations and held without charge. It's like, when they want you, they'll keep on going until they find something, anything, to try to break you down. Anyway, the local bus depot arranged regular outings for the people on the estate, where a bus would arrive at a certain time and the people could pay a small fare and be taken to seaside towns like Hastings or Brighton – we called these outings 'beanos', which means a merry time or a spree. On this particular day, we all went to a place called Dymchurch, on the Romney Marshes in Kent, and the double-decker bus was packed. Shelley was about fourteen or fifteen then, and she came with me, as well as John and Daniel.

Well, Dymchurch was exactly like the name said – Dym. The place was deserted and there was nothing to do, so everyone went into the local pubs. Now, I'm not a drinker and me and Shelley went for a walk along the beach and to look at the shops and it was arranged that we'd all meet back at the bus at 5.00 p.m. By the time I got back there, everyone was pissed, and I mean everyone! Only the children and the bus driver were sober. The driver was absolutely fucking mortified and I was trying to keep Shelley away from the fuckers, so I decided to sit downstairs because it was far too rowdy on the top deck. Eventually they all managed to put one foot in front of the other and get on the bus, and we all set off back to Catford. It was like a scene from a *Carry On* film, because they needed to stop every five fucking minutes for a piss and the only places with public toilets were pubs along the way. They'd all get off the bus and go into the pubs and the driver wouldn't be able to get them back out again. The driver was doing his nut and, eventually, I decided to go in after them and drag the fuckers back out.

They were falling up and down the stairs and bumping into each other and knocking each other over and, when we finally arrived back to the estate, the driver heaved a sigh of relief and threw us all off. However, the police were waiting for us and tried to arrest Daniel again. When I asked them for what, they said for dangerous driving. Well, he wasn't driving the fucking bus, that's for sure, but it didn't matter to them and they tried to grab hold of him. Now, Daniel is the biggest of my boys, at six foot seven, and he worked out with the weights and was proper built and was into martial arts and he wasn't taking too kindly to being manhandled by them. So they called up reinforcements and a couple of vanloads soon arrived. Don't forget, there were all these drunken people about and a mini-riot broke out, with women hitting the coppers with their shoes and blokes tripping them up and dogs being set on them. The police were trying to physically lift Daniel to the Maria, to take him to the station. There were four coppers with one leg and five with the other and loads more with hold of his arms, but they still couldn't move him.

In the background, the drunken crowd was going fucking mad, birds were now jumping on coppers' backs and blokes were knocking their hats off and dogs hanging on to their fucking ankles. It was comical to behold and I would have laughed myself sick if it hadn't been Daniel they were after. In the end, I persuaded Daniel to go with them, because I knew they'd only get more and more coppers and, in the end, someone would get hurt. Or they'd get him down to the station and lay into him in the cells, which they were quite happy to do once there was a bunch of them against one bloke.

Daniel was taken to the station and charged and I decided to go there too and try to find out when he'd be released. But I couldn't shake off the drunken rabble and they all followed me. The police didn't like it and threatened to arrest everybody, but they knew it would be impossible to take everybody in, the cells would have been full to bursting and there was young children there as well. So they released Daniel on police bail and the crowd dispersed. Later, when we were preparing his case for court, a police statement said they went to arrest Daniel Mackenney and were met by a seven-foot giant and several hundred drunken football hooligans, which was a slight exaggeration. The end result was, I took photographs of the bruises that came out on Daniel's body and sent them, with a complaint, to Scotland Yard. The case was dropped.

I remember going to visit Harry-Boy in Suffolk Prison once and there was a coach that took us there from New Cross, picking people up on the way. Anyway, I was waiting this day with Benny and Shelley and I got talking to this big-built blonde bird. She had a right chatty personality and was smoking and yapping away all the time we were waiting for the coach. Anyway, the coach never turned up and I didn't want to let Harry-Boy down, so I rang Daniel and asked him to come drive us up there. I couldn't leave the blonde bird there after being talking to her, so we took her with us in the car. She was hilarious and she was talking ten to the dozen, nobody could get a word in edgeways. She was rolling fags and she offered one to Daniel. What we didn't know was, she was smoking spliffs, and my family ain't no angels, but they never touched drugs. Anyway, Daniel gets a fit of the giggles and he loses his way and we end up going round and round this fucking roundabout about four or five times. When we finally got there, Daniel and the bird were laughing at fuck all and the screws thought they were taking the piss. It turned out she was Harry Roberts's wife, who was labelled the 'cop-killer' when he shot three policemen back in the sixties. Harry's still in prison today and he's not laughing.

Then, one Christmas Eve, I heard the dogs barking and howling in the night, so I got out of bed to investigate. I saw smoke billowing out from the bathroom and it looked like the boiler was on fire. I got everyone out and called the fire brigade, who put the fire out and told me that the flames had almost reached the gas supply to the boiler and, if that had happened, it could have blown the fucking house up. So it looked like the dogs saved us all from becoming the first cockney astronauts that night. I wonder what MI5 would have made of it?

Another Christmas Eve night and the water tank in the loft broke – notice how it was always at night that these fucking things happened. Anyway, the water came through the ceiling and down on top of me while I was asleep in bed. I woke up coughing and spluttering and thinking I was on the fucking *Titanic*, before I realised what was happening. Before I knew it, the whole top floor was flooded and water was running down the stairs. I had to go turn all the electrics off at the mains, before running round to Harry-Boy's for help. It turned out that the ballcock in the tank had broken and the water just kept flowing until Harry got up there and shut it off.

I love antiques and have always been a bit of a hoarder. Anyway, I went down to Bellingham neighbourhood office in Lewisham once to sort out a problem with my rent. At the time, I had an antique table I liked with carved, ornamental legs. One of the legs got broke and I was taking it to a local antique furniture shop where I originally bought the table. I only took the leg because the table was far too big and I wanted to see if they'd be able to fix it. I had the table leg in a bag and I brought it into the rent office with me. The next thing the police had surrounded the place and I heard them shouting on a loudspeaker: 'Come out with your hands up!'

You what? Shelley was with me and she was only a kid, yet I had to walk out of the rent office, with my hands in the air and the bag over my shoulder. Then I had to lie on the ground while they searched me and found the fucking table leg. Someone had seen me go in with the bag and assumed I had a fucking sawn-off and was going in to do the fucking place over. There was loads of fucking grasses about, so-called 'do-gooders' who rang the police at every opportunity, even when I wasn't doing anything wrong. I had a little chuckle about it later, remembering the embarrassed looks on the faces of the coppers when they found nothing but a fucking broken table leg. I hope they gave the fucking grass a mouthful for wasting their time.

After Harry-Boy got out of prison, he came round to see me at 49 Crutchley Road. John happened to come round at the same time and he'd been out all day drinking – like I said, the Joiner's Arms changed the way the family worked, things were never the same again – anyway, Harry-Boy and John got into an argument over something and it was getting a bit heated. I tried to get in between them, as it was bad enough my family fighting outsiders without fighting amongst themselves. All my children have very strong personalities and, like me, they don't back down from no one. Anyway, it came to blows and it reminded me of when I was growing up, watching my brothers fighting. In the kerfuffle, which wasn't too bad at this stage, I copped a clout and was bleeding from the lip – both Harry-Boy and John were big men, six-five and built with it. When they saw me bleeding, it really kicked off into a full-scale ruck, I thought they were going to fucking kill each other. It spilled out into the garden and all my little ornaments got broken, the hedge was knocked down, along with a wall I had running round my flower beds. It was madness. Now, you might not think this was amusing, but I'd been asking the boys to do something with my garden for ages and, when it was all over, they had to sort it out and it looked much better than it did before they demolished it.

Another time a bunch of coppers came to my house and said they were checking the area because there'd been a spate of burglaries. They asked if I'd seen anything suspicious and

I told them to go ahead and check out the garden if they wanted to – I did like to cooperate with the police whenever I could, as you know, and I was surprised they weren't trying to arrest me for the fucking burglaries instead of warning me about them. I'd been at 49 Crutchley Road for many years by then and I had a fully grown hedge that was about ten feet tall and it had an arch cut through the middle of it for a wrought-iron gate. There was also a huge fir tree in the garden and a giant pampas-grass plant, so there was plenty of shadows for them to investigate. Anyway, I went back inside and let them get on with it but, no sooner than I was sitting down, when a knock came to the door again. I opened it and there were the coppers with their uniforms all soaking wet. I had an old hair-trigger sprinkler thing in the garden by then that would go off if anyone came near it. The coppers must have tripped over it in their search. I just said: 'I see you've found my burglar alarm, then.'

They weren't best pleased.

When Shelley was fifteen, she had to do work experience for her school. A place was arranged for her to do this at Lewisham police station, of all places. A few days before she was due to begin, the police contacted the school and told them she wouldn't be able to do her work experience with them because 'it would be a conflict of interest'. A couple of years later when Shelley was seventeen, one of the coppers got his son to go spy on her while she was working for a bank in Catford. The boy developed an obsession for Shelley and went back and told his father that he fancied her. The copper came to me, would you believe it, all nice as fucking pie like he was my best mate or something and asked if I could arrange a date for his son with Shelley. I told him it was up to Shelley. If she wanted to go out with the boy, then it was between the two of them. But Shelley wasn't interested, so the geezer went back to being his old nasty self again, only worse than ever. However, it was worth it for the Mackenneys to be able to get one back at the cunts for a change.

Back in 2004, I was coming home from shopping in Catford. When I got to my house, there was some madwoman in the front garden and John was there too, trying to stop her getting near the house. I didn't know what the fuck was going on and John was in front of her, waving his arms up and down and she had stuff all over her hands. I knew this bird from somewhere, but I couldn't remember her name; she was an acquaintance from a long time ago, and I mean a long time!

She was shrieking like a fucking banshee and I had no idea what was going on. Then I noticed this slimy stuff smeared on the windows. She was holding a pack of butter in her hand and John was trying to stop her from plastering it on the fucking house. There was fucking butter all over the windows and the door. What the fuck was going on? The bird was making no sense at all and, no matter what I did, I couldn't get her away from the house, she wouldn't fucking budge.

Anyway, it was raining out, so I ended up whacking her over the head with my umbrella. This took her by surprise and she spun round with a look of disbelief on her mad fucking face. So I carried on hitting her till she ran out of the garden and off down the road, still shrieking like a fucking lunatic. To this day, I still don't know what her fucking problem was.

It wasn't the first time some mad fucking bird had come round my house. One night, this complete fucking alcoholic woman turned up and said she was Harry-Boy's girlfriend. She was drunk as a fucking skunk, but I let her in, just in case she was telling the truth. I told her Harry wasn't here, but I didn't tell her where she could find him, in case he didn't want to know. Anyway, she was wearing this full-length fur coat and she kept going on about how Harry-Boy had packed her in and she just wanted to talk to him. Sixer was in the house, visiting at the time, and he was still quite ill, so I was getting a bit fed up with her and was just about to sling her out, when she stumbled and fell over and lay sprawled on the floor on her back. Well the coat fell open and it turns out she was completely naked underneath. She was a big bird and I couldn't move her for love nor fucking money. I told Sixer to keep an eye on her while I ran round for Harry and he just stood there looking down at her, like he'd never seen a naked woman before in his life. Harry-Boy came round and it took the three of us to lift her into his car so he could get her home. We laughed about it later.

Some people don't have the same sense of humour as me and there's lots who wouldn't laugh at what I'd laugh at. It's probably because of what I've been through in my life and the situations I've found myself in. Like the time when Little-Legs broke his leg and was on crutches, I think I already mentioned it. Well, it was summertime and it was hot and loads of kids from the estate were playing outside on the grass. John was out walking one of my dogs and, as he passed the neighbours opposite, a bloke came out and he was ranting and raving and shouted at John that he was gonna cut the fucking dog's head off. He was a crazy fucker and I'm sure he was on drugs or something. A fight started between this geezer and John and I ran over to try to break it up. Harry-Boy was in prison at the time. Next thing I see is this mad fucker pulled out a machete and went for John with it. John had nothing to defend himself with and I was sure he was gonna get hurt. Then Little-Legs comes out of nowhere, hobbling on his crutches. He starts to like swordfight this mad fucker with one of his crutches and the mad geezer is swinging the machete.

All the kids in the road stopped playing football or whatever it was they were doing and just stood there, watching this crazy fight going on. Little-Legs was trying to balance on one crutch and fend off the machete with the other, hobbling round between the parked cars like it was some mad fucking game or something. It was fucking comical and it was like something people would film with their cameras and put on fucking YouTube today. But it was serious too, because the geezer could have killed Little-Legs, but Little-Legs was even fucking madder than he was. While this was going on, John ran into my house and came back out with an iron bar. When the crazy cunt saw John coming at him, he turned and ran away, leaving Little-Legs so fucking exhausted he fell down onto the ground and I thought he was going to have a fucking heart attack.

John was like a fucking raging bull and if he'd got his hands on the cunt I'm sure he would've killed him. The geezer ran into his house and tried to slam the door, with John following close behind. He couldn't get the door shut in time and John disappeared in after him. Next thing I seen, was the geezer coming flying back out of the house, jumped over Little-Legs lying on the ground and legged it off down the road. John came back out with the iron bar, but the geezer was too far away for him to chase. He stepped over Little-Legs and went inside our house. All the kids were just standing there with their mouths open. I helped Little-Legs back to his feet and he went back to where he was sitting, on a chair outside his flat. The kids started playing again after a minute or two and it was like nothing had happened.

17

THE PRESENT AND THE FUTURE

Finally, Bert Wickstead, the 'Old Grey Fox', died and evidence emerged that he was aware of the fact that Terence Eve wasn't dead when Harry was supposed to have murdered him, on the orders of Terry Pinfold. This evidence was covered up while Wickstead was alive, but now it came out that Eve was on some sort of fucking witness-protection programme for turning supergrass, after the Hertfordshire wages blag. There were a lot of geezers who were wrongly put away by Commander Wickstead but, when he was alive, he was revered in the press as the epitome of fair play and incorruptible justice in the police force. In actual fact, the man was a manipulator, who was prepared to do anything and frame up anyone to further his own career and any clean copper who went up against him was soon dealt with.

The revelation about Eve being alive was enough to open the case again. It was the breakthrough I'd given up hoping for and I was over the fucking moon. The discrediting of Bruce Childs as a witness proved that we weren't the family of a murderer. We, along with Big H, had been found guilty for all these years – before finally being proven innocent!

Big H was released in 2003, the same year Sixer died, after serving twenty-four years for crimes he didn't commit. His conviction was quashed by the Court of Appeal. I didn't go to the court, just in case it went wrong again, like it had before. Loveinia had been going to see her father and she knew what was going on and she told me before it went on the news. When the time actually came for him to be released, I just couldn't believe it. I was so happy for him, I really was. I saw him for the first time in years on the news and he looked old – he didn't look like the Harry I remembered. He was diagnosed with emphysema in prison and the standard of care he received in there left a lot to be desired. It had taken its toll on him. He was standing with that Pinfold geezer, who I never liked, and it all seemed so long ago – when we were young and fucking crazy and in love and afraid of fuck-all.

The woman he married in prison was waiting for him and, after he got out, I spoke to him a couple of times on the telephone and Harry-Boy and Loveinia had some contact with him for a time. But it stopped after a while and I don't have any contact with him now. I thought a few times about trying to get in touch, but I don't think I'd know what to say to him. Maybe he wants to be left alone and not have to remember anything that might remind him of the past, of the horrendous miscarriage of justice that happened to him. Even though I had nothing to do with that and might have been able to steer him away from it if we'd stayed together – maybe the past is somewhere he doesn't want to go. As far as I know, his 'aqua valve' is still used by divers to this day.

Harry winning the long war was a vindication. It was as if a huge weight had been lifted from my shoulders. But, although Big H was a free man, there were still court cases pending for Harry-Boy and John and the fight, for them, still wasn't over. It took many more visits to court before they finally got free of the system. It may seem different now, but the years of abuse and torment have taken their toll. I can never get those wasted years back, but there were some good times in there as well. I never let the system grind me down, whether it was the slums, or the war, or the care homes, or borstal, or the law courts, or the police, or the newspapers. I was born a fighter and I'm still one to this day.

Sixer was seventy-three when he died and he outlived all the doctors who said he'd never recover. His mother had died a while back, before he had his accident, and the rest of the family had disowned him for living with me. I went to his funeral, but the fuckers reclaimed him when he was dead and made me wait outside the cemetery – me and his children weren't allowed inside with the rest of the self-righteous cunts.

All my brothers, except for Ronnie, died of prostate cancer, Tommy in 1999, Johnny in 2002 and Jimmy in 2005. Gracie died in 2001, she had osteoporosis and her legs became really weak. I went to see her in hospital and she told me she'd only be in there till she got her legs back again. She looked terrible; she used to be a big woman but she lost so much weight and had wasted away. She never did come out again, I don't think it was the osteoporosis that killed her, but some complication did. It came as a great shock to me when Gracie died. We may not have always seen eye to eye, but she looked out for me as best she could when I was young and she was more like a step-mother than a sister. I miss her and wish I hadn't caused so much grief in her life.

Shelley left me in 2002. She was twenty-two and work-ing in a bank at the time. Don't forget, her mother had walked out on her when she was only three and she'd lived with me ever since. I took her everywhere with me and she went to every police station and courthouse and prison with me. She witnessed every raid and police attack and I think it all just got too much for her in the end. She left without telling me where she was going; she just disappeared one day and I didn't get to speak to her again for a year and a half. I hired a private detective and used some connections to try to find out where she'd gone and I eventually discovered that she was living in Birmingham and she'd had a nervous breakdown – and a daughter.

It was very lonely without Shelley. Me and her were very close and we'd been everywhere together for so many years. I went up to see her and we tried to repair our rela-tionship and it all came back, the closeness we had for all them years while she was growing up. Then Shelley was diagnosed with early-stage cancer and I knew that I couldn't leave her. Big H was free and Sixer was gone and I decided I didn't want to live in Catford any more, the area was changing and, anyway, it held too many bad memo-ries for me. I wanted to live with Shelley, so that's what I did – I moved up to Birmingham.

I've been living in Birmingham a while now and, what can I say, I'm still a south-east Londoner and I don't like it up here. At first it was all right, but I miss London, where I lived all my life – I'm a cockney and I'll always be a cockney. I've already had four fights in Birmingham and I'll be eighty by the time this book comes out – not bad going, eh? I'll still step into the ring with a bird a third of my age if she wants to try her luck.

Listen, I learned a lot in my life and I don't trust people easily no more. Mistakes can fucking kill you and I try not to make them if I can help it, at least not like I used to make them when I was younger. You might think I hate the police, but I don't – we all need the coppers to keep order, especially these days with everyone out to kill someone, but we need good coppers, straight coppers, not the bent, dodgy fuckers of the seventies and eighties.

And things ain't like they used to be when I was young and nobody seems to have any respect for anything any more. Thing is, they come fucking unstuck when they give me any fucking lip, because I give them what for in a language they understand. I may be an old biddy, but my fighting spirit's still here and, if you ain't careful, you might get a punch in the fucking throat!

What do I think of society today? In some ways it's good, but in other ways it's gone to fucking pot. We got gobshites running the country who're more interested in lining their own pockets, but I suppose that's nothing new, is it? The poor seem to be getting poorer and the rich getting richer. Soon it'll be back like it was in the Middle fucking Ages, with people working for starvation wages and the lords and ladies of the new aristocracy swanning around with their painted faces and their private fucking jets. I suppose you'll say that's a fucking liberty, coming from me, who stole her way through life. But I never stole from the poor people, like the cunts are doing now – legally. The ones I stole from could well afford it and they were the same ones who exploited people like me and my family and kept us down in the gutter. So fuck them!

The street crime of today is different from when I was young. We had a kind of unspoken code then, no muggings and no burglaries in your own area. Yes, we were thieves, but we didn't steal from the people next door, all the nicking I did was from businesses – or a good old-fashioned con. But it's every fucker for himself or herself these day, you can't even walk down the street without watching your back in case some fucking smack-head does you over for your last forty quid. And even then it ain't entirely the smack-head's fault, it's the people who control him or her, the people at the top who control everything. Then, I suppose it's always been like that, the thing that's different is respect – there ain't none no more.

Teenagers will always be teenagers; you can't stop them having sex, but you'd think that in these days of contraceptives none of them would be having unwanted babies. They have kids and still expect to be able to go out and enjoy themselves and change partners like they change fucking knickers and expect their parents to look after the babies for them. Then they have another baby with another partner and all the fucking kids are related to each other and none of them knows who their fucking half-brothers and half-sisters are and they grow up and have babies with each other. Is it any fucking wonder the *Jeremy Kyle Show* does so fucking well, society's fucked up in the head, like Sixer used to be.

I don't like that fucking rapping hip-hop music neither – that ain't proper music, it's like some kind of street poetry with a bad attitude, like calling women bitches and stuff like that. If they called me a bitch, they'd be picking their fucking teeth up off the floor. I don't care what colour they are, nor how big they are neither. And the clothes – what do they fucking look like? You can't tell the girls from the boys! In my day, men wore suits and women wore dresses – men were men and not these silly new-man fuckers, trying to get in touch with their fucking feminine side. I ask you! In my day, men didn't have no fucking feminine side, where the fuck did that come from? And, if the men want to be women nowadays, the women want to be fucking men. I ain't against women's lib and that, but you can take it too far – and then they complain they're not treated like ladies no more. You can't act like a man and expect to be treated like a fucking lady – can you? If you want to be a man, then you gotta take it like a man!

The other thing is, every cunt wants to be famous these days, and they'll do anything to get that fucking fifteen minutes. All this shit on the television, all these reality shows and fucking talent shows, full of fucking halfwits and idiots with no talent at all. It's like television is brainwashing people into thinking all this bollocks is real life. It ain't real life and the reality shows should be called 'unreality shows'. Life is out there on the street, not inside the fucking television box. They used to say once that religion is the opium of the people – nowadays, television is the fucking opium of the people. They're all sitting there in a semi-coma, looking at the shit, instead of getting up and doing something.

I think I should have been born a man. Actually, no, that wouldn't have been a good idea. If I was a man, I'd have killed someone by now. If I was a man, I'd have been unstoppable. If I was a man today, I'd carry a gun and I'd blast any cunt who tried it on with me. I wouldn't kill them, because that would be stupid and I'd only go away for life, like Big H. No, I'd shoot them in the fucking knee-caps and there'd be a lot of people going around on fucking crutches.

People sometimes say to me 'You must've seen a lot in your day, Eileen.'

But the stuff I saw and went through was over a long period of time – eighty years. Thing is, people today see so much, it's like things change so quickly, much quicker than they used to and people don't know the fuck where they are half the fucking time. Everyone wants a quick fix for whatever ails them – drink or drugs or money or their fifteen minutes of fucking fame or whatever. There used to be things like morals and values and respect – I keep going on about respect and you're probably saying, 'Eileen, you didn't have much respect when you were younger.'

But I did. I respected true people, people who didn't pretend and had the backbone to say it how it was. God gave everyone a mouth to use and you should use it to say what you really feel, what you really mean – that way, we all know where we stand. Don't we?

Everything's about image these days, and nothing's what it seems to be. One time you knew where you fucking stood, good or bad, now you don't know what's good or who's bad and everyone's being fucking manipulated by some cunt in the shadows who has his hand up their fucking jacksie. You can't tell friend from foe these days, so it's better to trust no one and just keep your own counsel. And there's no fight left in anybody, no drive, no lust for life – people are just contented to doss and make do. I don't believe in that, I'll rest when I'm fucking dead; until then, I'll keep fighting on.

I definitely need to move back to London. I'm a Londoner born and bred, born and raised. It's in my blood and it's who I am and it'll never change and, to be honest, I don't want it to change. I don't want to have to be politically correct, like every other fucker. What the fuck does 'politically correct' mean anyhow? It's just a fucking shallow modern term that means fucking nothing, like a lot of other stuff these days. It's a fucking cotton-wool society, with every cunt getting counselling for this and that and the fucking other. If you ask me, it's all a load of bollocks – in my day you got over it and moved on, you had no fucking choice. When it comes down to it, we're all animals and life is just survival of the fucking fittest.

My family are scattered all over the country now and I'm not used to living like that. I'd like it if we were all living close together in London again. I know London's not like it used to be any more, but we could find a place where we could belong, where we could be close and everyone could pull together. We might fall out every now and then but, in the end, family is family and blood is thicker than water and, when it comes down to the crunch, we all stand by our own. That's the way I was raised and how I raised my children.

Although I don't lift no more, I still check out the shops when I walk into them. It's like second nature to me, I always case the place, looking for little weaknesses in the security and, even though they have CCTV and security tags and guards all over the place, I could still do it – if I wanted to. And I went back to visit Holloway once, just to see what it was like now – it was a lot nicer, with TV and telephones and therapy and toilets. For fuck's sake, I wish it was like that when I was in there – I wouldn't have wanted to fucking leave.

We take peace for granted nowadays too. I know there's small wars going on all over the fucking world, but here in this country we live in so-called luxury, with more things than we actually need. We want more things than we can use and we have a little fucking tantrum if we don't get them. I can still remember waking up freezing cold in the dead of night to run to an overcrowded shelter in the pouring rain, hoping that I wouldn't get killed and that I'd live to see one more fucking day. I'm not saying that makes me better than anyone else, but it kinda focuses the fucking mind, wouldn't you say?

There are two things you don't want to get me started on – immigration and homosexuality. Don't get me wrong, I got a lot of friends in both camps, and my own mother was second-generation Irish, but I don't want to live in fucking Saudi Arabia nor America nor South Africa nor Japan – but, if I did, I'd respect their way of life there. And some of my best mates when I was rolling the toffs up West were gay men, they were fucking fantastic, and they dressed better than I did. No, I only had a problem with the big butch dykes who tried it on with me – I didn't fight them because they were gay, I fought them because they pissed me off and thought they could take liberties with me. Live and let live, I say, I don't care what people get up to, as long as they have respect and don't try to take liberties.

That's my rant over. And I know some people say I'm a self-opinionated old fucking villain, and maybe I am. I have an attitude problem, I know that – always have had. I don't like losing; it's not in my nature to lie down and give up. But I am who I am and I can't change now, and if people don't like me, I don't give a fuck! I wasn't put on this earth to be liked.

Despite all that, I'm optimistic for the future of my granddaughter Shelley and my great granddaughter Alyssia. I hope they never have to go through what I've been through but, although I regret some things, life has made me the person I am today. I wouldn't have had it any other way – well, nearly any other way. I'd do it all again if I was given the chance and I'd probably do some things differently. But I experienced more in my lifetime than most would experience in ten – and I ain't finished yet!

I still can't be told what to do, no more than I ever could, and I don't take kindly to piss-taking cunts. I still don't back down from a fight and I still ain't scared of nothing. If people want to have a go at me, then fucking let them. But, be warned, I'll fucking have a go back. My body might be older, but I ain't changed one little bit, and the time I'll stop fighting is when I'm fucking dead and buried.

End of story!